Applied
Time Series Analysis
For
Managerial
Forecasting

Applied
Time Series Analysis

For
Managerial
Forecasting

Charles R. Nelson

Graduate School of Business
University of Chicago

Holden–Day, Inc.

San Francisco

Düsseldorf   Johannesburg   London
Panama   Singapore   Sydney   Toronto

APPLIED TIME SERIES ANALYSIS
For Managerial Forecasting

Library of Congress Catalog Card Number: 72-88942
ISBN: 0-8162-6366-3

67890 CO 8079876

Printed in the United States of America

To Katy

Preface

This book was written with the objective of making recent developments in applied time series analysis, particularly those due to Box and Jenkins, accessible to students in business, economics, management science, and industrial engineering at the master's level. The need for such a text became evident to me when I undertook development of a forecasting course for MBA students at the Graduate School of Business of the University of Chicago. Although univariate time series analysis offers a powerful tool for forecasting in many operational settings, and should, I felt, constitute the core of such a course, it became apparent that little of what has been written in that area may be read and understood by students lacking substantial preparation in statistics. Nevertheless, I became convinced that much of the substance of what is important for application could be communicated to a less-sophisticated audience. For example, presentation of the theory of linear stochastic processes is greatly facilitated by use of the algebra of backshift operators. Unfortunately, some considerable investment in time, relative to that available in a single academic term, is required before most students are sufficiently comfortable and skilled in using backshift algebra to benefit from the investment. Consequently, in this text many general results that are readily proved using backshift algebra are simply stated after their plausibility and intuitive appeal have been established by simple examples. Experimentation with this approach, combined with heavy emphasis on first-hand data analysis, led to a workable program that equips the student to make intelligent use of time series analysis and provides him with a base for further reading or formal study in the area.

Chapter 1 reviews the primary methodological alternatives open to the operational forecaster and establishes the motivation for putting particular emphasis on univariate time series analysis. The introductory discussion goes on to consider why there is a payoff to good forecasting in the context of a profit-maximizing firm and the relationship between the forecaster and the decision-maker. Chapter 2 begins the formal study of time series analysis with the concepts of stationarity and autocorrelation. Models for stationary time series are presented in Chapter 3. The moving-average model is introduced as a special case of the general discrete linear stochastic process, after which autoregressive models and mixed autoregressive–moving-average models are seen to be natural conceptual extensions. Considerable attention is given to derivation of the autocorrelation structures of these models and the observational characteristics for the data that those structures imply. Chapter 4 widens the scope of the linear models to include nonstationary behavior by entertaining the stationary models of Chapter 3 as models for the differences or successive changes occurring in nonstationary series. With this extension, the linear models are seen to offer a very flexible framework in which to describe the behavior of a wide range of stationary and nonstationary series. Chapter 5 takes up the problem of statistical inference—namely, choice of a model appropriate to a particular time series ("identification") and use of the data at hand to estimate the parameters of the model. Considerable emphasis is placed on understanding the limits of precision encountered in practical application and on interpretation of results obtained in illustrative examples. Chapter 6 completes the model-building sequence with computation of forecasts and confidence intervals and derivation of rules for adaptive revision of forecasts. Seasonality is a property of many time series of interest to the operational forecaster, and a special class of linear models is required to model such series. These are discussed in Chapter 7, where their basic stochastic properties are developed and identification and estimation are illustrated by application to monthly auto registrations in the United States. No forecasting strategy should proceed in a critical vacuum. Rather, alternative techniques should be subjected to comparison with a view toward discovering their relative strengths and weaknesses and, ultimately, revision of forecasting strategy. Chapter 8 is addressed to the question of forecaste evaluation, offering a methodological approach that emphasizes optimal weighting of alternative forecasts in composite forecasts. Evaluation of forecasts of major macro-economic variables by the Federal Reserve Board-MIT-Penn econometric model of the United States economy on the one hand, and by simple linear univariate time series models on the other, provides a case study of forecast evaluation, illustrating basic principles.

In Chapters 5 to 7, discussion of illustrative applications is accompanied by output from computer programs entitled PDQ, ESTIMATE, and FORECAST corresponding to the three basic stages in the implementation of linear models for forecasting. These programs are written in Fortran IV for the IBM 360 and are designed to allow the nonprogramming user maximum flexibility in performing the complex computational procedures required by the technique. Inquiries concerning availability of the programs should be directed to me at the Graduate School of Business, University of Chicago, Chicago, Ill. 60637.

Writing any text, particularly one in a relatively new area, is very much an iterative process with feedback from students providing much of the input for successive revisions. I owe a great deal, therefore, to my students in Business 354 for the constructive quality of the feedback that they supplied and for the impetus which their enthusiasm for the subject gave me in pursuing the project to its end. Their equanimity in the face of the uncertainty presented by a new course based on a provisional text in a state of flux has been most admirable. I am also indebted to colleagues at the University of Chicago and others whose comments on various drafts and general encouragement have been invaluable: in particular, Robert Blattberg, Phillip Cooper, Katherine Dusak, John Gould, and Harry Roberts. Hernan Cortes-Douglas helped with preparation of homework problems and figures and was the source of many useful suggestions. Steven Beveridge and Mohan Bhandiwad did most of the programming. Permission from the Cambridge University Press to reproduce figures from Aitchinson and Brown, "The Lognormal Distributions," as Figure 6.5 of this book and from the *American Economic Review* to reprint in Chapter 8 sections from my article, in the December 1972, issue is gratefully acknowledged.

Charles R. Nelson

Contents

6

FORECASTING ARIMA PROCESSES   143

7

MODELS FOR SEASONAL TIME SERIES   168

8

FORECAST EVALUATION: A CASE STUDY   202

Appendix

COMPUTER PROGRAMS FOR IDENTIFICA-
TION, ESTIMATION, AND FORECASTING   222

Applied
Time Series Analysis
For
Managerial
Forecasting

1
Forecasting Methods and Objectives

Forecasting is one of the most pervasive and important elements of managerial decision-making because the ultimate effect of a decision generally depends on the outcome of factors that cannot be foreseen at the time the decision is made. The role of forecasting cuts across all fields of management—finance, marketing, production, operations research, business economics, and public administration. This text is concerned primarily with the contribution that time series analysis can make to operational forecasting, particularly in the light of recent developments due primarily to G. E. P. Box and G. M. Jenkins. In order to orient the reader with respect to alternative approaches to forecasting it is useful to begin with a typological breakdown of forecasting methodology into five fairly distinct categories.

1.1 A Typology of Forecasting Methods

subjective forecasting

The forecasting approach followed in the great majority of day-to-day decisions, both managerial and personal, is an intuitive or subjective one. Most often the need for short-term response and the unfavorable ratio of prospective benefits to the cost of sophisticated techniques dictate a seat-of-the-pants procedure. Furthermore, the decision-maker may believe that his intuition in a particular setting is more reliable than any mathematical forecasting function, and this may in fact be the case. The factors taken into account in forming an intuitive forecast may be few or many, but its essential characteristic is that it is not reproducible; rather, it is unique to the individual forecaster. We may get some qualitative idea of how intuitive forecasts are formed by interviewing the forecaster. If we are primarily concerned with his performance, then the most illuminating approach may be to regard the forecaster as a "black box," the reliability of which may be assessed from a record of forecasts accumulated over time.

structural and econometric models

If considerable time and resources are available, the manager might choose to employ mathematical and statistical methods to assist in the preparation of forecasts. One such method is to build a *structural model*, that is, a set of mathematical functions which purport to represent causal relationships descriptive of his organization's environment. For example, suppose that evaluation of prospective investment projects requires evaluation of future revenue and hence a forecast of the future price of the good being produced. In the simplest model of the firm's environment that price would be determined in a competitive market by supply-and-demand functions. The first step in building such a model is the *specification* of the model, that is, deciding on the factors affecting supply and demand to be included in the model and on the particular functional form to describe their influence.

In a very simple example, we might have the quantity supplied to the market at time t, Q_t^s, depending on price P_t and the hourly wage paid in the industry W_t with the quantity demanded Q_t^d depending on price and consumer's income Y_t. The model then would be

$$Q_t^s = f_s(P_t, W_t)$$
$$Q_t^d = f_d(P_t, Y_t) \tag{1.1.1}$$

where the mathematical functions f_s and f_d describe the relationship between supply and demand and their respective determinants. To complete the specification of the model it is necessary to give specific form to f_s and f_d, which in practice would probably be assumed to be linear. In that case the model becomes

$$Q^s = \alpha_0 + \alpha_1 P_t + \alpha_2 W_t$$
$$Q^d = \beta_0 + \beta_1 P_t + \beta_2 Y_t \tag{1.1.2}$$

where the α's and β's are fixed but unknown coefficients. The next stage in building the model is parameter inference, that is, estimation of values for the unknown coefficients from historical data on the variables. The data will certainly not satisfy Eqs. (1.1.2) exactly, no matter what coefficient values are inserted; therefore, it will be necessary to introduce unobserved disturbance terms into the model to allow for the inevitable discrepancies. These disturbance terms are interpreted as random variables subject to a probability distribution having mean value zero. The model becomes then a *statistical model* and is given by

$$Q_t^s = \alpha_0 + \alpha_1 P_t + \alpha_2 W_t + \epsilon_{s,t}$$
$$Q_t^d = \beta_0 + \beta_1 P_t + \beta_2 Y_t + \epsilon_{d,t}$$

(1.1.3)

Because the model arises in an economic context, it is referred to as an *econometric model*, and estimation of the coefficient parameters is a problem in the application of the *theory of econometrics*.

Suppose now that the coefficients of the model have been estimated. How do we proceed to exploit the model to forecast future prices? Clearly, if we were given the future values of wages W_t, income Y_t, and disturbances $\epsilon_{s,t}$ and $\epsilon_{d,t}$, then using the market clearing condition

$$Q_t^s = Q_t^d$$

(1.1.4)

we could solve Eqs. (1.1.3) for future values of price and quantity. In effect, by knowing W_t and Y_t as well as the disturbance terms we are able to position the supply-and-demand curves and solve for equilibrium price and quantity. The catch, of course, is that in practice we do not have the information required to solve the system. Although it would seem sensible to set the future disturbances at zero, their expected values, we are faced still with the problem of forecasting wages and income before we can use the model to present price and quantity. Furthermore, the model offers no assistance here since wages and income are determined outside the model; that is, they are *exogenous* to the model. It would appear that the structural model has transformed rather than solved the forecasting problem, that is, transformed it into the problem of forecasting wages and income. We could use intuitive forecasts of wages and income as inputs to the model, but if it comes to that we might prefer to rely directly on intuitive forecasts of price since we probably have greater confidence in our "feel" for our own market than for relatively remote magnitudes much as consumers' income.

As a means of summary, it is useful to list the sources of forecast error associated with the structural model. First, future wages and income will undoubtedly differ from whatever values were assumed when the model was solved to obtain forecasts. Second, realized values of future disturbances will differ from zero. The forecast error will also be affected by the sampling error present in our estimates of the α and β coefficients. Finally, the model itself may be subject to specification error; that is, the structure itself may be deficient in some respect: for example, demand-and-supply relations might not be linear as we have assumed.

It is worth noting that under some circumstances exogenous variables are known at the time a forecast is prepared. For example, a model of a firm's market share might include among determinants its advertising expenditures that are under direct control of the firm. Many other important determinants of market share, however, will still remain unknown until future periods. The fact, then, that structural models generally transform rather than solve forecasting problems has motivated the search for forecasting techniques which rely only on information available when the forecast is made. Sample surveys of buyers' intentions certainly fall into this category. Surveys of consumers' intentions are often used in practice as *leading indicators* of consumer expenditures, and surveys of businessmen's intentions are being widely used in forecasting business investment, raw materials purchases, and so forth. One set of information that is always available to the forecaster, however, and at very low cost, is the past history of the variable being forecast. If that history spans any considerable length of time, we might reasonably entertain the possibility of inferring from it the path which the variable is most likely to follow in the future. Let us consider then some of the *extrapolative* techniques that have been suggested.

deterministic models

A class of models which yield extrapolative forecasts are those that treat the variable of interest as a deterministic function of time. Thus, if the time series of observations on the variable at times $1, 2, \ldots, t, \ldots$, are denoted $z_1, z_2, \ldots, z_t, \ldots$, then it is assumed that

$$z_t = f(t) \tag{1.1.5}$$

where $f(t)$ is some function of time to be chosen from among plausible candidates. A popular choice for $f(t)$ in practice is a polynomial in time. For example, if the polynomial were of degree K, we would have

$$z_t = \alpha_0 + \alpha_1 t^1 + \alpha_2 t^2 + \cdots + \alpha_K t^K \tag{1.1.6}$$

where the coefficients α_i are to be inferred somehow from past history that, if the current period is period T, consists of observations $z_1, \ldots, z_T$ on the time series z_t. We know that if we allow K to be large enough, in particular to be equal to $(T-1)$, the number of available observations less 1, then the coefficients may be chosen so that the model accounts exactly for every observation. This is because if we write out (1.1.6) for each observation we have a set of T equations in the T unknowns $\alpha_0, \ldots, \alpha_{T-1}$. Following that approach would seem to be unsatisfactory for a number of reasons. First of all, we probably are not prepared to believe that very high powers of t are really important in the evolution of z_T. Second, if we use the resulting polynomial to forecast beyond the sample period, we know perfectly well that forecast errors will occur, although the model gives us no clue as to how large those errors are likely to be.

Alternatively, suppose that we truncate the polynomial at something less than degree $(T - 1)$. Now the model can no longer account exactly for all observations, and it is necessary to introduce a disturbance term into the model to account for discrepancies. Choice of coefficient values then becomes a problem in statistical inference. Furthermore, the forecasting properties of the model will depend crucially on the choice of degree for the polynomial and on the statistical properties of the resulting disturbance term. We must be wary particularly in choosing the degree of the polynomial since polynomials of high degree tend to imply forecast profiles that become nonsensical as the horizon of forecast becomes large. This is because as the model is evaluated at successively larger values of t, as we project further into the future, the terms in the highest powers of t dominate the whole expression. It is apparent that in application the polynomial model loses much of the appeal it had at first blush to deterministic simplicity.[1]

Another deterministic model often used in practice is the exponential growth model

$$z_t = A e^{rt} \tag{1.1.7}$$

where A = constant given by initial conditions

      e = natural number

      r = continuous growth rate of z_t through time

The actual historical observations will, of course, never conform exactly to the exponential function, so again a disturbance term must be introduced to account for discrepancies. These discrepancies are likely to be substantial and to persist in one direction or the other for considerable periods of time, thus casting doubt on the usefulness of the model for short-term forecasting.

Perhaps the most fundamental objection to any model which represents a variable as a deterministic function of time is the implication of the model that the long-term evolution of the time series is completely systematic and therefore highly predictable. This is difficult to swallow as a characterization of

---

[1] Pitfalls in the use of polynomials as forecasting models have been discussed by D. J. Cowden in The Perils of Polynomials, *Management Science*, **9**(4):546–550 (July 1963).

such economic variables as prices, sales, profits, interest rates, etc., and we should be reasonably suspicious of the quality of the forecasts that will result from application of such a model.

ad hoc forecasting formulas

Another class of forecasting techniques that depend only on past history are what we might characterize as ad hoc forecasting formulas. All such formulas are of the form

$$\hat{z}_t(l) = f_l(z_1, \ . \ . \ . \ ,z_{t-1},z_t) \tag{1.1.8}$$

where $\hat{z}_t(l)$ denotes the forecast made at time t of z_{t+l} and $f_l(\ )$ is a function of past history depending only on the forecast horizon l. The "naïve" models often used to establish standards of accuracy for other forecasting techniques belong to this class; for example, we might prefer that the next observation on z will be equal to the previous one so that

$$\hat{z}_t(1) = z_t \tag{1.1.9}$$

or that the next change in z will be equal to the previous change so that

$$\hat{z}_t(1) = z_t + (z_t - z_{t-1}) \tag{1.1.10}$$

Because of the strong tendency economic time series have to maintain their level or rate of change, these naïve predictors are often hard to beat. For example, it is well known that (1.1.9) is the best extrapolative forecast of stock-market prices (see Fama 1965).

If we wanted to draw on information from the more distant past of the variable, we could use *moving averages* of past observations; for example,

$$\hat{z}_t(1) = \tfrac{1}{10}(z_t + \ \cdot \ \cdot \ \cdot \ + z_{t-9}) \tag{1.1.11}$$

would just take a simple average of the last 10 observations as a forecast of the next. The difficulty with a forecast such as (1.1.11) is that it seems implausible that z_{t-9} would be able to tell us as much about the likely value of z_{t+1} as would z_t, and it is therefore undesirable to give it as much weight. Intuitively, it seems more reasonable to put most weight on the most recent observation and let the weights decline as we go further back into the past. There are, of course, numerous such weighting schemes, but the one which has received the most attention (see particularly Brown 1962) is that of the *exponential smoothing model*. To see how an exponential smoothing forecast is constructed, consider the set of weights $(1 - \beta)$, $(1 - \beta)\beta$, $(1 - \beta)\beta^2$, . . . , where β is a fraction between 0 and 1. Since the ratio of any adjacent pair of weights is the fraction β, they are said to decline exponentially. The forecast one period ahead is then

$$\hat{z}_t(1) = (1 - \beta)z_t + (1 - \beta)\beta z_{t-1} + (1 - \beta)\beta^2 z_{t-2} + \cdots \quad (1.1.12)$$

which is referred to as an *exponentially weighted moving average* (EWMA). The weighting pattern may be adjusted by selecting different values of β. If β is small, then the weight given to the current observation is large and successive weights decline rapidly. On the other hand, if β is large, then little weight is given to the current observation and subsequent weights decay slowly. We note that the EWMA is a true average since the weights sum to unity.

What about forecasts for longer horizons? If we construct the l-step-ahead forecast by the most natural extension of (1.1.12), applying the exponentially declining weights successively to forecasts of horizons $(l - 1)$, $(l - 2)$, . . . , then

$$\hat{z}_t(l) = (1 - \beta)\hat{z}_t(l - 1) + \cdots + (1 - \beta)\beta^{(l-2)}z_t(1)$$
$$+ (1 - \beta)\beta^{(l-1)}z_t + \cdots \quad (1.1.13)$$

Then it is easy to show that the l-step-ahead forecast reduces to just

$$\hat{z}_t(l) = (1 - \beta)z_t + (1 - \beta)\beta z_{t-1} + (1 - \beta)\beta^2 z_{t-2} + \cdots \quad (1.1.14)$$

The EWMA in the form so far presented is obviously not yet suitable for application because computation of forecasts requires an infinite number of previous observations. Fortunately, a convenient computational device that requires only the previous forecast and the current observation is easily derived. Namely, from (1.1.14) it is apparent

$$\hat{z}_t(l) = (1 - \beta)z_t + \beta \hat{z}_{t-1}(l) \quad (1.1.15)$$

so that the new forecast is simply computed by taking fraction β of the old forecast plus fraction $(1 - \beta)$ of the current observation.

Generally, the primary virtue of exponentially weighted moving averages is their great computational convenience. Their most obvious weakness is the lack of a general methodology of selection among alternative schemes, hence our characterization of them as ad hoc. When we use one of the formulas, how do we know that the one we have chosen is most appropriate? How do we know whether it is providing good forecasts or poor ones?

time series analysis

The final approach to forecasting, which we outline here, is that of *time series analysis*, which is the primary subject of most of this text. The distinguishing feature of time series analysis is that the sequence of observations on a given variable is viewed as a realization of *jointly distributed random variables.* That is, there is presumed to be some joint distribution function on the sequence of observations $z_1, \ldots, z_N$, say,

$$p_{1, \ldots, N}(z_1, \ldots, z_N) \tag{1.1.16}$$

The subscripts $1, \ldots, N$ on the density function call attention to the fact that in general the parameters or even form of the density function may depend on the particular time points in question. Now, if we knew the density function (1.1.16), we could readily make statements about the *probable* outcome of as yet unrealized observations. This kind of model is referred to as a *stochastic process* since it says that the sequence of observations evolves through time according to a probability law.

As a simple example of a stochastic process, consider the *random walk,* in which each successive *change* in the variable is drawn *independently* from a probability distribution with mean zero. The variable z_t then evolves according to

$$z_t - z_{t-1} = u_t \tag{1.1.17}$$

or
$$z_t = z_{t-1} + u_t \tag{1.1.18}$$

where u_t is a random variable with mean zero and is drawn independently every period, thus making each successive step taken by z random. For example, u_t might be generated by the flips of a fair coin, and so

$$u_t = \begin{cases} +1 & \text{with probability } \frac{1}{2} \\ -1 & \text{with probability } \frac{1}{2} \end{cases} \tag{1.1.19}$$

If we think of the process as starting at some origin z_0, then the process evolves with the addition of successive steps as follows:

$$
\begin{aligned}
z_1 &= z_0 + u_1 \\
z_2 &= z_0 + u_1 + u_2 \\
&\cdots \cdots \cdots \cdots \\
z_t &= z_0 + u_1 + \cdots + u_t
\end{aligned}
\tag{1.1.20}
$$

Figure 1.1 shows the realization of a random walk for which the u_t are normally distributed and drawn independently by a computer using a so-called random-number generator. It is interesting to note how much this realization is like a piece of stock-market history (look at the back page of the *Wall Street Journal*). This is not surprising since stock prices are known to conform well to the random-walk model in the sense that successive price changes are essentially independent (see again Fama 1965).

If we have a time series that seems to be well described by the random-walk model and for which we wish to prepare forecasts, what form will those

figure 1.1 Realization of a random walk with forecasts and 95 percent confidence intervals.

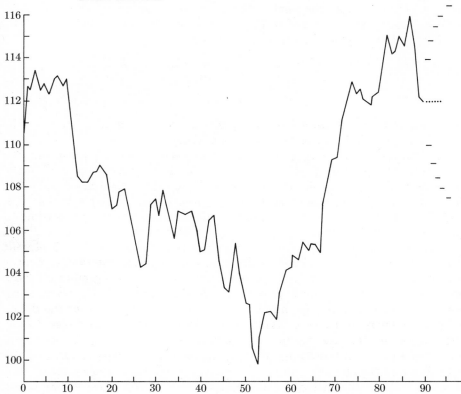

forecasts take and how will they be derived? Let us start with the history of observations $z_1, \ldots, z_T$, and suppose that we want to forecast the future realization z_{T+1}. We note first that z_{T+1} is a random variable. Why? Because it is made up of the number z_T, now fixed by virtue of having been observed, plus the random variable u_{T+1}. Furthermore, we may easily describe the probability distribution of z_{T+1} given the past history; for instance, the mean is shown by [where $E(X|Y)$ denotes the expectation of random variable X given information Y]

$$
\begin{aligned}
E(z_{T+1}|\ldots,z_{T-1},z_T) &= E(z_T + u_{T+1}|\ldots,z_{T-1},z_T) \\
&= E(z_T|\ldots,z_{T-1},z_T) + E(u_{T+1}|\ldots,z_{T-1},z_T) \\
&= z_T + E(u_{T+1}) \\
&= z_T \qquad\qquad\qquad\qquad\qquad\qquad (1.1.21)
\end{aligned}
$$

so that the *expected* position of the series in the next period is just its current position. Note in derivation (1.1.21) we use the fact that the past history of z tells us nothing about the next independent drawing on u. We may also easily calculate the variance of z_{T+1} given the past history since [where $V(X|Y)$ denotes the variance of X given information Y]

$$
\begin{aligned}
V(z_{T+1}|\ \ldots\ ,z_{T-1},z_T) &= V(z_T + u_{T+1}|\ \ldots\ ,z_{T-1},z_T) \\
&= 0 + V(u_{T+1}) \\
&= \sigma_u{}^2
\end{aligned}
\tag{1.1.22}
$$

where again we make use of the independence of u_{T+1}, and $\sigma_u{}^2$ denotes the variance of any of the u_t, in this case the variance of u_{T+1}.

Our knowledge about z_{T+1} then takes the form of knowledge about the probability distribution from which it will be drawn, allowing us to make probability statements concerning its realization. For example, if u_t is normally distributed, we can say that the distribution of z_{T+1} given history through time T is a bell-shaped curve centered on the center z_T [its mean according to (1.1.21)] with 95 percent of the probability enclosed in the interval $z_T \pm 1.96\sigma_u$ as illustrated in Fig. 1.1. We can say then that there is only a 5 percent chance that the next observation will lie outside the given interval. What is our *forecast* of z_{T+1}? Clearly we have already provided much more information than could be provided by any single-point forecast. However, if we insist on designating a single number as our forecast, the mean of the distribution, namely z_T in this case, would seem to be the appropriate choice. It is, after all, the modal value for z_{T+1} if the distribution of z_{T+1} is symmetric as in the normal case, but more important the mean has the property of being the *minimum mean-square-error* forecast. That is, there is no other forecast conditioned just on the history of the series which can produce errors whose squared values will on the average be smaller.

Extension of the forecasting horizon to more than one period is straightforward. We note that the expected value of z_{T+2} given the history $(.\ .\ .\ ,z_{T-1},z_T)$ is

$$
\begin{aligned}
\hat{z}_T(2) = E(z_{T+2}|\ \ldots\ ,z_{T-1},z_T) &= E(z_T + u_{T+1} + u_{T+2}|\ \ldots\ ,z_{T-1},z_T) \\
&= z_T + E(u_{T+1}) + E(u_{T+2}) \\
&= z_T
\end{aligned}
\tag{1.1.23}
$$

so that our two-period-ahead forecast will also be just the present location of the series. The variance of z_{T+2} given the history is then

$$
\begin{aligned}
V(z_{T+2}|\ \ldots\ ,z_{T-1},z_T) &= V(z_T + u_{T+1} + u_{T+2}|\ \ldots\ ,z_{T-1},z_T) \\
&= 0 + \sigma_u{}^2 + \sigma_u{}^2 \\
&= 2\sigma_u{}^2
\end{aligned}
\tag{1.1.24}
$$

so the probability that z_{T+2} will lie outside the interval $z_T \pm 1.96 \sqrt{2}\sigma_u$ illustrated in Fig. 1.1 is only 5 percent. It is now clear that the forecast for all horizons will be just z_T and that the variance of successively more distant realizations simply $l\sigma_u{}^2$, where l is the forecast horizon. Since the corresponding standard deviation is $\sqrt{l}\sigma_u$, the size of confidence intervals will increase with the square root of horizon (see again Fig. 1.1, where successive intervals are indicated for $l = 1, \ldots , 5$)—equivalently we might say that our knowledge about the future decreases with the square root of horizon.

Clearly, z_{T+1} and z_{T+2} are nonindependent jointly distributed random variables since they share the term u_{T+1}. Their covariance is easily derived as follows [where $C(X, Y|W)$ denotes the covariance between random variables X and Y conditional on information W]:

$$C(z_{T+1}, z_{T+2} | \ldots , z_{T-1}, z_T)$$
$$= C[(z_T + u_{T+1}), (z_T + u_{T+1} + u_{T+2}) | \ldots , z_{T-1}, z_T]$$
$$= V(u_{T+1}) + C(u_{T+1}, u_{T+2})$$
$$= \sigma_u{}^2 \tag{1.1.25}$$

using the independence of u_{T+1} and u_{T+2}. If u_t is normal, then z_{T+1}, z_{T+2} are joint normally distributed and expressions (1.1.21) to (1.1.25) are sufficient to specify the joint distribution completely.

We note that a *drift* is easily built into the random-walk model by adding a constant, say, δ, each period; that is,

$$z_t = z_{t-1} + u_t + \delta \tag{1.1.26}$$

meaning that on the average the process will tend to move in the direction given by the sign of δ. The constant term does not affect expressions for variance and covariance—only the means are shifted by the amount of the constant each period. The reader is encouraged to check these conclusions as an exercise.

The random-walk model has provided a simple example of how a model of a time series as a stochastic process can be utilized to provide information about the future evolution of the time series. How can we determine that a particular stochastic process is appropriate as a model for a particular data series? This can be done primarily by studying the structure of correlation over time evident in the historical data; the techniques for accomplishing this will occupy much of our attention in later chapters.

1.2 Why Does Good Forecasting Pay Off?

It is an eminently plausible proposition that the better the forecasts available to management are, the better their performance as measured by the outcomes of decisions will be. The purpose of this section is to illustrate the validity of this proposition in a rather general setting of production planning.

Suppose a firm produces a product by using manufacturing processes that require enough time so that the sale price of the product may change materially between the time production begins and the time the output is ready for sale. The profits of the firm will then depend on the uncertain outcome of changes in price. We assume for simplicity that the final product is of such a nature that it cannot be stored for future sale. The effect of this assumption is that a "myopic" choice of production plans to maximize profit from each production cycle is also consistent with maximization of the present value of all future profits.

We divide time into periods equal to the length of the production cycle and denote by π_t profits in period t, by Q_t quantity produced during period t, by P_t price at which Q_t is sold at the end of the period, and by $C(Q)$ the cost of producing Q units. Profit is given by

$$\pi_t = P_t Q_t - C(Q_t) \tag{1.2.1}$$

and must be a random variable at the time of the production decision (i.e., the choice of Q_t) because P_t is at that time a random variable. Now firms in the industry are not completely ignorant about P_t; in particular, let us imagine that P_t may be decomposed into the components

$$P_t = \bar{P}_t + u_t + v_t \tag{1.2.2}$$

such that $\bar{P}_t$ is known to both the *identical* firms A and B, and u_t is known to B but not to A, and v_t is known to neither. We further assume that u_t and v_t are uncorrelated over time so that B cannot use its knowledge of u_t to predict v_t and that their mean values are zero. If we again refer to expected values as forecasts, then firm A's forecast of P_t is $\bar{P}_t$ (the expectation of P_t given only $\bar{P}_t$) and firm B's forecast is $(\bar{P}_t + u_t)$ (the expectation of P_t given both $\bar{P}_t$ and u_t). The extra information which B has means that its forecasts are more accurate since the errors made by A and B will be $(u_t + v_t)$ and v_t, respectively, which differ in mean square by the amount of the variance of u_t.

The objective of firm A is to maximize the expected average profits from the production process by choosing Q_t appropriately. Expected profit for A is given by

$$E_A(\pi_t) = E_A[(\bar{P}_t + u_t + v_t)Q_t - C(Q_t)]$$
$$= \bar{P}_t Q_t - C(Q_t) \tag{1.2.3}$$

Maximizing $E_A(\pi_t)$ with respect to Q_t, differentiating (1.2.3) with respect to Q_t, and setting the resulting expression equal to zero provides the optimal production run, denoted Q_t^A, as the solution to

$$\bar{P}_t = C'(Q_t^A) \tag{1.2.4}$$

where $C'(Q_t^A)$ denotes the derivative $dc(Q)/dQ$ evaluated at Q_t^A. Hence firm A chooses a level of output that equates marginal cost with its forecast of price or expected price. Firm B goes through similar calculations, except that since it knows u_t, the condition for maximum expected profit is

$$(\bar{P}_t + u_t) = C'(Q_t^B) \tag{1.2.5}$$

where $(\bar{P}_t + u_t)$ is B's forecast of price. Given the particular values of $\bar{P}_t$ and u_t for a period, firm B has therefore maximized expected profit, and this expected profit must be greater than that of A, which has proceeded in ignorance of u_t. Clearly then, over a number of periods the average profits of B will exceed those of A, although the particular values of $\bar{P}_t$, u_t, and v_t will vary.

To get an intuitive grasp on this result, note that if both firms had perfect foresight, they would solve the profit-maximization problem by using the price which will actually prevail in the next period. Neither firm, however, has such foresight, although the price forecast used by firm B is closer, on the average, to the actual future price. In other words, B comes closer to solving the "correct" maximization problem, that is, the one which both will wish they had been able to solve when they are confronted with the realized price next period.

We have assumed for the sake of exposition that A and B are identical firms, but this may also be regarded simply as a convenient device for examining the effect on the performance of a single firm of the quality of forecasts available to it. How much would the firm be willing to pay to have the better forecast? The most it would pay is the difference between the level of expected profit resulting from the production plan implied by (1.2.5) and that resulting from (1.2.4).

To see just what the effect of better forecasts on profits might be in a specific example, consider a firm with the quadratic cost function

$$C(Q_t) = \alpha + \beta Q_t + \gamma Q_t^2 \tag{1.2.6}$$

when α, β, and γ are fixed parameters. If the firm used the A forecast, then it would choose Q_t^A, satisfying

$$\bar{P}_t = \beta + 2\gamma Q_t^A \tag{1.2.7}$$

or

$$Q_t^A = \frac{\bar{P}_t - \beta}{2\gamma} \tag{1.2.8}$$

On the other hand, if it were in possession of additional information u_t, it would set production according to

$$(\bar{P}_t + u_t) = \beta + 2\gamma Q_t^B \tag{1.2.9}$$

or

$$Q_t^B = \frac{(\bar{P}_t + u_t) - \beta}{2\gamma} \tag{1.2.10}$$

Now, given the values of $\bar{P}_t$ and u_t in the current period, the difference between the expected profit associated with (1.2.10) and with (1.2.8) is

$$(\bar{P}_t + u_t)(Q_t{}^B - Q_t{}^A) - [C(Q_t{}^B) - C(Q_t{}^A)] = \frac{u_t{}^2}{4\gamma} \qquad (1.2.11)$$

which depends on the square of the additional piece of information u_t that is incorporated in forecast B.

Presumably the magnitude of u_t varies from period to period, and if we take the expectation of the profit differential (1.2.11) over the distribution from which u_t is drawn, we obtain

$$E\left(\frac{u_t{}^2}{4\gamma}\right) = \frac{V(u_t)}{4\gamma} \qquad (1.2.12)$$

that is, the average profit differential over time depends on the *variance* of u_t. Thus, the more the variation in $\bar{P}_t$ is due to variation in u_t, the more valuable it is to know u_t and to incorporate that knowledge in the production decision. It is interesting to note again that the variance of u_t is the difference between the variances of the forecast errors for A and B. Thus, the greater accuracy of forecast B as measured by forecast-error variance is reflected directly in the profit results of the firm. Finally, note that (1.2.12) gives the firm the value of having knowledge of u_t and is the maximum amount it would pay to acquire that information.

1.3 The Relationship between the Forecaster and the Decision-maker

Although the operational functions of forecasting and decision-making are often combined in a single individual, the use of technically sophisticated techniques generally results in their being delegated to separate units within an organization. The feasibility of this functional dichotomy becomes apparent when we consider the general structure of the decision process.

The ultimate outcome of a decision, as measured by some appropriate criterion, will depend on the setting chosen for the decision variable, say, D, and on the outcome of factors not under control of the decision-makers, say, Z. In the example of Sec. 1.2, results were measured in terms of profits, D was quantity produced, and Z was the price that confronted the firm when output was ready for sale. The outcome of the decision, its *utility* to the decision-maker, may be expressed then in general as a function of variables D and Z, say, $U(Z,D)$, and is a random variable at the time the decision is made simply because Z is a random variable. Now if the objective of the decision-maker is to maximize expected utility (or profit), the problem may be expressed as the maximization of

$$E[U(D,Z)] = \int U(D,Z)P(Z|I) \, dZ \qquad (1.3.1)$$

where $P(Z|I)$ is the probability density function for Z given the information set I that is available to the firm. In the example of Sec. 1.2, I consisted of $\bar{P}_t$ for firm A and of u_t as well as $\bar{P}_t$ for firm B. The role of the forecaster may be interpreted as that of supplying the density function $P(Z|I)$ and the role of the decision-maker as that of combining that input with the objectives of the firm or organization to arrive at an optimal setting for D.

In a fundamental sense, the information set I is also under control of the organization since it may purchase more or less information as it sees fit. For example, a firm might hire consultants, increase the sophistication of its forecasting effort, subscribe to advisory services, etc. Since the purchase of information is costly, I must be included as an argument in the criterion function, and expected utility becomes

$$E[U(D,I,Z)] = \int U(D,I,Z)P(Z|I) \, dP \qquad (1.3.2)$$

in which now both D and I are decision variables. Clearly, the optimal choices for D and I must be determined jointly, and hence at this level the forecasting and decision-making functions are interdependent.[1] It seems implausible, however, that the optimal setting of I will vary a great deal over time. The gain in expected profits resulting from the additional information available to firm B in the example of Sec. 1.2, given by expression (1.2.12), depended only on the variance of u_t and a parameter of the production-cost function, both of which are constant over time. Under such circumstances the level of expenditure on forecasting may be fixed, establishing the dichotomy between the jobs of the forecaster and the decision-maker on a routine basis. However, as the structure, environment, and objectives of the organization change and as new techniques of forecasting and new information sources become available, policy and strategy in the forecasting area should come under periodic review.

---

[1] The trade-off between forecast accuracy and the costs of alternative forecasts is discussed by Chambers, Mullich, and Smith (1971) in the context of sales forecasting in the glass industry. In chap. 8 of this text the trade-off is illustrated by comparison of the forecasting performance of a complex and expensive econometric model of the United States economy with that of simple and relatively inexpensive time series models.

Exercises

1.1 Confirm that the weights given past observations in the EWMA forecast sum to unity, that is,

$$(1 - \beta) + (1 - \beta)\beta + (1 - \beta)\beta^2 + \cdots = 1 \qquad \text{for } 0 < \beta < 1$$

(Note that $1 + \beta + \beta^2 + \cdots$ is a geometric series.)

1.2 Show that exponential smoothing forecasts for horizons one and two periods ahead are equivalent by substituting (1.1.12) into (1.1.13) for $l = 2$.

1.3 Defining the revision of EWMA forecasts from period $t - 1$ to period t as the change $[\hat{z}_t(1) - \hat{z}_{t-1}(1)]$, using expression (1.1.15), show that this revision is a constant fraction of the most recent forecast error. Why does this result generalize to the revision of forecasts of any horizon?

1.4 Starting at $z_0 = 100$, generate a realization $z_1, \ldots, z_{20}$ for the random-walk model (1.1.18) with u_t distributed according to (1.1.19). A coin will serve as your random-number generator. Graph the realization. Provide forecasts of $z_{21}, \ldots, z_{25}$. What is the probability that z_{25} will lie *within* $z_{20} \pm 6$? *Within* $z_{20} \pm 5$?

1.5 Rederive expressions (1.1.21) to (1.1.25) for the case of a random walk with drift as given by (1.1.26).

1.6 The film division of Acme Chemical Corporation produces a line of high-speed films used in industrial applications. Deterioration of the emulsion on the film precludes storage for more than a few weeks. The film is produced in monthly batches and sold in a competitive market where price often varies enough to affect profitability materially. The cost structure of the film division is approximately

$$C = \$10{,}000 + \$(10Q) + \$(.001Q^2) \text{ per month}$$

where Q is the number of film packs produced.

Using current price-forecasting procedures, the film division in a particular month regards expected price to be \$20 per film pack. *If* more sophisticated techniques were employed in price forecasting, the firm *would* regard expected price to be \$18 in that particular month.

(a) Evaluate the expected profit of the film division for the month in question under each of the two alternative sets of expectations.

(b) Derive the optimal production runs implied by each of the expected prices, assuming that the objective of the division is to maximize expected profits. Sketch the marginal-cost schedule, and show how your solutions correspond to the intersections of the marginal-cost schedule and the two levels of expected price.

(c) Given the forecast that would be provided by the more sophisticated technique, what would be the expected profit resulting from the production plan associated with the less sophisticated technique? What is the difference between the expected profit just computed and that resulting from the production plan associated with the more sophisticated forecast?

(*d*) If the average over time of the square of the difference between the two price forecasts were $3, what is the most Acme Chemical Corporation would pay per month to have the more sophisticated technique in use at the film division?

Additional Readings

Brown, R. G.: "Smoothing, Forecasting, and Prediction of Discrete Time Series," Prentice-Hall, Inc., Englewood Cliffs, N.J., 1962. The primary reference on exponential smoothing.

Chambers, J. C., S. K. Mullich, and D. D. Smith: How to Choose the Right Forecasting Technique, *Harvard Business Review*, **49**:45–74 (July–August 1971). A review and evaluation of alternative forecasting techniques and their relative costs in the context of sales forecasting in the glass industry.

Fama, E. F.: Random Walks in Stock Market Prices, *Financial Analysts Journal*, pp. 3–7 (September–October 1965). A discussion of the random-walk model of stock-price behavior, the empirical evidence supporting it, and its implications for attempts by "chartists" to forecast price movements.

Theil, H.: "Applied Economic Forecasting," North-Holland Publishing Company, Amsterdam, 1966. An introduction to fundamental concepts in forecasting is given in chap. 1, pp. 1–14, with particular reference to regression analysis.

2
Fundamental Concepts in Time Series Analysis

The cornerstone of time series analysis is the concept of the sequence of observations making up a time series as a realization of jointly distributed random variables. That is, the sequence of observations $z_1, \ldots, z_N$ taken at the discrete and equally spaced time intervals $1, \ldots, N$ is thought of as being drawn from a probability distribution, say,

$$p_{1,\ldots,N}(z_1, \ldots, z_N)$$

where $p(\ )$ is a probability density function, the subscripts $1, \ldots, N$ on p indicate that the distribution is associated with those time periods and the random variables in question are $z_1, \ldots, z_N$.

Our ultimate objective will be to use this joint distribution to make probability statements about future observations. For example, suppose that we knew the joint distribution function for $N = T + 1$ and that we were at time T having observed $z_1, \ldots, z_T$. Then from knowledge of $p_{1,\ldots,T+1}(z_1, \ldots, z_{T+1})$ and our knowledge of the observed values of $z_1, \ldots, z_T$ we would be able to construct the *conditional* distribution function for the *future* observation z_{T+1}, namely,

$$p_{T+1|1, \ldots, T}(z_{T+1}|z_1, \ldots, z_T)$$

where, as in Chap. 1, the vertical line precedes the conditioning information. In other words, the information that we have about the relationship between $z_1, \ldots, z_T$ and z_{T+1} from their joint distribution function permits us to use $(z_1, \ldots, z_T)$ to make statements about the likely outcome of z_{T+1}.

Although it may seem difficult to envision a concrete application of such a procedure, we have in fact already carried one out in the random-walk example of Chap. 1. There we constructed the first and second moments of the conditional distribution $p_{T+1,T+2|1, \ldots, T}(z_{T+1}, z_{T+2}|z_1, \ldots, z_T)$, the conditional expectations of z_{T+1} and z_{T+2} and their conditional variances and covariance, and showed how these conditional moments imply forecasts and confidence intervals for z_{T+1} and z_{T+2}. The information which allowed us to do this was knowledge that future observations would be generated by the particular stochastic process given by (1.1.17). This illustrates a basic feature of the approach: We shall almost never actually bother to write down a specific joint distribution function; rather, we shall find that it is much easier to deal directly with the *mechanism* of the stochastic process generating our observations and to derive from it the conditional distribution of future realizations. In practice, of course, we must first attempt to infer from the data what mechanism it is that generated the data. Thus the past history of the time series is called upon to do double duty: First, it must inform us about the particular mechanism which describes its evolution through time, and, second, it allows us to put that mechanism to use in forecasting the future.

2.1 The Concept of Stationarity

The notion of a joint distribution function for a time series is nevertheless essential for understanding time series analysis, for example, in grasping the important concept of *stationarity*.[1] To motivate our concern with stationar-

---

[1] In the discussion which follows it is very important that the reader be familiar with the concepts of joint, marginal, and conditional distributions. Very briefly, if x and y are jointly distributed random variables and if the variables are continuous, $p(x^*, y^*)$ is the probability density at the point $x = x^*$, $y = y^*$. Or, if the variables assume only discrete values, the probability of the joint event $x = x^*$, $y = y^*$. The marginal distribution of either x or y is the probability distribution of one without regard to the particular outcome of the other, that is, is the marginal distribution $p(x)$, which is given by

$$p(x) = \int p(x,y) \, dy$$

in the continuous case, or

$$p(x) = \sum_y p(x,y)$$

in the discrete case [where Σ_y denotes summation of $p(x,y)$ over all values of y]. The con-

ity, consider the problem of describing the first two moments of the joint distribution function: the means, variances, and covariances of the random variables $z_1, \ldots, z_N$. This means may be displayed simply as the vector of N individual expected values, namely,

$$(Ez_1, \ldots, Ez_N) \tag{2.1.1}$$

The variances and covariances may be displayed in a symmetric matrix of N^2 elements as follows:

$$\begin{bmatrix} V(z_1) & C(z_1z_2) & \cdots & C(z_1z_N) \\ C(z_2z_1) & V(z_2) & C(z_2z_3) & C(z_2z_N) \\ & \cdot & & \\ & & \cdot & \\ & & & \cdot \\ & & & \cdot \\ & & \cdot & \\ C(z_Nz_1) & \cdots \cdots \cdots & V(z_N) \end{bmatrix} \tag{2.1.2}$$

We see that in order to describe just the first two moments of the joint distribution, we already require, in general, N expectations and $\frac{1}{2}(N^2 + N)$ variances and covariances. [Note that although there are N^2 elements in matrix (2.1.2), only $1(N^2 + N)$ of them are distinct because of the symmetry of the matrix.] In the practical situation where observations $z_1, \ldots, z_N$ are in hand and we wish to *infer* their joint distribution, any attempt to estimate the $\frac{3}{2}N + \frac{1}{2}N^2$ elements of (2.1.1) and (2.1.2) is clearly hopeless. Some simplifying structure must be imposed on the joint distribution if it is to be the basis for an operational forecasting technique.

Considerable simplification is achieved if we require that the joint distribution be invariant with regard to a displacement in time; that is,

$$p(z_t, \ldots, z_{t+k}) = p(z_{t+m}, \ldots, z_{t+k+m}) \tag{2.1.3}$$

---

ditional distributions $p(x|y)$ or $p(y|x)$ are the distributions of one of the random variables given a particular outcome for the other. Thus, in the continuous case the distribution of x conditional on $y = y^*$ is

$$p(x|y^*) = \frac{p(x,y^*)}{\int p(x,y^*) \, dx}$$

and in the discrete case

$$p(x|y^*) = \frac{p(x,y^*)}{\Sigma_x \, p(x,y^*)}$$

Suggestions for background reading on the basic concepts of joint distributions are given in the Additional Readings at the end of this chapter.

chap. 2 fundamental concepts in time series analysis

where t is any point in time and k and m are any pair of integers. The subscripts on the distribution function have been dropped since location in time is no longer relevant. The property defined by (2.1.3) is known as *stationarity*.[1] To demonstrate the simplification effected by stationarity and its implications for the behavior of the time series, we note, for k equal to zero, (2.1.3) becomes

$$p(z_t) = p(z_{t+m}) \qquad m = \pm 1, \pm 2, \ldots \tag{2.1.4}$$

that is, the *marginal* distribution functions for any two observations are the same. It follows directly that their expected values are the same

$$E(z_t) = E(z_{t+m}) \tag{2.1.5}$$

and that their variances are the same

$$V(z_t) = V(z_{t+m}) \tag{2.1.6}$$

Similarly, for $k = 1$ we have

$$p(z_t, z_{t+1}) = p(z_{t+m}, z_{t+m+1}) \qquad m = \pm 1, \pm 2, \ldots \tag{2.1.7}$$

which means that the covariances between z_t and z_{t+1} and between z_{t+m} z_{t+m+1} must be the same. These covariances may be denoted simply by γ_1 since their value depends only on the fact that the observations in question are separated by one period. Thus,

$$C(z_t, z_{t+1}) = C(z_{t+m}, z_{t+m+1}) = \gamma_1 \tag{2.1.8}$$

Similarly, for any pair of observations separated by, say, j periods, we have

$$p(z_t, z_{t+j}) = p(z_{t+m}, z_{t+m+j}) \tag{2.1.9}$$

and therefore the covariance between any such pair depends only on j; that is,

$$C(z_t, z_{t+j}) = C(z_{t+m}, z_{t+m+j}) = \gamma_j \tag{2.1.10}$$

We shall refer to γ_j as the *autocovariance* at lag j (the prefix "auto" is used because it is the covariance between different observations in the same series).

---

[1] More precisely, (2.1.3) defines *strict* stationarity. Weaker forms of stationarity require only that moments through some specified order be invariant over time. For example, covariance stationarity requires only that the mean and covariance matrix be invariant. Of course, covariance stationarity implies strict stationarity if the joint distribution is normal.

Now if we denote $E(z_t)$ in general by μ and $V(z_t)$ by γ_0, then the first and second moments (2.1.1) and (2.1.2) become simply

$$(\mu, \ldots, \mu) \tag{2.1.11}$$

and

$$\begin{bmatrix} \gamma_0 & \gamma_1 & \cdots & \gamma_{N-1} \\ \gamma_1 & \gamma_0 & \gamma_1 & \cdots & \gamma_{N-2} \\ & & \cdot & & \\ & & & \cdot & \\ & & & & \cdot \\ & & & & \cdot \\ & & & & \cdot \\ \gamma_{N-1} & & \cdots & & \gamma_0 \end{bmatrix} \tag{2.1.12}$$

which involve now "only" $N+1$ distinct terms, which is still quite a few! Clearly, we must find a way to reduce the dimensionality of the problem even further—that problem is set aside for Chap. 3.

Meanwhile, we note that stationarity has a number of general implications for the behavior of a time series. The condition that the expectation of z_t does not depend on t but rather is a constant serves to locate the time series in space in the neighborhood of that mean value. The series will take trips away from the mean, but it will return repeatedly during its history. One way to visualize this is to imagine that a stationary stochastic process is evolving over time and you are asked to guess the probable value of, say, z_{2068} without having seen the previous history of the series. Your best guess would clearly be μ; that is, it would be sensible to start looking for z_{2068} in the neighborhood of its expectation. In the case that z_t is normally distributed [that is, $p(z_1, \ldots, z_N)$ is a multivariate normal distribution], you could state further that there is a probability of only .05 that z_{2068} will be found outside the interval $\mu \pm 1.96\sqrt{\gamma_0}$ since $\sqrt{\gamma_0}$ is the standard deviation of z_{2068}. Thus stationarity in the technical sense implies stationarity in the intuitive sense of locating the process within a region from which it will only rarely depart.

Looking ahead to Figs. 3.2 to 3.4, 3.6, and 3.7 (Chap. 3), we see displayed fairly long realizations of various stationary stochastic processes, all of which manifest an affinity to a mean value. Figure 2.1 is the plot of 80 observations on quarterly sales of an established line of machine tools (tool sales series A). Although we would have no strong prior reasons to expect such a series to be stationary, casual visual assessment certainly reveals no tendency to wander away from its historical mean of about $666 thousand. On the other hand, quarterly sales of another product line (tool sales series B plotted in Fig. 2.2) has exhibited what might be described as a distinct change in level over the

figure 2.1 Tool sales series A in thousands of dollars, 80 quarters.

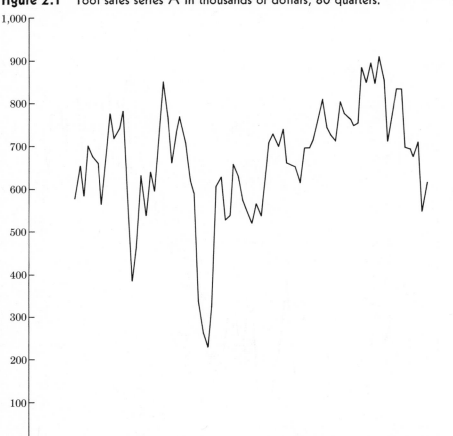

sample period—compelling us to characterize its behavior as nonstationary. Finally, the unemployment rate in the United States 1948–01 through 1966–04 plotted in Fig. 2.3 appears to fluctuate around a historical mean of about 4.6 percent. Our economic knowledge about the nature of this series would lead us to expect that it would behave in an essentially stationary fashion, albeit with fairly lengthy trips from the mean.

2.2 Autocorrelation

Another implication of stationarity which has an important interpretation in terms of the behavior of a time series derives from the fact that the autocovari-

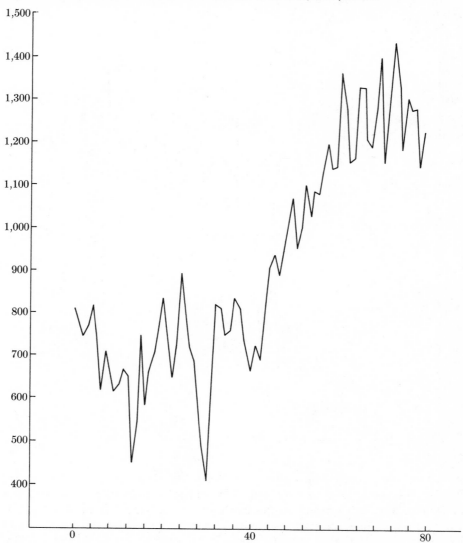

figure 2.2 Tool sales series B in thousands of dollars, 80 quarters.

ance between any two observations depends *only* on the number of time periods separating them. Recalling the definition of autocovariance, we have

$$\gamma_j = C(z_t, z_{t+j})$$
$$= E[(z_t - Ez_t)(z_{t+j} - Ez_{t+j})] = E[(z_t - \mu)(z_{t+j} - \mu)] \qquad (2.2.1)$$

chap. 2 fundamental concepts in time series analysis

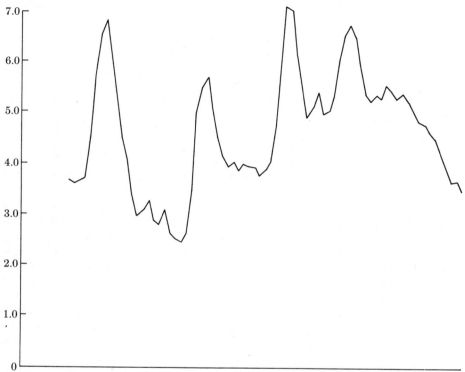

which says that the covariance between observations z_t and z_{t+j} is the *expected* product of their deviations from the mean of the process. In other words, if a higher-than-average observation *tends* to be followed by another higher-than-average observation j periods later, and likewise for lower-than-average observations, the autocovariance between z_t and z_{t+j} is positive. But if a higher-than-average observation tends to be followed by a lower-than-average observation j periods later and vice versa, then the autocovariance is negative.

For example, it is obvious from inspection of Figs. 3.2 and 3.6 that γ_1 is positive in both cases since successive observations are most often in the same side of the mean. In Fig. 3.6 it also appears that γ_2, γ_3, and γ_4 are positive because once the process has crossed the mean it tends to stay there for a while. The signs of the autocovariances become less apparent from mere inspection as we consider successively longer lags. For Fig. 3.2 the tendency to persist on one side of the mean is so short-lived that the signs of γ_2, γ_3, and so forth, are not at all obvious from inspection. We shall see in Chap. 3 that all the γ_j of the latter series except for γ_1 are in fact zero. If the sign of γ_1 were negative for some process, its behavior clearly would be marked by frequent passages across the mean, high observations followed by low and vice versa. This kind of pattern is evident in Figs. 3.4 and 3.7. Our two economic series, tool sales series A and the unemployment rate, clearly have autocovariances which are positive out to quite long lags; that is, each takes rather lengthy trips away from the mean.

It is obvious that the autocovariance structure of a time series will play a crucial role in the time series analysis approach to forecasting. For series such as tool sales series A, the unemployment rate, and the ones in Figs. 3.2 and 3.6, we would clearly predict that z_{T+1} would be above the mean μ if we had observed that z_T was above the mean. In comparison, for the series illustrated in Figs. 3.4 and 3.7 a value of z_T above the mean would certainly lead us to predict a value below the mean for z_{T+1}.

The fact that the autocovariances γ_j seem to determine the appearance of a time series suggests that a stationary process will display the same general pattern of behavior no matter when we observe it. The realization $(z_{100}, \ldots, z_{200})$ will not be exactly the same as $(z_{800}, \ldots, z_{900})$, but its general appearance will be very similar. Thus in a probabilistic sense history repeats itself in stationary time series. It might seem appropriate then to characterize a process simply by displaying the set of covariances $\gamma_0, \gamma_1, \ldots$. For purposes of comparing different series, however, this is not entirely satisfactory since a difference in the dispersion of the processes, perhaps caused by different scales of measurement, would lead to very different autocovariances. For example, if sales are measured in hundreds of thousands instead of millions of dollars, all second moments are increased by a factor of 100. Because variance is a measure of dispersion, comparability is achieved if we standardize the autocovariances by dividing them all by γ_0, that is, by transforming them to correlations. Such correlations are referred to as *autocorrelations*. If we denote the correlation between z_t and z_{t+j} by ρ_j, then the set of autocorrelations, often referred to collectively as the *autocorrelation function*, is given by

$$\rho_0 \equiv \frac{\gamma_0}{\gamma_0} = 1$$

$$\rho_1 \equiv \frac{\gamma_1}{\gamma_0} \qquad\qquad (2.2.2)$$

$$\rho_2 \equiv \frac{\gamma_2}{\gamma_0}$$

$$\cdot \ \cdot \ \cdot \ \cdot \ \cdot \ \cdot$$

A graph of the autocorrelation function is called the *correlogram*. The first two correlograms displayed in Fig. 3.1 are those of the processes that generated the realizations in Figs. 3.2 and 3.4, respectively. Similarly, the first two correlograms in Fig. 3.5 correspond to Figs. 3.6 and 3.7, respectively. These correlograms confirm our visual assessment of the autocovariance or, equivalently, autocorrelation structure in each case.

2.3 Estimation of the Autocorrelation Function from Sample Data

Estimates of the autocorrelations of any time series are readily computed from a data sample, applying first the sample analog of Eq. (2.2.1) to obtain estimates of the autocovariances. A natural estimate of γ_j, the *expected* product of the deviations of z_t and z_{t+j} from the mean of the series, is the *average* product of the deviations of z_t and z_{t+j} from the *sample* mean. Denoting this estimate of γ_j by c_j, we have then from data $z_1, \ldots, z_T$ the estimates

$$c_j = \frac{1}{T} \sum_{t=1}^{T-j} [(z_t - \bar{z})(z_{t+j} - \bar{z})] \qquad j = 1, 2, \ldots \dagger \tag{2.3.1}$$

where $\bar{z}$ denotes the sample mean

$$\bar{z} = \frac{1}{T} \sum_{t=1}^{T} z_t \tag{2.3.2}$$

and Σ denotes the summation of the terms indicated. Using relations (2.2.2), estimates of the autocorrelations (denoted γ_j) are given then by

$$r_j = \frac{c_j}{c_0} \qquad j = 1, 2, \ldots \tag{2.3.3}$$

A graph of the r_j is referred to as the *sample correlogram*.

As we shall see in later chapters, the sample correlogram serves much the same function in time series analysis as does the histogram in sampling problems; namely, it is not the final objective of the analysis but rather provides the basis for choice of a model, in this case a stochastic process, suitable to the data at hand.

2.4 Analysis of Nonstationary Time Series

Finally, we should note that many time series of interest for operational forecasting are quite obviously nonstationary. For example, stock prices certainly

---

† Some authors have preferred to divide the sum of cross products by $T - j$, the number of terms in the sum. Clearly, in large samples, choice between divisors T and $T - j$ will make little difference.

display no affinity for a mean value; instead, they appear to wander freely in either direction. Likewise, many output measures, such as sales of a firm or gross national product (GNP), tend to display such behavior. Are we left defenseless under such circumstances? Definitely not. Fortunately, the differences, that is, successive changes, in many nonstationary series are stationary. For example, the random-walk model accounts very well for stock-price behavior, and the differences $(z_t - z_{t-1})$ are certainly stationary since [from (1.1.17)] they are just the independently distributed random steps generated identically through time according to (1.1.19). In Chap. 3 we shall study a class of stationary stochastic processes that is proving to be very useful in forecasting a wide range of stationary time series, and in Chap. 4 we shall show how the same class of processes may be applied to nonstationary time series if we assume that the time series of differences is stationary.

Exercises

2.1 List three time series that are of an economic nature and could be characterized as stationary in their behavior. List three that would seem to be nonstationary.

2.2 Stationarity implies that the covariance between any two observations depends only on the span of time between them. Using the definition of autocovariance (2.2.1), show that in particular it does not matter whether we look backward or forward in time; that is,

$$C(z_t, z_{t+j}) = C(z_t, z_{t-j}) = \gamma_j$$

How does this imply that the autocorrelation function is symmetric; that is,

$$\rho_j = \rho_{-j}$$

2.3 Consider the stochastic process

$$z_t = u_t$$

where u_t is drawn independently each period from

$$u_t = \begin{cases} +1 & \text{with probability } \frac{1}{2} \\ -1 & \text{with probability } \frac{1}{2} \end{cases}$$

(a) Is the process z_t stationary? Why?
(b) What are the values of the parameters μ, γ_0, γ_1, and γ_j, with $j > 1$, for this process?

2.4 Let u_t be defined as in Exercise 2.3, and let the observed series z_t be generated according to

$$z_t = u_t + u_{t-1}$$

(a) Is z_t stationary? Why?
(b) Derive the mean of the process μ.
(c) Derive the second moments γ_0, γ_1, and γ_j for $j > 1$ by direct application of the definition of autocovariance (2.2.1), substituting $(u_t + u_{t-1})$ for z_t and making use of the fact that since $E(u_t) = 0$, we have $E(u_t^2) = V(u_t)$.

chap. 2 fundamental concepts in time series analysis

(d) Write down the autocorrelation function of the process. Sketch the correlogram.

2.5 Rework Exercise 2.4 under the assumption that the u_t are normally distributed with mean 0 and variance 4.

2.6 Acme Chemical Corporation finds that monthly sales of its paint division are well described by the model

$$z_t = u_t - u_{t-1} + 6$$

where z_t is sales in millions of dollars and the u_t are generated as in Exercise 2.5.

(a) Is this sales series stationary? Why?

(b) Derive the mean of the process μ.

(c) Derive the second moments γ_0, γ_1, and γ_j for $j > 1$ by direct application of definition (2.2.1).

(d) Write down autocorrelation function of the process. Sketch the correlogram.

(e) Use a coin to generate discretely distributed values of u_t, letting $u_t = 2$ for a head and $u_t = -2$ for a tail. From a sample of such u_t's, produce an artificial realization of sales $(z_1, \ldots, z_{10})$.

(f) For the observations generated in part (e), compute the *sample* autocovariances for $j = 0, 1, \ldots, 4$ and the *sample* autocorrelations for $j = 0, 1, \ldots, 4$. Sketch the sample correlogram.

2.7 The following data are annual sales of Acme Chemical Corporation in millions of dollars:

Period	Sales
1	695
2	691
3	687
4	687
5	690
6	689
7	694

Compute $c_0, \ldots, c_4, r_0, \ldots, r_4$, and graph the sample correlogram for lags 1 through 4.

Additional Readings

Box, G. E. P., and G. M. Jenkins: "Time Series Analysis, Forecasting and Control," Holden-Day, Inc., San Francisco, 1970. The concepts of stationarity and autocorrelation are discussed in chap. 2, sec. 2.1.

Freeman, H.: "Introduction to Statistical Inference," Addison-Wesley Publishing Company, Inc., Reading, Mass., 1963. Chapters 2 through 5 are suggested as a review of basic concepts in probability theory and an introduction to joint distributions.

Hogg, R. V., and A. T. Craig: "Introduction to Mathematical Statistics," 3d ed., The Macmillan Company, New York, 1970. Chapters 1 and 2 review basic concepts in probability theory and give an introduction to joint distributions.

3
Models
for
Stationary
Time Series

From studying the concept of a joint distribution for the observations from a stationary time series in Chap. 2, it became apparent that the number of parameters required to describe just the mean and variance of the distribution generally exceeds the number of observations. Since in practice the parameters of the distribution must be inferred from the data at hand, it is clear that operationality requires the imposition of some simplifying structure so that statistical inference is confined to only a few fundamental parameters. This will be accomplished by postulating that the data have been generated by a linear stochastic process of autoregressive, moving-average, or mixed auto-regressive–moving-average form. These processes are capable of accounting for a wide range of patterns of autocorrelation and therefore a wide range of behavior in stationary time series. Their flexibility makes them a very useful class of models for many time series encountered in practice.

3.1 Discrete Linear Stochastic Processes

All the models for stationary time series that we shall be studying belong to the general class of discrete linear stochastic processes. A stochastic process is a discrete linear process if each observation z_t may be expressed in the form

$$z_t = \mu + u_t + \Psi_1 u_{t-1} + \Psi_2 u_{t-2} + \cdots \qquad (3.1.1)$$

where μ and the Ψ_i are fixed parameters and the time series $(\ldots, u_{t-1}, u_t, \ldots)$ is a sequence of *identically* and *independently* distributed random disturbances with mean zero and variance σ_u^2, often referred to as *white noise*. The process (3.1.1) is discrete because observations z_t are taken at discrete and equally spaced intervals and linear because the z_t are a linear combination of the current and past disturbances.

Given a particular linear process, that is, particular values for the parameters, how can we verify that the process is stationary? First of all, the mean and variance-covariance matrix of the process must exist and be invariant with respect to time. The mean of the process is simply given by

$$E(z_t) = \mu + E(u_t + \Psi_1 u_{t-1} + \cdots) \qquad (3.1.2)$$

Now, it is tempting to evaluate the expectation of the infinite sum by taking the sum of expectations of individual terms as one would take the expectation of a finite sum of random variables. This, however, is not a generally valid procedure; rather, it requires (from integral calculus) that

$$\sum_{i=0}^{\infty} \Psi_i = K \qquad (3.1.3)$$

where Σ = summation operator
$\quad \Psi_0 = 1$
$\quad K$ = some finite number

If condition (3.1.3) is satisfied, then the summation $\Sigma_{i=0}^{\infty} \Psi_i$ is said to converge and the mean of the process is

$$E(z_t) = \mu \qquad (3.1.4)$$

If we observed the evolution of the process over time, we would notice that it fluctuated around the value μ, taking trips away from that value but always returning to that neighborhood. Note that the mean of the process does not depend on t, which satisfies one requirement of stationarity.

The variance of the process is easily derived directly from its definition as follows:

$$\gamma_0 = E[z_t - E(z_t)]^2$$
$$= E[u_t + \Psi_1 u_{t-1} + \cdots]^2$$
$$= E[u_t^2 + \Psi_1^2 u_{t-1}^2 + \cdots]$$
$$\quad + E \text{ (cross-product terms)}$$
$$= \sigma_u^2 \sum_{i=0}^{\infty} \Psi_i^2 \qquad (3.1.5)$$

The derivation is meaningful only if the mean of the process exists and the sum $\Sigma_{i=0}^{\infty} \Psi_i^2$ converges. It is important to see why only the square terms contribute to the final answer and the expectation of the cross-product terms is zero. Since the mean of any u_{t-i} is zero, $E(u_{t-i}^2)$ is the variance of u_{t-i}, namely, σ_u^2, and $E(u_{t-i}u_{t-j})$, when $i \neq j$, is the covariance between u_{t-i} and u_{t-j} and therefore zero by the independence of the disturbances.

The covariance between z_t and, say, z_{t-j}, is easily derived in a similar fashion; namely,

$$\begin{aligned}
\gamma_j &= E[z_t - E(z_t)][z_{t-j} - E(z_{t-j})] \\
&= E[(u_t + \Psi_1 u_{t-1} + \cdots)(u_{t-j} + \Psi_1 u_{t-j-1} + \cdots)] \\
&= E[(\Psi_j u_{t-j}^2) + (\Psi_1 \Psi_{j+1} u_{t-j-1}^2) + \cdots)] \\
&\quad + E \text{ (cross-product terms)} \\
&= \sigma_u^2 (\Psi_j + \Psi_1 \Psi_{j+1} + \cdots) \\
&= \sigma_u^2 \sum_{i=0}^{\infty} \Psi_i \Psi_{i+j}
\end{aligned} \tag{3.1.6}$$

which is meaningful only if the sum $\Sigma_{i=0}^{\infty} \Psi_i \Psi_{i+j}$ exists. Note that neither the variance nor the covariances depend on t, again a requirement of stationarity.

A few simple examples will clarify the points made so far. Consider the process

$$z_t = \mu + u_t + \phi u_{t-1} + \phi^2 u_{t-2} + \cdots \tag{3.1.7}$$

where ϕ is some fraction, that is, $|\phi| < 1$. Does (3.1.7) satisfy the stationarity condition $\Sigma_{i=0}^{\infty} \Psi_i = K$? Yes, it does since $\Psi_i = \phi^i$ and

$$\sum_{i=0}^{\infty} \Psi_i = \sum_{i=0}^{\infty} \phi^i = \frac{1}{1 - \phi} \tag{3.1.8}$$

The mean of the process then is μ. The variance is readily shown to be

$$\gamma^2 = \frac{\sigma_u^2}{1 - \phi^2} \tag{3.1.9}$$

and similarly the autocovariances are

$$\gamma_j = \frac{\phi^j \sigma_u^2}{1 - \phi^2} \tag{3.1.10}$$

Now suppose that the absolute value of ϕ is 1 or greater, say, equal to 1 exactly, so that (letting $\mu = 0$ for convenience),

$$z_t = u_t + u_{t-1} + u_{t-2} + \cdots \tag{3.1.11}$$

Clearly, the process is nonstationary since the sum $\Sigma_{i=0}^{\infty} \Psi_i = (1 + 1 + \cdots)$ does not converge, and it is also clear that there is no point in attempting to compute variance or autocovariances since $\Sigma_{i=0}^{\infty} \Psi_i \Psi_{i+j} = (1 + 1 + \cdots)$ also does not converge. A realization of this process will take ever more lengthy trips from any given reference point and exhibit no affinity for a particular neighborhood. We have seen this process before in slightly different guise; namely, it is the random-walk process (1.1.17). The equivalence is apparent from the substitutions

$$z_t = z_{t-1} + u_t$$
$$z_t = u_t + u_{t-1} + z_{t-2} \tag{3.1.12}$$
$$z_t = u_t + u_{t-1} + u_{t-2} + z_{t-3}$$

and so forth, which if continued indefinitely would produce (3.1.11). The behavior of this process was illustrated in Fig. 1.1.

3.2 Moving-average Processes

Although any linear process may be written in the general form (3.1.1), we shall only be interested for practical purposes in processes for which the Ψ_i weights may be expressed in terms of a small number of fundamental parameters. One way this may occur is when $\Psi_i = 0$ for $i > q$; that is,

$$z_t = \mu + u_t + \Psi_1 u_{t-1} + \cdots + \Psi_q u_{t-q} \tag{3.2.1}$$

which is referred to as a moving-average process of order q because the observations are a moving average in the disturbances reaching back for q periods. In order to distinguish the moving-average case from linear processes in general, there is a shift in notation for the weights; namely,

$$z_t = \mu + u_t - \theta_1 u_{t-1} - \cdots - \theta_q u_{t-q} \tag{3.2.2}$$

and the minus signs are introduced by convention. A convenient shorthand to denote the qth-order–moving-average process is MA (q). Note that the process is fully described by $q + 2$ parameters: σ_u^2, μ, θ_1, $\ldots$, θ_q. Any moving-average process is stationary since the condition $\Sigma_{i=0}^{\infty} \Psi_i$ translates into $1 - \Sigma_{i=0}^{\infty} \theta_i$, which must always be finite because there are a finite number of terms in the sum.

the first-order–moving-average process

As an example, consider the very important first-order–moving-average, or MA (1), process, which is

$$z_t = \mu + u_t - \theta_1 u_{t-1} \tag{3.2.3}$$

The mean of the process is

$$E(z_t) = \mu + E(u_t) - \theta_1 E(u_{t-1})$$
$$= \mu \tag{3.2.4}$$

and the variance is

$$\gamma_0 = E(u_t - \theta_1 u_{t-1})^2$$
$$= \sigma_u^2 (1 + \theta_1^2) \tag{3.2.5}$$

The autocovariance of lag 1 period is

$$\gamma_1 = E[(u_t - \theta_1 u_{t-1})(u_{t-1} - \theta_1 u_{t-2})]$$
$$= \sigma_u^2 (-\theta_1) \tag{3.2.6}$$

autocovariances for lags greater than one period are

$$\gamma_j = E(u_t - \theta_1 u_{t-1})(u_{t-j} - \theta_1 u_{t-j-1})$$
$$= 0 \qquad j > 1 \tag{3.2.7}$$

and the autocorrelation function is just

$$\rho_1 = \frac{-\theta_1}{1 + \theta_1^2} \tag{3.2.8}$$
$$\rho_j = 0 \qquad j > 1$$

Note that (3.2.4) to (3.2.7) are just the expressions previously obtained for moments of linear processes, except that the Ψ_i weights take on the values $\Psi_1 = -\theta_1$, $\Psi_j = 0$ for $j > 1$.

A very important property of MA (1) is apparent from the autocorrelation function, namely, that its "memory" is only one period long. A given observation, say, z_{53}, is correlated with its predecessor z_{52} and its successor z_{54} but not with any other members of the series because the moving average carries along only one previous disturbance. Thus, z_{53} shares u_{52} with z_{52} and u_{53} with z_{54} but has no disturbances in common with any other z_t.

As a specific illustration, let $\mu = 5$, $\sigma_u^2 = 1$ and $\theta_1 = -.9$ so that

$$z_t = 5 + u_t + .9u_{t-1} \tag{3.2.9}$$

Then

$$E(z_t) = 5$$
$$\gamma_0 = 1.81$$
$$\gamma_1 = .9 \tag{3.2.10}$$
$$\gamma_j = 0 \qquad j > 1$$
$$\rho_1 = .50$$
$$\rho_j = 0 \qquad j > 1$$

figure 3.1 Autocorrelation functions of three moving-average processes.

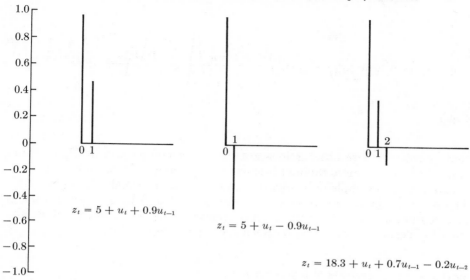

$$z_t = 5 + u_t + 0.9u_{t-1}$$

$$z_t = 5 + u_t - 0.9u_{t-1}$$

$$z_t = 18.3 + u_t + 0.7u_{t-1} - 0.2u_{t-2}$$

The correlogram for this process is plotted in Fig. 3.1 and consists of a single spike equal to .50 at $j = 1$. Figure 3.2 shows a realization of this process using disturbances drawn independently from a normal distribution with mean 0 and variance 1. It is instructive to observe how high observations tend to be followed by high observations and low observations by low observations although, as we would expect from the correlogram, there is no very long-lived persistence on one or the other side of the mean. The disturbances

figure 3.2 Realization of the process $z_t = 5 + u_t + .9u_{t-1}$, $\sigma_u^2 = 1$.

figure 3.3 Disturbances u_t corresponding to realization of Fig. 3.2.

that generated these observations are shown for comparison in Fig. 3.3 and indeed look much more random because they are not autocorrelated.

Altering the example only slightly, let $\theta_1 = +.9$, in which case $\rho_1 = -.50$. The correlogram for this process is illustrated in Fig. 3.1, and a realization is pictured in Fig. 3.4. Note the choppy appearance of the series, which results from the negative correlation between successive observations.

moving-average processes of higher order

The moments of any MA (q) process are easily obtained by direct application of formulas (3.1.4) to (3.1.6); that is, the mean is given by

$$E(z_t) = \mu \qquad (3.2.11)$$

and the variance by

$$\gamma_0 = \sigma_u^2 \sum_{i=0}^{q} \theta_i^2 \qquad (3.2.12)$$

figure 3.4 Realization of the process $z_t = 5 + u_t - .9u_{t-1}$, $\sigma_u^2 = 1$.

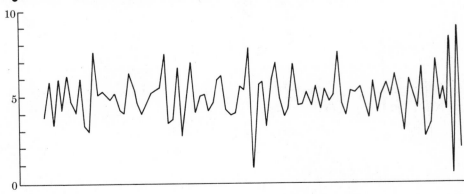

chap. 3   models for stationary time series

where θ_0 is understood to be 1, and the autocovariances by

$$\gamma_j = \begin{cases} \sigma_u{}^2(-\theta_j + \theta_1\theta_{j+1} + \cdots + \theta_{q-j}\theta_q) & j = 1, \ldots, q \\ 0 & j > q \end{cases} \quad (3.2.13)$$

The autocorrelation function is therefore

$$\rho_j = \begin{cases} \dfrac{-\theta_j + \theta_1\theta_{j+1} + \cdots + \theta_{q-j}\theta_q}{1 + \theta_1{}^2 + \cdots + \theta_q{}^2} & j = 1, \ldots, q \\ 0 & j > q \end{cases} \quad (3.2.14)$$

so that the correlogram consists of q spikes at lags $1, \ldots, q$, and 0, thereafter. The memory of MA (q) is q periods long since z_t shares in common no disturbances with members of the series separated from it by more than q periods.

For a numerical example, take the MA (2) process with $\mu = 18.3$, $\sigma_u{}^2 = 2$, and $\theta_1 = -.7$, $\theta_2 = .2$, which has the moments

$$\begin{aligned}
E(z_t) &= 18.3 \\
\gamma_0 &= 2(1 + .49 + .04) \\
&= 3.06 \\
\gamma_1 &= 2(.7 - .14) \\
&= 1.12 \\
\gamma_2 &= 2(-.2) \\
&= -.4 \\
\gamma_j &= 0 \quad j > 2 \\
\rho_1 &= .37 \\
\rho_2 &= -.13 \\
\rho_j &= 0 \quad j > 2
\end{aligned} \qquad (3.2.15)$$

The correlogram for this process is illustrated in Fig. 3.1 with a spike of .37 at lag 1 period and a spike of $-.13$ at lag 2 periods. It indicates that if a given observation is above the mean of the process, its successor will tend to be above the mean but following two periods later will tend to be *below* the mean.

3.3 Autoregressive Processes

To introduce the idea of autoregressive processes, we go back to (3.1.1), which expresses z_t in terms of the current disturbance and all past disturbances. An alternative way of expressing z_t is in terms of the current disturbance and *all past observations.* This is easily demonstrated by rearranging (3.1.1) so that u_t appears on the left and everything else on the right; thus

$$u_t = z_t - \mu - \Psi_1 u_{t-1} - \Psi_2 u_{t-2} - \cdots \qquad (3.3.1)$$

Now (3.3.1) holds for any time subscript, for example, for $t - 1$:

$$u_{t-1} = z_{t-1} - \mu - \Psi_1 u_{t-2} - \Psi_2 u_{t-3} - \cdots \qquad (3.3.2)$$

Substituting (3.3.2) into (3.3.1) to eliminate u_{t-1} yields

$$z_t = \mu(1 - \Psi_1) + \Psi_1 z_{t-1} + u_t + (\Psi_2 - \Psi_1{}^2)u_{t-2}$$
$$+ (\Psi_3 - \Psi_1\Psi_2)u_{t-3} + \cdots \qquad (3.3.3)$$

Similarly, u_{t-2}, u_{t-3}, and so forth may be successively eliminated from (3.3.3), leaving an expression for z_t of the form

$$z_t = \pi_1 z_{t-1} + \pi_2 z_{t-2} + \cdots + \delta + u_t \qquad (3.3.4)$$

where the weights π_i on past observations are functions of the Ψ_i weights and δ is constant, which is also a function of μ and the Ψ_i weights.

If it is the case that $\pi_i = 0$ for $i > p$, then the process is just

$$z_t = \pi_1 z_{t-1} + \cdots + \pi_p z_{t-p} + \delta + u_t \qquad (3.3.5)$$

and is referred to as an *autoregressive process* of order p or just AR (p). In order to distinguish the AR case from the general form (3.3.4), the coefficients are denoted ϕ_i instead of π_i; hence AR (p) is written

$$z_t = \phi_1 z_{t-1} + \phi_2 z_{t-2} + \cdots + \phi_p z_{t-p} + \delta + u_t \qquad (3.3.6)$$

The term *autoregressive* comes from the fact that (3.3.6) is essentially a regression equation in which z_t is related to its own past values instead of to a set of independent variables.

To recap briefly, any linear process may be written in the form (3.1.1) as a weighted sum of the current and all past disturbances. If that weighted sum has only a finite number of nonzero terms, then the process is a moving-average process. Likewise, any process may be written in the form (3.3.4) as the current disturbance plus a weighted sum of all past observations. If the number of nonzero terms is finite, then the process is an autoregressive process.

the first-order autoregression

The simplest example of an autoregressive process and one which is very important in practice is the first-order autoregressive process AR (1), which is

$$z_t = \phi_1 z_{t-1} + \delta + u_t \qquad (3.3.7)$$

Since z_t depends only on the previous observation, it is referred to as a *Markov process*. Higher-order AR processes are not Markov processes since they depend on previous observations two or more periods in the past.

Is the process stationary, and if so, what are its moments? One way of answering this question is to write (3.3.7) in terms of past disturbances only by substituting for z_{t-1} and z_{t-2} and so forth successively, a procedure which provides

$$z_t = \frac{\delta}{1 - \phi_1} + u_t + \phi_1 u_{t-1} + \phi_1^2 u_{t-2} + \cdots \qquad (3.3.8)$$

Thus, when AR (1) is written in terms of past disturbances, it is seen to be, loosely speaking, an MA process of infinite order. Furthermore, the particular MA process obtained is one that we have seen before, namely, (3.1.7), with $\phi_1 = \phi$ and $\delta/(1 - \phi_1) = \mu$. Therefore, we may draw on the results for (3.1.7); in particular, stationarity for the AR (1) process requires that

$$|\phi_1| < 1 \qquad (3.3.9)$$

that the mean of the process is

$$E(z_t) = \frac{\delta}{1 - \phi_1} \qquad (3.3.10)$$

and that the variance and autocovariances of the process are given by

$$\gamma_j = \phi_1^j \frac{\sigma_u^2}{1 - \phi_1^2} \qquad (3.3.11)$$

For example, if

$$z_t = .8z_{t-1} + 6 + u_t$$
$$\sigma_u^2 = 5 \qquad (3.3.12)$$

then

$$E(z_t) = 30$$
$$\gamma_j = (.8)^j (13.9) \qquad (3.3.13)$$

The autocorrelation function for the AR (1) process, which is easily derived from (3.3.11), is simply

$$\rho_j = \phi_1^j \qquad (3.3.14)$$

indicating that the correlation between observations declines exponentially with the number of periods separating them. For example, in the case of (3.3.12), we would have

$$\rho_j = (.8)^j \qquad (3.3.15)$$

The correlogram for the example (3.3.12) is given in Fig 3.5, and a realization of it is pictured in Fig. 3.6. The realization confirms the pattern of correlation

figure 3.5 The autocorrelation functions of autoregressive processes.

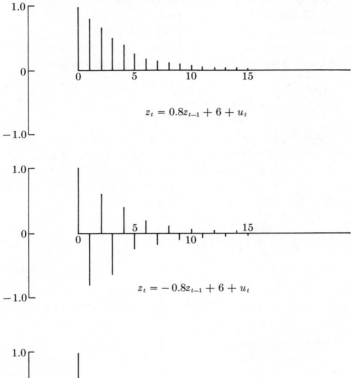

$$z_t = 0.8z_{t-1} + 6 + u_t$$

$$z_t = -0.8z_{t-1} + 6 + u_t$$

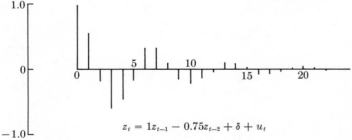

$$z_t = 1z_{t-1} - 0.75z_{t-2} + \delta + u_t$$

indicated by (3.3.15); that is, a high observation will tend to be followed by another high observation, not only in the next period, but in the next few periods.

As a contrasting illustration, the correlogram for AR (1) with $\phi_1 = -.8$ is shown in Fig. 3.5, and a realization appears in Fig. 3.7. The autocorrelations of this process are, from (3.3.14), negative for odd lags and positive for even lags, giving rise to the very jagged appearance of the correlogram and hence the series itself.

figure 3.6 Realization of the process $z_t = .8z_{t-1} + 6 + u_t,\ \sigma_u^2 = 5.$

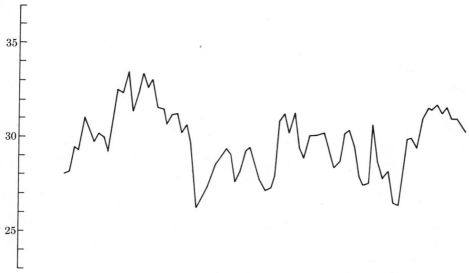

Another way of computing the moments of AR (1), which will be very useful with AR processes of higher order, is as follows. The expectation of the process is

$$E(z_t) = E(\phi_1 z_{t-1} + \delta + u_t)$$
$$= \phi_1 E(z_{t-1}) + \delta + 0 \qquad (3.3.16)$$

figure 3.7 Realization of the process $z_t = -.8z_{t-1} + 6 + u_t,\ \sigma_u^2 = 5.$

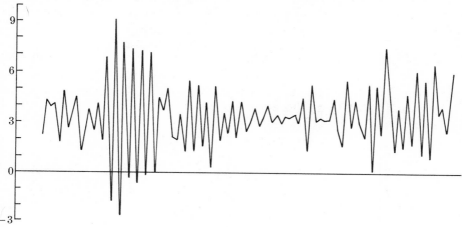

but if the process is stationary, $E(z_{t-1}) = E(z_t)$, and so

$$E(z_t) = \frac{\delta}{1 - \phi_1} \tag{3.3.17}$$

which is the result obtained before. The variance of the process is most easily obtained if we denote by $\tilde{z}_t$ the deviation of the process from its mean; that is,

$$\tilde{z}_t = z_t - \frac{\delta}{1 - \phi_1} \tag{3.3.18}$$

which is easily shown to follow the process

$$\tilde{z}_t = \phi_1 \tilde{z}_{t-1} + u_t \tag{3.3.19}$$

which is just (3.3.7) without the constant—a sensible result, since $\tilde{z}_t$ is nothing but a rescaling of the process such that the mean $E(\tilde{z}_t)$ is zero. The variance of z_t is then

$$\begin{aligned}
\gamma_0 = E(\tilde{z}_t{}^2) &= E[\tilde{z}_t(\phi_1 \tilde{z}_{t-1} + u_t)] \\
&= \phi_1 E(\tilde{z}_t \tilde{z}_{t-1}) + E(\tilde{z}_t u_t) \\
&= \phi_1 \gamma_1 + E[(\phi_1 \tilde{z}_{t-1} + u_t) u_t] \\
&= \phi_1 \gamma_1 + \phi_1 E(\tilde{z}_{t-1} u_t) + E(u_t{}^2) \\
&= \phi_1 \gamma_1 + \sigma_u{}^2
\end{aligned} \tag{3.3.20}$$

which involves the autocovariance of lag 1 period and the variance of the disturbances. Note that $E(\tilde{z}_{t-1} u_t)$ is zero because $\tilde{z}_{t-1}$ involves only disturbances occurring prior to period t, which are all independent of u_t. Now, γ_1 is given by

$$\begin{aligned}
\gamma_1 = E(\tilde{z}_t \tilde{z}_{t-1}) &= \phi_1 E(\tilde{z}_{t-1}^2) + E(u_t \tilde{z}_{t-1}) \\
&= \phi_1 \gamma_0
\end{aligned} \tag{3.3.21}$$

Equations (3.3.20) and (3.3.21) may be solved then for the values of γ_0 and γ_1. Substituting (3.3.21) into (3.3.20), we have

$$\begin{aligned}
\gamma_0 &= \phi_1{}^2 \gamma_0 + \sigma_u{}^2 \\
&= \frac{\sigma_u{}^2}{1 - \phi_1{}^2}
\end{aligned} \tag{3.3.22}$$

Then

$$\gamma_1 = \phi_1 \left(\frac{\sigma_u{}^2}{1 - \phi_1{}^2} \right) \tag{3.3.23}$$

Autocovariances for lags 2, 3, . . . , are obtained recursively from the relationship

$$\gamma_j = E(\tilde{z}_t \tilde{z}_{t-j})$$
$$= \phi_1 E(\tilde{z}_{t-1} \tilde{z}_{t-j}) + E(u_t \tilde{z}_{t-j})$$
$$= \phi_1 \gamma_{j-1} \qquad j = 1, 2, 3, \ldots \qquad (3.3.24)$$

which implies
$$\gamma_j = \phi_1^j \gamma_0 \qquad j = 1, 2, \ldots \qquad (3.3.25)$$

and hence
$$\rho_j = \phi_1 \rho_{j-1}$$
$$= \phi_1^j \qquad\qquad\qquad (3.3.26)$$

all of which we have derived by the first method as well.

Before leaving the AR (1) process, it is instructive to consider why the stationarity requirement that $|\phi_1| < 1$ makes sense. First suppose that $\phi_1 = 1$. This special case of AR (1) is just (1.1.18), the nonstationary random walk. Now suppose that $\phi_1 > 1$, say, $\phi_1 = 2$. The history of z_t would exhibit not only nonstationarity but explosive growth. In fact, after any length of time the series would really cease to be stochastic in the sense that the magnitude of the observations would become so large that the disturbance u_t would become, in comparison, negligible. This suggests that there is something rather special about the value of 1 for ϕ_1; that is, there is something rather special about first differences since the random walk is nonstationary yet retains its stochastic character. We shall return to this theme in Chap. 4 when differencing is used as the basis for models of nonstationary series.

the second-order autoregression

The virtues of the second approach taken to derivation of the moments of AR (1) become apparent when we examine the second-order autoregression

$$z_t = \phi_1 z_{t-1} + \phi_2 z_{t-2} + \delta + u_t \qquad (3.3.27)$$

The reader may easily verify that if AR (2) is written in MA form, it is of infinite order, although the coefficients Ψ_i are not simple functions of ϕ_1 and ϕ_2. How then to check for stationarity? Fortunately, it turns out that stationarity is assumed if the roots of the *characteristic equation* $(1 - \phi_1 B - \phi_2 B^2) = 0$, where B is simply a "stand-in" algebraic symbol, lie outside of the unit circle (in the complex plane). This is equivalent to requiring that

$$\phi_1 + \phi_2 < 1$$
$$\phi_2 - \phi_1 < 1 \qquad (3.3.28)$$
$$|\phi_2| < 1$$

After checking to see that (3.3.28) is satisfied, we proceed to take the expectation of the process

$$
\begin{aligned}
E(z_t) &= E(\phi_1 z_{t-1} + \phi_2 z_{t-2} + \delta + u_t) \\
&= \phi_1 E(z_{t-1}) + \phi_2 E(z_{t-2}) + \delta + E(u_t) \\
&= \frac{\delta}{1 - \phi_1 - \phi_2}
\end{aligned}
\tag{3.3.29}
$$

It is easily verified that deviations from the mean of the process, $\tilde{z}_t = z_t - \delta/(1 - \phi_1 - \phi_2)$, follow the same AR (2) process without a constant. Hence

$$
\begin{aligned}
\gamma_0 = E(\tilde{z}_t{}^2) &= \phi_1 E(\tilde{z}_t \tilde{z}_{t-1}) \\
&\quad + \phi_2 E(\tilde{z}_t \tilde{z}_{t-2}) \\
&\quad + E(\tilde{z}_t u_t) \\
&= \phi \gamma_1 + \phi_2 \gamma_2 + \sigma_u{}^2
\end{aligned}
\tag{3.3.30}
$$

and
$$
\begin{aligned}
\gamma_1 = E(\tilde{z}_t \tilde{z}_{t-1}) &= \phi_1 \gamma_0 + \phi_2 \gamma_{-1} \\
&= \phi_1 \gamma_0 + \phi_2 \gamma_1
\end{aligned}
\tag{3.3.31}
$$

since $\gamma_{-1} = \gamma_1$ and

$$
\gamma_2 = E(\tilde{z}_t \tilde{z}_{t-2}) = \phi_1 \gamma_1 + \phi_2 \gamma_0
\tag{3.3.32}
$$

so that the set of equations

$$
\begin{aligned}
\gamma_0 &= \phi_1 \gamma_1 + \phi_2 \gamma_2 + \sigma_u{}^2 \\
\gamma_1 &= \phi_1 \gamma_0 + \phi_2 \gamma_1 \\
\gamma_2 &= \phi_1 \gamma_1 + \phi \gamma_0
\end{aligned}
\tag{3.3.33}
$$

may be solved (given values of ϕ_1, ϕ_2, and $\sigma_u{}^2$) for γ_0, γ_1, and γ_2. For $j > 2$, γ_j is given by

$$
\begin{aligned}
\gamma_j &= E(\tilde{z}_t \tilde{z}_{t-j}) \\
&= \phi_1 \gamma_{j-1} + \phi_2 \gamma_{j-2} \quad j > 2
\end{aligned}
\tag{3.3.34}
$$

allowing recursive computation of autocovariances of successively higher order. The autocorrelation function may be computed from (3.3.33) and (3.3.34), or, alternatively, note that if we divide (3.3.31) to (3.3.33) by γ_0, we have the two equations

$$
\begin{aligned}
\rho_1 &= \phi_1 + \phi_2 \rho_1 \\
\rho_2 &= \phi_1 \rho_1 + \phi_2
\end{aligned}
\tag{3.3.35}
$$

referred to as the *Yule–Walker equations*, which may be solved for ρ_1 and ρ_2. Autocorrelations of higher order are given then by successive application of

$$
\rho_j = \phi_1 \rho_{j-1} + \phi_2 \rho_{j-2} \quad j > 2
\tag{3.3.36}
$$

The range of patterns that the autocorrelation function may assume in the AR (2) case is clearly more complicated than for AR (1); nevertheless, it is possible to make some general observations. For both AR (1) and AR (2) *the autocorrelations follow the same dynamic relationship as does the process itself* [compare (3.3.7) with (3.3.26) and (3.3.27) with (3.3.36)]. If the roots of the characteristic equation $(1 - \phi_1 B - \phi_2 B^2) = 0$ are real and $(\phi_1{}^2 + 4\phi_2 \geq 0)$, then the autocorrelation function will either be positive as it damps out to zero or it will alternate in sign as it damps to zero. However, if the roots are complex $(\phi_1{}^2 + 4\phi_2 < 0)$, then the autocorrelation function will be a damped sign wave as illustrated in Fig. 3.5 for parameter values $\phi_1 = 1.0$, $\phi_2 = -.75$.

autoregressive processes of higher order

The results obtained for AR (1) and AR (2) are now readily extended to AR processes of arbitrary order p. Any AR process may be written in terms of disturbances only, and of course stationarity requires convergence of the infinite sum of the coefficients Ψ_i. This would be assured if AR processes could be written as MA processes of finite order. As observed for AR (1) and AR (2) and as is readily verified by the reader, AR processes in general lead to an infinite string of coefficients Ψ_i; that is, AR processes are equivalent to MA processes of infinite order. Stationarity may be determined, however, by a generalization of the condition for AR (1) and AR (2); namely, the roots of the characteristic equation $(1 - \phi_1 B - \cdots - \phi_p B^p) = 0$ must lie outside the unit circle.

The mean of AR (p) is

$$E(z_t) = \phi_1 E(z_{t-1}) + \cdots + \phi_p E(z_{t-p}) + \delta + E(u_t)$$

$$= \frac{\delta}{1 - \phi_1 - \cdots - \phi_p} \qquad (3.3.37)$$

Following the procedure used for AR (1) and AR (2), the equations

$$\gamma_0 = \phi_1 \gamma_1 + \cdots + \phi_p \gamma_p + \sigma_u{}^2$$
$$\gamma_1 = \phi_1 \gamma_0 + \cdots + \phi_p \gamma_{p-1}$$
$$\cdots \cdots \cdots \cdots \cdots \cdots \cdots \qquad (3.3.38)$$
$$\gamma_p = \phi_1 \gamma_{p-1} + \cdots + \phi_p \gamma_0$$

given parameters $\phi_1, \ldots, \phi_p$ and $\sigma_u{}^2$, may be solved $(p + 1$ linear equation) for the $p + 1$ unknown $\gamma_0, \ldots, \gamma_p$. For lags greater than p, the covariances γ_j may be computed recursively from

$$\gamma_j = \phi_1 \gamma_{j-1} + \cdots + \phi_p \gamma_{j-p} \qquad j > p \qquad (3.3.39)$$

The autocorrelation function may be computed directly because if the last p equations of (3.3.38) are divided through by γ_0, they become the Yule–Walker equations for AR (p), namely,

$$\rho_1 = \phi_1 + \phi_2\rho_1 + \cdot\;\cdot\;\cdot + \phi_p\rho_{p-1}$$

$$\cdot\;\cdot\;\cdot\;\cdot\;\cdot\;\cdot\;\cdot\;\cdot\;\cdot\;\cdot\;\cdot\;\cdot\;\cdot\;\cdot\;\cdot\;\cdot\;\cdot\;\cdot \qquad (3.3.40)$$

$$\rho_p = \phi_1\rho_{p-1} + \phi_2\rho_{p-2} + \cdot\;\cdot\;\cdot + \phi_p$$

a system of p linear equations in the p unknowns $\rho_1, \ldots, \rho_p$. Autocorrelation coefficients for longer lags may then be computed recursively from

$$\rho_j = \phi_1\rho_{j-1} + \cdot\;\cdot\;\cdot + \phi_p\rho_{j-p} \qquad j > p \qquad (3.3.41)$$

3.4 Invertibility of Moving-average Processes

The determination of conditions for the stationarity of autoregressive processes helps to motivate the concept of *invertibility* for moving-average processes. Stationarity for an AR process requires that when z_t is written in terms of past disturbances, the sum of coefficients Ψ_i converge. For this to be the case, the individual coefficients Ψ_i must become smaller as i increases and fast enough so that their sum converges to a finite number, which may be determined by examination of the roots of $(1 - \phi_1 B - \cdot\;\cdot\;\cdot - \phi_p B^p) = 0$.

Now consider the result of writing an MA process in the form (3.3.4), that is, in terms of the current disturbance only and past observations. This may be accomplished by substituting successively for u_{t-1}, then u_{t-2}, and so forth. The reader may easily convince himself that any MA process when written in this form involves observations back into the infinite past, that is, becomes an AR process of infinite order. Invertibility requires that the coefficients π_i on past disturbance ultimately become small as i gets large and do so rapidly enough so that the sum $\sum_{i=1}^{\infty} \pi_i$ converges. Thus invertibility is the *algebraic* analog of stationarity for MA processes, and it is not surprising that the conditions in the parameters $\theta_1, \ldots, \theta_q$ are also analogous; namely, the roots of the equation $(1 - \theta_1 B - \cdot\;\cdot\;\cdot - \theta_q B^q) = 0$ must lie outside the unit circle.

To illustrate, in the case of the MA (1) process the autoregressive version of the process is obtained by the substitutions

$$z_t = \mu + u_t - \theta_1 u_{t-1}$$
$$= (\mu + \theta_1\mu) + u_t - \theta_1 z_{t-1} - \theta_1^2 u_{t-2} \qquad (3.4.1)$$

and so forth, so that the process becomes

$$z_t = -\theta_1 z_{t-1} - \theta_1^2 z_{t-2} - \theta_1^3 z_{t-3} - \cdot\;\cdot\;\cdot + \frac{\mu}{1 - \theta_1} + u_t \qquad (3.4.2)$$

Now, if $|\theta_1| > 1$, then the weight given to a past observation would increase exponentially with the time that had lapsed since its occurrence, or, speaking loosely, the greatest weight in the determination of z_t would be given to the most distant past. If this unsatisfactory state of affairs is to be avoided, it must be that $|\theta_1| < 1$, that is, the root of $(1 - \theta_1 B) = 0$ is greater than 1.

3.5 Mixed Autoregressive–Moving-average Processes

A natural extension of the AR and MA models would be a class of models having both autoregressive and moving-average terms, that is, processes of the form

$$z_t = \phi_1 z_{t-1} + \cdots + \phi_p z_{t-p} + \delta + u_t - \theta_1 u_{t-1} - \cdots - \theta_q u_{t-2} \quad (3.5.1)$$

Such mixed processes are referred to as *autoregressive–moving-average processes* of orders p and q or just ARMA (p,q). For many series encountered in practice, the inclusion of both autoregressive and moving-average terms results in a model that has fewer parameters than would be necessary for a satisfactory model of pure AR or pure MA form.

the ARMA (1,1) process

The simplest mixed process is the ARMA (1,1) process

$$z_t = \phi_1 z_{t-1} + \delta + u_t - \theta_1 u_{t-1} \quad (3.5.2)$$

which may be written in pure moving-average form by the sequence of substitutions

$$
\begin{aligned}
z_t &= \phi_1^2 z_{t-2} + (\delta + \phi_1 \delta) + u_t + (\phi_1 - \theta_1)u_{t-1} - \phi_1 \theta_1 u_{t-2} \\
&= \phi_1^3 z_{t-3} + (\delta + \phi_1 \delta + \phi_1^2 \delta) + u_t + (\phi_1 - \theta_1)u_{t-1} \\
&\qquad\qquad + \phi_1(\phi_1 - \theta_1)u_{t-2} - \phi_1^2 \theta_1 u_{t-3}
\end{aligned}
$$

$$\cdots \cdots \cdots \cdots \cdots \cdots \cdots \cdots \cdots \cdots \cdots \cdots \cdots \cdots \cdots$$

$$
\begin{aligned}
&= \frac{\delta}{1 - \phi_1} + u_t + (\phi_1 - \theta_1)u_{t-1} + \phi_1(\phi_1 - \theta_1)u_{t-2} \\
&\qquad\qquad\qquad\qquad + \phi_1^2(\phi_1 - \theta_1)u_{t-3} + \cdots \quad (3.5.3)
\end{aligned}
$$

If the process is to be stationary, the sum of coefficients $\sum_{i=0}^{\infty} \phi_1^i(\phi_1 - \theta_1)$ must converge, thus requiring $|\phi_1| < 1$, as in the case of the AR (1) process.

Although ARMA (1,1) is an MA process of infinite order, we might imagine trying to approximate it with an MA process of finite order by dropping terms after the point where coefficients $\phi_1^i(\phi_1 - \theta_1)$ become smaller than some arbitrary amount. Suppose, for example, that $\phi_1 = .9$ and $\theta_1 = -.9$; that is,

$$z_t = .9z_{t-1} + \delta + u_t + .9u_{t-1} \tag{3.5.4}$$

Then

$$\Psi_i = \phi_1^{i-1}(\phi_1 - \theta_1)$$
$$= (.9)^{i-1}(1.8) \tag{3.5.5}$$

and hence

$$\Psi_1 = 1.8$$
$$\Psi_2 = 1.62 \tag{3.5.6}$$
$$\Psi_3 = 1.46$$

and so forth. Clearly, a moving-average process of very high order would be required to approximate this ARMA (1,1) process. This illustrates the *parsimony* achieved by mixed models in the sense that the mixed model has only two coefficients, but the moving-average approximation to it requires many coefficients.

The ARMA (1,1) process may also be written in autoregressive form following the substitutions

$$z_t = \phi_1 z_{t-1} + \delta + u_t - \theta_1 u_{t-1}$$
$$= u_t + (\delta + \theta_1 \delta) + (\phi_1 - \theta_1)z_{t-1} + \theta_1 \phi_1 z_{t-2} - \theta_1^2 u_{t-2}$$
$$\cdots \cdots \cdots \cdots \cdots \cdots \cdots \cdots \cdots \cdots \cdots \cdots \cdots \cdots \cdots$$
$$= (\phi_1 - \theta_1)z_{t-1} + \theta_1(\phi_1 - \theta_1)z_{t-2}$$
$$+ \theta_1^2(\phi_1 - \theta_1)z_{t-3} + \cdots + \frac{\delta}{1 - \theta_1} + u_t \tag{3.5.7}$$

Invertibility of the process requires that the sum $\Sigma_{i=1}^{\infty} \pi_i = \Sigma_{i=1}^{\infty} \theta_1^{i-1}(\phi_1 - \theta_1)$ converge and hence that $|\theta_1| < 1$ as in the case of an MA (1) process.

Since the coefficients of past observations become small at large lags, it is clear that an autoregressive approximation to ARMA (1,1) could be obtained by truncation of the autoregression where π_i becomes sufficiently small. Assuming once more that $\phi_1 = .9$ and $\theta_1 = -.9$, we have

$$\pi_i = \theta_1^{i-1}(\phi_1 - \theta_1)$$
$$= (-.9)^{i-1}(1.8) \tag{3.5.8}$$

and so

$$\pi_1 = 1.8$$
$$\pi_2 = -1.62 \tag{3.5.9}$$
$$\pi_3 = 1.46$$

from which the parsimony of the mixed model is again apparent since the autoregressive approximation will require many coefficients compared with the two coefficients of the ARMA (1,1) process.

The mean of the ARMA (1,1) process is given by

$$E(z_t) = \phi_1 E(z_{t-1}) + \delta + E(u_t) - \theta_1 E(u_t \delta_1)$$

$$= \frac{\delta}{1 - \phi_1} \qquad (3.5.10)$$

the same result as was obtained for AR (1). To obtain the variance of the process, we note that $\tilde{z}_t = z_t - \delta/(1 - \phi_1)$, the deviations of the process from its mean, generated by

$$\tilde{z}_t = \phi_1 \tilde{z}_{t-1} + u_t - \theta_1 u_{t-1} \qquad (3.5.11)$$

so that the variance of the process is

$$\gamma_0 = E(\tilde{z}_t^2) = \phi_1 E(\tilde{z}_t \tilde{z}_{t-1}) + E(\tilde{z}_t u_t) - \theta_1 E(\tilde{z}_t u_{t-1}) \qquad (3.5.12)$$

Now $E(\tilde{z}_t u_{t-1})$ is the covariance between $\tilde{z}_t$ and the previous disturbance and

$$E(\tilde{z}_t u_{t-1}) = \phi_1 E(\tilde{z}_{t-1} u_{t-1}) + E(u_t u_{t-1}) - \theta_1 E(u_{t-1}^2)$$

$$= \phi_1 \sigma_u^2 - \theta_1 \sigma_u^2 \qquad (3.5.13)$$

Hence $\qquad \gamma_0 = \phi_1 \gamma_1 + \sigma_u^2 - \theta_1(\phi_1 - \theta_1)\sigma_u^2 \qquad (3.5.14)$

This differs from the result for AR (1) because of the last term, which arises from the fact that u_{t-1} is a component of $\tilde{z}_t$. Now, for γ_1 we have

$$\gamma_1 = E(\tilde{z}_t \tilde{z}_{t-1}) = \phi_1 E(\tilde{z}_{t-1}^2) + E(u_t \tilde{z}_{t-1}) - \theta_1 E(u_{t-1} \tilde{z}_{t-1})$$

$$= \phi_1 \gamma_0 - \theta_1 \sigma_u^2 \qquad (3.5.15)$$

which differs from γ_1 for AR (1), again because u_{t-1} is a component of $(\tilde{z}_t)$. Next, we have for γ_2

$$\gamma_2 = E(\tilde{z}_t \tilde{z}_{t-2}) = \phi_1 E(\tilde{z}_{t-1} \tilde{z}_{t-2}) + E(u_t \tilde{z}_{t-2}) - \theta_1 E(u_{t-1} \tilde{z}_{t-2})$$

$$= \phi_1 E(\tilde{z}_{t-1} \tilde{z}_{t-2})$$

$$= \phi_1 \gamma_1 \qquad (3.5.16)$$

which does *not* differ from the AR (1) result because the moving-average part of ARMA (1,1) reaches back only one period. It is apparent, then, that for longer lags

$$\gamma_j = \phi_1 \gamma_{j-1} \qquad j = 2, 3, \ldots \qquad (3.5.17)$$

as in the AR (1) case.

To compute the autocovariances given the parameters of the process, Eqs. (3.5.14) and (3.5.15) are solved first for γ_0 and γ_1, resulting in

$$\gamma_0 = \frac{(1 + \theta_1^2 - 2\phi_1\theta_1)}{1 - \phi_1^2}$$

$$\qquad (3.5.18)$$

$$\gamma_1 = \frac{(1 - \phi_1\theta_1)(\phi_1 - \theta_1)}{1 - \phi_1^2}$$

sec. 3.5   autoregressive–moving-average processes   49

Then the rest of the covariances are computed recursively from (2.5.17). The autocorrelation at lag 1 is therefore given by

$$\rho_1 = \frac{\gamma_1}{\gamma_0} = \frac{(1 - \phi_1\theta_1)(\phi_1 - \theta_1)}{1 + \theta_1{}^2 - 2\phi_1\theta_1} \tag{3.5.19}$$

and then dividing (3.5.17) through by γ_0 we have for longer lags

$$\rho_j = \phi_1\rho_{j-1} \qquad j = 2, 3, \ldots \tag{3.5.20}$$

In summary, we see that the presence of the moving-average term in the ARMA (1,1) process enters into the determination of ρ_1. The remaining part of the autocorrelation function is determined just by the autoregressive part of the model. Thus, the autocorrelation function combines characteristics of both MA (1) and AR (1). As a numerical example, let $\phi_1 = .5$, $\theta_1 = -.9$, and $\sigma_u{}^2 = 1$. Then

$$\begin{aligned} \gamma_0 &= (.5)\gamma_1 + 1 - (-.9)(1.4)(1) \\ &= .5\gamma_1 + 2.26 \end{aligned} \tag{3.5.21}$$

$$\gamma_1 = .5\gamma^2 + .9 \tag{3.5.22}$$

and so

$$\gamma_0 = 3.61$$

$$\gamma_1 = 2.7 \tag{3.5.23}$$

$$\gamma_j = (.5)^{j-1}(2.7) \qquad j = 2, 3, \ldots$$

and

$$\rho_1 = .75$$

$$\rho_2 = .375 \tag{3.5.24}$$

$$\rho_j = (.5)^{j-1}(.75) \qquad j = 2, 3, \ldots$$

Now, in the absence of the moving average, we would have had $\rho_1 = .5$, $\rho_2 = (.5)^2$, and so forth, so the effect of the moving-average term is to alter the value of ρ_1, after which the autocorrelations decay at the same rate they would for an AR (1) process with $\phi_1 = .5$. Alternatively, let θ_1 be $+.9$. Then

$$\gamma_0 = 1.21$$

$$\gamma_1 = -.3 \tag{3.5.25}$$

$$\gamma_j = (.5)^{j-1}(-.3)$$

and

$$\rho_1 = -.25$$

$$\rho_j = (.5)^{j-1}(-.25) \qquad j = 2, 3, \ldots \tag{3.5.26}$$

Now, in the first example z_t was positively correlated with all its predecessors and its successors and the correlation decayed at the rate (.5) with increasing lag. In the second example, z_t is negatively correlated with its predecessors and successors and the correlation decays at the rate (.5). In both examples, the moving-average part of the model provides the initial conditions (ρ_1) for computation of the autocorrelation function but in the second case actually induces negative correlation where, for a pure AR (1) process with $\phi_1 = .5$, there would be positive correlation. The two autocorrelation functions are pictured in Fig. 3.8.

figure 3.8 Autocorrelation functions of mixed autoregressive–moving-average processes.

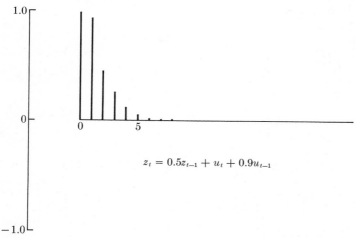

$$z_t = 0.5z_{t-1} + u_t + 0.9u_{t-1}$$

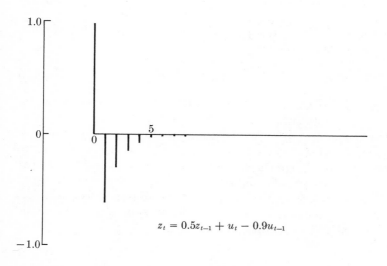

$$z_t = 0.5z_{t-1} + u_t - 0.9u_{t-1}$$

mixed processes of higher order

The results obtained for ARMA (1,1) generalize to mixed processes of arbitrary order. Any ARMA process may be written as an MA process of infinite order. The stationarity condition that $\Sigma_{i=0}^{\infty} \Psi_i$ converge is satisfied if the roots of the equation $(1 - \phi_1 B - \cdots - \phi_p B^p) = 0$ lie outside the unit circle. Similarly, the autoregressive form of the process is of infinite order and the invertibility condition $\Sigma_{i=1}^{\infty} \pi_i$ converge is satisfied if the roots of the equation $(1 - \theta_1 B - \cdots - \theta_q B^q) = 0$ lie outside the unit circle.

The mean of the process is

$$E(z_t) = \phi_1 E(z_{t-1}) + \cdots + \phi_p E(z_{t-p}) + \delta + E(u_t)$$
$$- \cdots - \theta_q E(u_{t-q})$$

$$= \frac{\delta}{1 - \phi_1 - \cdots \phi_p} \tag{3.5.27}$$

The covariances are evaluated by a set of equations of the form

$$\gamma_j = E(\tilde{z}_t \tilde{z}_{t-j}) = \phi_1 E(\tilde{z}_{t-1} \tilde{z}_{t-j}) + \cdots + \phi_p E(\tilde{z}_{t-p} \tilde{z}_{t-j}) + E(u_t \tilde{z}_{t-j})$$
$$- \theta_1 E(u_{t-1} \tilde{z}_{t-j}) - \theta_q E(u_{t-q} \tilde{z}_{t-j}) \tag{3.5.28}$$

Now, if $j < q$, then the terms involving $\tilde{z}_{t-j}$ and past disturbances will be nonzero since $\tilde{z}_{t-j}$ is correlated with all disturbances occurring through period $t - j$. Thus the equations for $\gamma_0, \gamma_1, \ldots, \gamma_q$ will involve the moving-average parameters $\theta_1, \ldots, \theta_q$. However, for $j > q$, we have

$$\gamma_j = \phi_1 \gamma_{j-1} + \cdots + \phi_p \gamma_{j-p} \qquad j > q \tag{3.5.29}$$

because then the terms involving $\tilde{z}_{t-j}$ and the disturbances are zero. Consequently, the ρ_j at longer lags are given by

$$\rho_j = \phi_1 \rho_{j-1} + \cdots + \phi_p \rho_{j-p} \qquad j > q \tag{3.5.30}$$

In summary, then, the autocorrelations for lags $1, \ldots, q$ will be affected by the moving-average part of the process. The remainder of the autocorrelation function will follow the pattern given by the autoregressive part of the process.

The autoregressive–moving-average processes described in this chapter provide a very powerful class of models for stationary time series encountered in practice because of their great flexibility in accounting for a wide range of autocorrelation functions and therefore for a wide range of time series behavior. In Chap. 4 the models are extended to accommodate nonstationarity of the type frequently encountered in operational contexts.

Exercises

3.1 Verify expressions (3.1.8) to (3.1.10) using the algebraic fact that for any x such that $|x| < 1$, then $1 + x + x^2 + \cdots = 1/(1 - x)$

3.2 Consider the MA (1) process

$$z_t = 6.8 + u_t - .7u_{t-1}$$
$$\sigma_u^2 = 1$$

where the u_t are independently and identically distributed.

(a) Is the process a discrete linear stochastic process? Why?

(b) Is the process stationary? Why?

(c) Derive directly (without using the formulas in the text) the moments

$$E(z_t)$$
$$\gamma_0, \gamma_1, \gamma_2, \gamma_{18}$$
$$\rho_0, \rho_1, \rho_2, \rho_{18}$$

(d) Graph the correlogram.

(e) Generate a realization of the process by tossing a coin ($H = +1$, $T = -1$). How does the appearance of the realization coincide with what you would expect from examination of the correlogram? If z_{82} were 7.7, would you expect z_{87} to be above or below the mean of the process?

(f) If the value of θ were $-.7$ instead of $+.7$, how would you expect the appearance of the realization to differ? Graph the correlogram for that case.

(g) Express the original process in autoregressive form providing numerical values for the constant and for π_1, π_2, and π_{99}. How is it apparent that the autoregressive form is of infinite order?

(h) Is the original process invertible? Why?

3.3 Now consider the MA (2) process

$$z_t = -1.7 + u_t - .6u_{t-1} + .3u_{t-2}$$
$$\sigma_u^2 = 3$$

(a) Is the process stationary? Why?

(b) Derive directly the moments

$$E(z_t)$$
$$\gamma_0, \gamma_1, \gamma_2, \gamma_3, \gamma_{23}$$
$$\rho_0, \rho_1, \rho_2, \rho_3, \rho_{23}$$

Graph the correlogram.

(c) If z_{93} were 3.8, would you expect z_{94} to be above the mean of the process or below?

(d) Express the process in autoregressive form providing numerical values for π_1, π_2, and π_3. How is it apparent from the sequence of substitutions that the autoregressive form is of infinite order?

(e) Is the process invertible? Why?

3.4   Now consider the AR (1) process

$$z_t = .5z_{t-1} + 10 + u_t$$
$$\sigma_u{}^2 = 4$$

(a)   Is the process a discrete linear stochastic process?   Why?
(b)   Is it invertible?   Why?
(c)   Is it stationary?   Why?
(d)   Derive directly the moments

$$E(z_t)$$

$\gamma_0, \gamma_1, \gamma_2$ and give an expression for γ_{150}

ρ_0, ρ_1, ρ_2 and give an expression for ρ_{150}

Graph the correlogram.
(e)   Generate a realization using your random-number generator ($H = +2$, $T = -2$).   How does its appearance agree with that suggested by the correlogram?   If z_{123} were 36, would you expect z_{124} to be above or below the mean of the process?   How about z_{125}?
(f)   For the same process (except $\phi_1 = -.5$), answer questions (d) to (f) again.   How does the realization of this process contrast with the original one?
(g)   Express the process in moving-average form providing numerical values for the constant and for Ψ_1, Ψ_2, and Ψ_3.   How is it apparent from your result that the process is stationary?

3.5   Now consider the AR (2) process

$$z_t = 1.5z_{t-1} - .75z_{t-2} + 4.1 + u_t$$
$$\sigma_u{}^2 = 2$$

(a)   Is the process stationary?   Why?
(b)   What is the mean of the process?
(c)   Set up and solve the Yule–Walker equations for the process, and then compute $\rho_3, \ldots, \rho_8$ using the appropriate recursion relationship.   Graph the correlogram.   If z_5 were 20.3, would you expect z_6 to be above or below the mean of the process?

3.6   Finally, consider the ARMA (1,1) process

$$z_t = .4z_{t-1} + u_t - .8u_{t-1}$$
$$\sigma_u{}^2 = 1$$

(a)   Is the process a discrete linear process?   Why?
      Is it stationary?   Why?   Is it invertible?   Why?
(b)   Derive directly

$$E(z_t)$$

$\gamma_0, \gamma_1, \gamma_2, \gamma_3$

$\rho_0, \rho_1, \rho_2, \rho_3$

Graph the correlogram.   If z_{71} were -5, would you expect z_{72} to be above or below the mean of the process?

(c) Rewrite the process in autoregressive form, giving numerical values for π_1, π_2, and π_3. What is the order of the autoregression?

(d) Rewrite the process in moving-average form, giving numerical values for Ψ_1, Ψ_2, and Ψ_3. What is the order of the moving average?

(e) For a stationary ARMA (1,7) process, provide an expression for ρ_{20} in terms of ϕ_1 and ρ_{10}.

3.7 While analyzing a set of data, Mr. Jones assumed that the observations had been generated by a stationary autoregressive process of order 6, namely,

$$z_t = \pi_1 z_{t-1} + \cdots + \pi_6 z_{t-6} + \delta + u_t$$

and by some appropriate procedure obtained parameter estimates

$$\pi_1 = .4$$
$$\pi_2 = -.36$$
$$\pi_3 = .32$$
$$\pi_4 = -.29$$
$$\pi_5 = .26$$
$$\pi_6 = -.23$$

(a) Applying the principle of parsimony, show how these six parameter values could be accounted for by the values of $\pi_1, \ldots, \pi_6$, implied by the two parameter processes ARMA (1,1). You may easily infer the value of θ_1 from his $\pi_2, \ldots, \pi_6$, and then using θ and his π_1 infer ϕ_1. In general, what could you say about the statistical efficiency of Mr. Jones' procedure requiring inference about six parameters as compared with one that focused only on ϕ_1 and θ_1?

(b) Using the parameters of the ARMA (1,1) obtained in part (a), compute ρ_1, ρ_2, ρ_3, ρ_4 and sketch the correlogram. If this correlogram had been presented to you, what would have tipped you off to the mixed nature of the process? On what basis could you have rejected an AR (1) specification immediately?

4
Models
for
Nonstationary
Time Series

Stationarity is a very strong condition to impose on a time series and is presumably never literally true of series encountered in practice; rather, it should be viewed as a useful working assumption. There are any number of ways in which departures from stationarity might occur, but the most apparent one in economic time series is the lack of affinity for a mean value. Examples would include most price series (we have already mentioned stock-market prices), most output series such as GNP or the sales of a firm, and expenditure series such as consumer expenditures on durable goods, capital expenditures by firms, or government expenditures.

The kind of nonstationarity displayed by such series may be characterized as being *homogeneous* in the sense that although the series moves freely without affinity for a particular location, its behavior at different periods in time is essentially the same. Fortunately, *homogeneous nonstationarity is displayed by series whose successive changes or differences are stationary*. Thus, the models for stationary series studied in Chap. 3 provide the basis for a highly flexible class of models for nonstationary series if we follow the simple expedient of working with their differences.

4.1 Differencing and Homogeneous Nonstationarity

The motivation for focusing on differencing as a means of accommodating homogeneous nonstationarity becomes evident by considering the first-order autoregressive process

$$z_t = \phi_1 z_{t-1} + u_t \qquad (4.1.1)$$

and the values that might be taken by the parameter ϕ_1. If ϕ_1 is less than 1 in absolute value, then the process is stationary, as we saw in Chap. 3. On the other hand, if ϕ_1 is greater than 1, then the behavior of the series will be explosive. That is, if we were to start the process off at, say, 0, the disturbances would be important in determining the first few values of the series; however, after a time the series would "take off," growing exponentially. The disturbances would become negligible relative to the level of the series, and hence the series would become essentially deterministic in its evolution. What about the case $\phi_1 = 1$? This is the random-walk process that, as we have seen in Chap. 3, is nonstationary. It is also, however, homogeneous in its behavior as inspection of Fig. 1.1 will indicate. It is homogeneous because the distribution of changes or differences in the process is unchanging; that is, the time series of differences is stationary because the differences are just

$$z_t - z_{t-1} = u_t \qquad (4.1.2)$$

and the distribution of u_t is fixed.

A natural generalization of the random walk is to consider the whole class of stationary ARMA processes as potential generating mechanisms for the differences of a nonstationary series. Thus, if we define w_t to be the sequence of differences

$$w_t = z_t - z_{t-1} \qquad (4.1.3)$$

then the general model may be written

$$w_t = \phi_1 w_{t-1} + \cdots + \phi_p w_{t-p} + u_t - \theta_1 u_{t-1} - \cdots - \theta_q u_{t-q} \qquad (4.1.4)$$

Replacing w_t with $(z_t - z_{t-1})$, we see that the observed series z_t is given directly by

$$z_t = z_{t-1} + \phi_1(z_{t-1} - z_{t-2}) + \cdots + \phi_p(z_{t-p} - z_{t-p-1})$$
$$+ u_t - \theta_1 u_{t-1} - \cdots - \theta_q u_{t-q} \qquad (4.1.5)$$

Note that z_t is just the sum of all past changes; that is,

$$z_t = w_t + w_{t-1} + w_{t-2} + \cdots \qquad (4.1.6)$$

Hence z_t is referred to as the integration of the w_t series and the process (4.1.4) as an *integrated autoregressive–moving-average process*.

In some cases, not common in economic contexts, it may be that even the first differences are nonstationary but that the second differences are stationary. The second differences are the differences of the first differences; that is, if the y_t are the second differences of the z_t, then

$$y_t = w_t - w_{t-1}$$
$$= (z_t - z_{t-1}) - (z_{t-1} - z_{t-2}) = z_t - 2z_{t-1} + z_{t-2} \qquad (4.1.7)$$

Denoting the degree of differencing by d, then an ARIMA process may be described by the dimensions p, d, and q. As a matter of convenience, an ARIMA process with no moving-average part may be referred to as ARI (p,d) and one with no autoregressive part as IMA (d,q).

To see why the ARIMA (p,d,q) process displays homogeneous behavior, that is, behavior which is independent of the level of z_t, consider the consequence of displacing the whole series by an arbitrary amount c through time $t - 1$. Now if $d = 1$ (4.1.5) determines the subsequent evolution of the process, and with the displacement of the series, z_t would be given by

$$z_t = (z_{t-1} + c) + \phi_1[(z_{t-1} + c) - (z_{t-2} + c)] + \cdots$$
$$+ \phi_p[(z_{t-p} + c) - (z_{t-p-1} + c)] + u_t - \theta_1 u_{t-1} - \cdots - \theta_q u_{t-q} \qquad (4.1.8)$$

which reduces immediately to

$$z_t = [z_{t-1} + \phi_1(z_{t-1} - z_{t-2}) + \cdots + \phi_p(z_{t-p} - z_{t-p-1})$$
$$+ u_t - \theta_1 u_{t-1} - \cdots - \theta_q u_{t-q}] + c \qquad (4.1.9)$$

which is just the value of z_t prior to the displacement plus the amount c. Thus the displacement does not alter the behavior of the series but rather just shifts its level in accordance with the property of homogeneity.

4.2 Other Transformations Useful in Achieving Stationarity

Differencing by itself is sometimes not sufficient to achieve stationarity for economic time series, particularly those spanning considerable lengths of time. For example, first differences of GNP from the turn of the century to the present become more disperse as time goes on; that is, the absolute magnitude of changes increases with time. This is as one would expect since it is probably relative or percentage changes that are homogeneous, and hence as the level of GNP rises the magnitude of changes increases. Now, changes in logs are essentially percentage changes. Thus, in a situation of this kind we could induce homogeneity by taking the natural logs of the raw data and then proceeding to examine differences in the logs.

To see why this transformation to natural logs would be appropriate, let z'_t be the raw data and z_t be

$$z_t = \ln(z'_t) \qquad (4.2.1)$$

If z'_t is, say, $x \times 100$ percent larger than z'_{t-1}, then the difference in logs is

$$
\begin{aligned}
z_t - z_{t-1} &= \ln(z'_t) - \ln(z'_{t-1}) \\
&= \ln \frac{z'_t}{z'_{t-1}} \\
&= \ln \frac{z'_{t-1}(1+x)}{z'_{t-1}} \\
&= \ln(1+x) \\
&\doteq x \qquad (4.2.2)
\end{aligned}
$$

which is the percentage change.

Although the log transformation may be appropriate in principle for many economic time series, as a practical matter it is generally necessary only for data records spanning more than a few decades.

4.3 The Difference-equation Form of the ARIMA Process

A given observation in a time series generated by an ARIMA (p,d,q) process may be expressed in terms of past observations and current and past disturbances, as in (4.1.5) for the case $d = 1$. Rearranging the terms in (4.1.5), we have

$$
\begin{aligned}
z_t = (1 + \phi_1)z_{t-1} + (\phi_2 - \phi_1)z_{t-2} + \cdots + (\phi_p - \phi_{p-1})z_{t-p} \\
- \phi_p z_{t-p-1} + u_t - \theta_1 u_{t-1} - \cdots - \theta_q u_{t-q} \quad (4.3.1)
\end{aligned}
$$

which is referred to as the *difference-equation* form of the ARIMA $(p,1,q)$ model. It is this form of the model that will ultimately be used in computing forecasts.

As an example, consider the difference-equation form of the ARIMA $(1,1,1)$ process

$$z_t = (1 + \phi_1)z_{t-1} - \phi_1 z_{t-2} + u_t - \theta_1 u_{t-1} \qquad (4.3.2)$$

which is seen to be a particular ARMA $(2,1)$ process with "ϕ_1" $= (1 + \phi_1)$ and "ϕ_2" $= -\phi_1$ and which does not satisfy stationarity conditions. Similarly, the difference-equation form of the very important ARIMA $(0,1,1)$, or simply IMA $(1,1)$, process is

$$z_t = z_{t-1} + u_t - \theta_1 u_{t-1} \qquad (4.3.3)$$

One way to view (4.3.3) is as a nonstationary ARMA (1,1) process for which "ϕ_1" $= 1$. Another way to view it is as a random walk to which a moving-average term $(-\theta_1 u_{t-1})$ has been added.

4.4 The Random-shock Form of the ARIMA Process

A second way of writing the ARIMA process is in terms of past disturbances only so that

$$z_t = u_t + \Psi_1 u_{t-1} + \Psi_2 u_{t-2} + \cdots \tag{4.4.1}$$

referred to as the *random-shock* form of the process. It may be obtained by successive substitution for z_{t-1}, z_{t-2}, and so forth, using the difference equation of the process. The specific values of weights Ψ_i then will depend on the order of differencing and values of the ϕ and θ coefficients. The random-shock form of a process will be very important in forecasting since it is the Ψ_i weights along with $\sigma_u{}^2$ that will be used for computation of standard errors and confidence intervals for future observations.

For example, the random-shock form of the IMA (1,1) model may be obtained by successive substitution for z_{t-1}, z_{t-2}, and so forth; hence

$$z_t = z_{t-1} + u_t - \theta_1 u_{t-1}$$
$$= (z_{t-2} + u_{t-1} - \theta_1 u_{t-2}) + u_t - \theta_1 u_{t-1}$$
$$\cdots\cdots\cdots\cdots\cdots\cdots\cdots\cdots$$
$$= u_t + (1 - \theta_1)u_{t-1} + (1 - \theta_1)u_{t-2} + \cdots \tag{4.4.2}$$

so that for IMA (1,1) we have

$$\Psi_i = (1 - \theta_1) \qquad i = 1, 2, \ldots \tag{4.4.3}$$

As expected, the IMA (1,1) process does not satisfy the stationarity condition for linear processes since $[1 + (1 - \theta_1) + (1 - \theta_1) + \cdots]$ does not converge.

The structure of the random-shock form of the IMA (1,1) process lends itself to an interesting interpretation of the evolution of the process. In particular, define the *level* of the process denoted $\bar{z}_t$ as

$$\bar{z}_t = (1 - \theta_1)u_{t-1} + (1 - \theta_1)u_{t-2} + \cdots \tag{4.4.4}$$

Then z_t is given by

$$z_t = \bar{z}_t + u_t \tag{4.4.5}$$

that is, by the sum of the level and the current disturbance. Now the level is itself a nonstationary process, which from (4.4.4) evolves according to

$$\bar{z}_t = \bar{z}_{t-1} + (1 - \theta_1)u_{t-1} \tag{4.4.6}$$

chap. 4 models for nonstationary time series

Thus fraction $(1 - \theta_1)$ of the disturbance u_{t-1} is absorbed each period into the level of the series. Following Muth, we might interpret $(1 - \theta_1)u_{t-1}$ as the "permanent" contribution of u_{t-1} and $\theta_1 u_{t-1}$ as its "transitory" contribution.[1] Furthermore, from (4.4.6) the level is seen to be a random walk with disturbance u'_t given by

$$u'_t = (1 - \theta_1)u_{t-1} \tag{4.4.7}$$

since

$$\bar{z}_t = \bar{z}_{t-1} + u'_t \tag{4.4.8}$$

The level of the series may also be expressed in terms of past observations, as we shall see in the next section.

4.5 The Inverted Form of the ARIMA Process

Starting with the difference-equation form of the process and substituting successively for $u_{t-1}, u_{t-2}, \ldots, z_t$ may be expressed in terms of the current disturbance and past observations only; that is,

$$z_t = \pi_1 z_{t-1} + \pi_2 z_{t-2} + \cdots + u_t \tag{4.5.1}$$

This form of the process is referred to as the *inverted* form of the process.

For the IMA $(1,1)$ process, the substitutions lead to

$$
\begin{aligned}
z_t &= z_{t-1} + u_t - \theta_1 u_{t-1} \\
&= z_{t-1} + u_t - \theta_1[(z_{t-1} - z_{t-2}) + \theta_1 u_{t-2}] \\
&= u_t + (1 - \theta_1)z_{t-1} + \theta_1 z_{t-2} - \theta_1{}^2[(z_{t-2} - z_{t-3}) + \theta_1 u_{t-3})] \\
& \cdots \cdots \cdots \cdots \cdots \cdots \cdots \cdots \cdots \cdots \cdots \cdots \\
&= (1 - \theta_1)z_{t-1} + \theta_1(1 - \theta_1)z_{t-2} + \theta_1{}^2(1 - \theta_1)z_{t-3} + \cdots + u_t
\end{aligned} \tag{4.5.2}
$$

so that the weights π_i are given by

$$\pi_i = \theta_1{}^{i-1}(1 - \theta_1) \qquad i = 1, 2, \ldots \tag{4.5.3}$$

Thus, as we look further into the past, each observation receives a weight that is fraction θ_1 as large as the weight given its successor in the determination of the current observation.

It may be shown that *generally* for ARIMA (p,d,q) processes with $d \geq 1$, the condition

$$\sum_{i=1}^{\infty} \pi_i = 1 \tag{4.5.4}$$

[1] See J. Muth, Optimal Properties of Exponentially Weighted Forecasts of Time Series with Permanent and Transitory Components, *Journal of the American Statistical Association*, **55**:299ff. (1960). Muth shows that the IMA $(1,1)$ process as a model of consumers' incomes is consistent with the formulation of "permanent" income as an EWMA of past incomes. This result is discussed further in Sec. 4.5.

holds. Verification of (4.5.4) for IMA (1,1) is left as an exercise for the reader.

If we compare expression (4.5.2) for the inverted form of the IMA (1,1) process with (4.4.6) for its random-shock form, we see that an alternative way of writing the level of the IMA (1,1) process $\bar{z}_t$ must be

$$\bar{z}_t = (1 - \theta_1)z_{t-1} + \theta_1(1 - \theta_1)z_{t-2} + \theta_1^2(1 - \theta_1)z_{t-3} + \cdots \quad (4.5.5)$$

which is equivalent to (4.4.4). The level of the process therefore may be viewed alternatively as an EWMA of past observations. The change in the level from period to period is then

$$\bar{z}_t = (1 - \theta_1)z_{t-1} + \theta_1\bar{z}_{t-1} \quad (4.5.6)$$

or

$$\bar{z}_t - \bar{z}_{t-1} = (1 - \theta_1)(z_{t-1} - \bar{z}_{t-1}) \quad (4.5.7)$$

Note that (4.5.7) is equivalent to our previous expression (4.4.6) for changes in the level since from (4.4.5) we see that u_{t-1} is just $(z_{t-1} - \bar{z}_{t-1})$.

Comparing expressions (4.5.5) and (4.5.6) with expressions (1.1.14) and (1.1.15), it becomes apparent that computation of exponential smoothing forecasts corresponds to computation of the level of a series if the series is generated by an IMA (1,1) process and the smoothing coefficient β is set equal to θ_1. Now, if in fact a particular series were generated by IMA (1,1), would the level or exponential smoothing forecast with $\beta = \theta_1$ provide a sensible forecast? To answer this, note that from (4.4.5) we have

$$E(z_t|H_{t-1}) = E(\bar{z}_t + u_t|H_{t-1})$$
$$= E(\bar{z}_t|H_{t-1}) + E(u_t|H_{t-1})$$
$$= \bar{z}_t \quad (4.5.8)$$

where H_{t-1} denotes past history through time $t - 1$, that is, $(\ldots, z_{t-2}, z_{t-1})$.

We have made use of the fact that $\bar{z}_t$ depends only on past history H_{t-1} and u_t which is independent of that past history. Hence the level $\bar{z}_t$ is the *conditional expectation of z_t given the preceding history of the series* at time $t - 1$. It is therefore the minimum mean-square-error forecast. The forecast error will be

$$z_t - \bar{z}_t = u_t \quad (4.5.9)$$

which has variance σ_u^2 and expectation zero. The error made by this forecast is the only component of z_t that is necessarily unknown at time $(t - 1)$. We conclude, then, that exponential smoothing yields optimal forecasts *if* the series is an IMA (1,1) process *and* the smoothing coefficient β is set equal to θ_1. What about the optimality of exponential smoothing for ARIMA (p,d,q) processes in general? It is quite apparent that generally it will not be optimal since the decomposition of z_t into the current disturbance and an EWMA of past observations is caused only by the particular structure of the IMA (1,1) process. Consequently, it is apparent that simple exponential smoothing will not provide optimal forecasts for series generated by ARIMA processes other than IMA (1,1).

4.6 Constant Terms in ARIMA Processes

The constant term μ has been omitted from the expressions for ARIMA processes presented so far in this chapter. In the absence of a constant term, the mean of the stationary processes generating the differences w_t is zero. Thus the average of differences over a long period of time will be approximately zero. What does this mean about the behavior of the undifferenced process z_t? It means simply that although the process exhibits no affinity for a mean value, it also exhibits no persistent tendency or "trend" in either the positive or negative direction.

Now consider the effect of a presence of a constant δ. The mean of the process of differences w_t is then

$$E(w_t) = \frac{\delta}{1 - \phi_1 - \cdots - \phi_p} \tag{4.6.1}$$

indicating that the average difference over a long period of time will be nonzero. For example, in the usual case where $d = 1$, if δ is positive, then the average change will be positive and the series z_t will tend to drift, or trend, upward. It is important to note that the presence of a constant term does not imply that the series follows a deterministic path through time as is the case for some of the models examined in Chap. 1, where the series was assumed to follow a polynomial or exponential function in time. Rather, the series will usually move in a positive direction, although it may take trips in the negative direction for a while. Conversely, it should be clear from the nature of nonstationary processes that what appears to be a trend to the human eye need not be owing to the presence of a constant. For example, trends of this sort are certainly present in Fig. 1.1, where no actual drift is present. How often one reads in the financial press that the stock market has been in an uptrend or downtrend, although these movements are simply the result of random changes! Consequently, we should be wary of concluding hastily that a particular nonstationary series exhibits real trend or drift merely from casual inspection.

This is more so the case if $d = 2$ so that the first differences are nonstationary. Since, then, the first differences would be free to wander without any tendency to revert to a mean value, the undifferenced series z_t might rise rapidly for long periods of time only to begin later a protracted negative movement. The tendency to see deterministic trends in such series is almost irresistible though none is present.

4.7 Examples of Nonstationary Processes: Gross National Product and Expenditures on Producers' Durables

The solid line in Fig. 4.1 is a plot of quarterly GNP in current dollars in the United States for 1947-01 through 1966-04. Neither what we know of the economic nature of this series nor what we see in Fig. 4.1 would tempt us to characterize it as stationary. The first differences of the series plotted in Fig. 4.2, however, are more deserving of that label. In Chap. 5 we find that

figure 4.1 Actual GNP in billions of current dollars (solid line) and two simulations of ARI (1,1) model, quarterly 1947-01 through 1966-04.

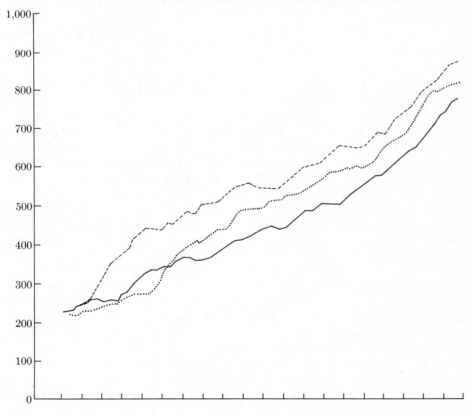

figure 4.2 Actual first differences of GNP in billions of current dollars, quarterly 1947-01 through 1966-04.

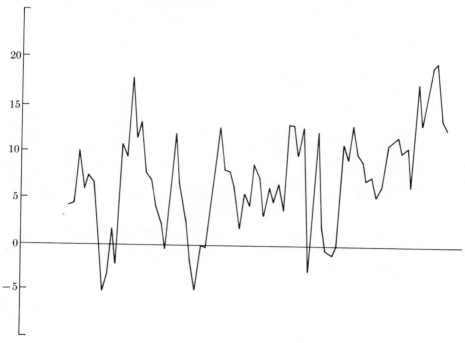

the ARI (1,1) model

$$(\text{GNP}_t - \text{GNP}_{t-1}) = .62(\text{GNP}_{t-1} - \text{GNP}_{t-2}) + 2.69 + u_t$$
$$\sigma_u{}^2 = 22.66 \tag{4.7.1}$$

(all quantities in billions of current dollars) is a very satisfactory model for GNP. That is, we shall model the first differences of GNP as a stationary first-order autoregression.

The dashed and dotted lines in Fig. 4.1 are two artificial realizations of GNP produced on a computer by successive drawings of normal disturbances with mean 0 and variance 22.66 from a random-number generator, using actual values of GNP in 1947-01 and 1947-02 as starting points for recursive computation of the GNP_t from (4.7.1). Note how the artificial series mimics the characteristics of the historical series, exhibiting the familiar features of business *cycles* with expansions and recessions meanwhile drifting upward through the postwar period.

Similarly, expenditures on producers' durables (EPD), which is one of the components of GNP, is plotted as the solid line in Fig. 4.3. The series exhibits no apparent affinity for a mean value, but its first differences plotted in Fig. 4.4 appear to be stationary. The model for EPD developed in the next chapter is the IMA (1,1) process

$$(\text{EPD}_t - \text{EPD}_{t-1}) = v_t + .35v_{t-1} + .52 \tag{4.7.2}$$
$$\sigma_v^2 = 1.12$$

(all quantities in billions of current dollars) where v_t is the disturbance process that drives the series. The dashed and dotted lines in Fig. 4.3 are artificial realizations generated by model (4.7.2) and are again difficult to distinguish in general character from the historical series. It would seem improbable that a Martian economist, unfamiliar with the details of United States economic

figure 4.3 Actual expenditures on producers' durables in billions of current dollars and two simulations of IMA (1,1) model, quarterly 1947-01 through 1966-04.

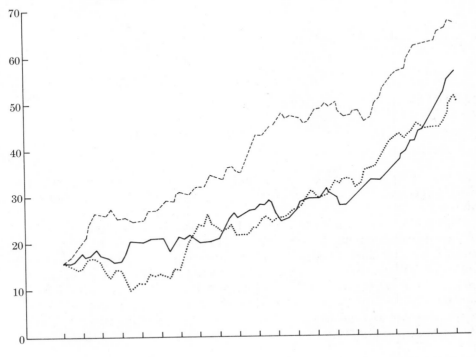

chap. 4 models for nonstationary time series

figure 4.4 Actual first differences of expenditures on producers' durables in billions of current dollars, quarterly 1947-01 through 1966-04.

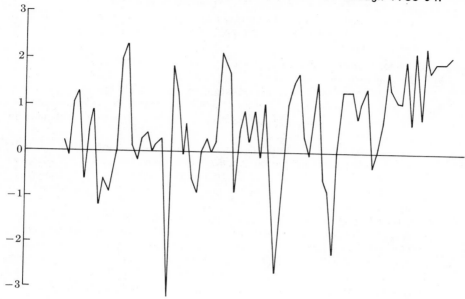

history, would be able to identify either GNP or EPD from among their artificial counterparts.

Exercises

4.1 Confirm that for any IMA (1,1) process

$$\sum_{i=1}^{\infty} \pi_i = 1$$

4.2 Explain why any ARIMA process $(d \geq 1)$ is invertible.

4.3 Mr. Smith looks at a particular time series and concludes that it is well represented by the AR (2) model

$$z_t = .88z_{t-1} + .10z_{t-2} + \delta + u_t$$

Mr. Jones looks at the same series and decides that an IMA (1,1) model radically different from that proposed by Mr. Smith is appropriate, namely,

$$z_t = z_{t-1} + u_t - .1u_{t-1}$$

(a) Write Mr. Jones' model in inverted form, evaluating π_1 and π_2 explicitly and providing a general expression for π_i.

(b) Confirm that $\Sigma_{i=1}^{\infty} \pi_i = 1$.

exercises

(c) What does comparison of the result obtained in (a) with Mr. Smith's model suggest about how radically different the two models really are?

(d) If forecasts of z_t were defined to be the conditional expectation $E(z_t|z_{t-1}, \ldots)$, how would you expect the two sets of forecasts to compare, using each model?

(e) How would you characterize the kind of long-run behavior implied by each of the models?

4.4 A consumer's income measured quarterly follows an IMA (1,1) process with $\theta_1 = .25$ and with no drift $(\delta = 0)$.

(a) Write the process in difference-equation, random-shock, and inverted forms.

(b) Provide two expressions for the "level" or "permanent" component of income. Describe in words the relationship between permanent income and past measured incomes.

(c) Each period the new value of permanent income may be expressed simply in terms of the most recent observation on measured income and the previous value of permanent income. Thus, consumer's measured income in period t was \$5,900 and his permanent income \$5,500. Compute his updated permanent income for period $t + 1$.

(d) Show why the consumer's permanent income in any period may be regarded as an optimal forecast of the measured income he is to receive that period.

(e) The permanent income theory of consumption behavior says that consumption expenditures during a given period are proportional to the permanent component of a consumer's income as of that period.[1] That is, if we denote measured income by z_t, permanent income by $\bar{z}_t$, and consumption by c_t, then

$$c_t = k\bar{z}_{t+1} \qquad k = \text{constant between 1 and 0}$$

describes consumption expenditures during period t. Explain in words the implied relationship between consumption and current and past values of measured income. How would this consumption hypothesis lend itself to interpretation as "forecasted income" consumption hypothesis? Taking $k = .8$, compute our consumer's consumption expenditures for the period t referred to in Exercise 4.4(c).

---

[1] The permanent income theory of consumption is put forth by M. Friedman, "A Theory of Consumption Function," Princeton University Press, Princeton, N.J., 1957. See particularly pp. 142–147, where the EWMA interpretation of permanent income is discussed.

chap. 4   models for nonstationary time series

5
Identification
and
Estimation
of
ARIMA
Models

In the preceding chapters we were concerned with the theoretical foundations of a very flexible class of models for stationary and nonstationary time series. We began our study of time series analysis with the ultimate objective of being able to forecast time series from their own past histories. In Chap. 2 we discussed how the behavior of a time series may be summarized by its autocorrelation function. In Chap. 3 stochastic processes of integrated auto-regressive–moving-average form were found to be capable of accounting for a very wide range of patterns of autocorrelation and therefore providing a very flexible class of models for stationary time series. The models were shown in Chap. 4 to be equally useful for the representation of nonstationary time series through the use of differencing.

In the next three chapters we reverse the logical sequence of the first four chapters to consider the problem of *statistical inference*. If we are given a set of observations on a time series, how do we go about estimating the autocor-relation function of the time series? How can that estimated autocorrelation function be used for *identification* of an appropriate ARIMA model for the series, that is, appropriate choices of p, d, and q? Once the model is identified, how might we proceed in *estimation* of parameter values, the ϕ's and the θ's? And finally, how may the model so obtained be used to *forecast* the future of the time series? Graphically, the first part of the text deals with the linkages moving from left to right in the following diagram:

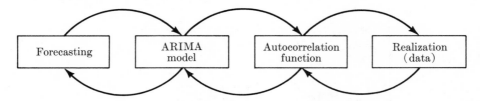

Chapters 5 to 7 then will deal with the reversal of that sequence, from right to left.

This chapter discusses procedures for identification and estimation. Chapter 6 is concerned with forecasting, that is, characterization of the conditional distribution of future observations given the past. Chapter 7 introduces a class of ARIMA models for seasonal time series, and Chap. 8 discusses techniques for forecast evaluation and illustrates them with a case-study application.

5.1   Estimation of the Autocorrelation Function

The first step in the chain of statistical inference is to provide an estimate of the autocorrelation function, which in turn will be the primary aid in model identification. Recall that the theoretical autocorrelation coefficient ρ_j is the ratio of the autovariance of lag j, γ_j to the variance of the process γ_0; that is,

$$\rho_j = \frac{\gamma_j}{\gamma_0} \tag{5.1.1}$$

The autocovariance γ_j is in turn the *expectation* of the cross product of the deviations from the mean of the process for a pair of observations separated by j periods

$$\gamma_j = E[(z_t - \mu)(z_{t+j} - \mu)] \tag{5.1.2}$$

A sensible estimate of γ_j would seem to be the *average* of such cross products in the data where the unknown mean μ is replaced by the sample mean. Denoting this estimate by c_j, as in Chap. 2, we have then

$$c_j = \frac{1}{T} \sum_{t=1}^{T-j} [(z_t - \bar{z})(z_{t+j} - \bar{z})] \tag{5.1.3}$$

where T is the number of observations in hand and $\bar{z}$ is given by

$$\bar{z} = \frac{1}{T} \sum_{t=1}^{T} z_t \tag{5.1.4}$$

Finally, in view of (5.1.1), a natural estimate of ρ_j, denoted r_j, would seem to be

$$r_j = \frac{c_j}{c_0} \tag{5.1.5}\dagger$$

Given sample data, then, an estimate of the autocorrelation function may be obtained by computing r_j for $j = 1, 2, 3, \ldots$. The largest possible subscript j would, of course, be $T - 1$, although in practice the computation is carried out to considerably less than that many lags. A visual device which is very useful in identification is the *sample correlogram*, that is, a graph of the sample autocorrelations. Our objective in studying the sample autocorrelations is to recognize in them a pattern typical of an ARIMA process with which we are familiar. This screening process is often facilitated by inspection of the sample correlogram.

It is very important to remember that sample autocorrelations are only *estimates* of the actual autocorrelations for the process which has generated the data at hand. The sample autocorrelations are therefore subject to sampling error and will never correspond in detail to the underlying true autocorrelations. Approximate expressions for the variance of r_j and the covariance between r_j and r_{j+s} for normal processes have been given by Bartlett.[1] In the particular case that the generating process is a moving-average process of order q, his formula for the variance of r_j reduces to

$$V(r_j) \approx \frac{1}{T} \left\{ 1 + 2 \sum_{i=1}^{q} \rho_i^2 \right\} \qquad j > q \tag{5.1.6}$$

In general, the approximate covarience between r_j and r_{j+s} at long lags is given by

$$\text{cov } (r_j, r_{j+s}) \approx \frac{1}{T} \sum_{i=-\infty}^{\infty} \rho_i \rho_{i+s} \tag{5.1.7}$$

† The properties of r_j as an estimate of ρ_j are discussed in G. M. Jenkins and D. G. Watts, "Spectral Analysis and Its Applications," pp. 174–189, Holden-Day, Inc., San Francisco, 1968.

[1] See M. S. Bartlett, On the Theoretical Specification of the Sampling Properties of Autocorrelated Time Series, *Journal of the Royal Statistical Society*, **B8**:27 (1946).

We note that $V(r_j)$ will decrease as the sample size T is increased; that is, the more data we have from a particular series the better will be our estimates of the true autocorrelations. It is apparent, however, that sampling error will generally be far from negligible for the sample sizes usually available in operational settings. Consequently, we would expect that large sample autocorrelations which are not indicative of the true autocorrelations will sometimes appear. Furthermore, since from (5.1.7) neighboring estimates of the autocorrelations generally covary, the sample autocorrelations may display rather smooth ripples at long lags that are not present in the true autocorrelation function.

The above considerations suggest that the practitioner must be on the look-out for general characteristics which are recognizable in the sample correlogram and not automatically attach significance to every detail. Thus, sample autocorrelations produced by a first-order autoregression will decline approximately, although not precisely, in an exponential fashion. To illustrate, Table 5.1 displays the theoretical autocorrelation function for the AR (1) process

$$z_t = .5z_{t-1} + u_t \qquad (5.1.8)$$

along with sample autocorrelations from 10 independent artificial realizations of the process, each containing 100 observations generated on a computer with the use of a random-number generator. Corresponding sample correlograms are displayed in Fig. 5.1. Although the sample estimates generally mimic the true values in general appearance, there are substantial departures from the theoretical autocorrelation function. Similarly, in Table 5.2 the theoretical

table 5.1 theoretical autocorrelations for the process $z_t = .5z_{t-1} + u_t$ and sample autocorrelations for 10 realizations of $T = 100$

Lag	ρ_i	Sample autocorrelations r_i for 10 independent realizations										Average of r_i over 10 realizations
1	.50	.53	.40	.50	.42	.30	.52	.47	.41	.67	.44	.465
2	.25	.26	.06	.19	.07	.15	.22	.27	.20	.40	.20	.203
3	.125	.20	−.14	.06	.08	.12	.11	.26	.06	.20	.09	.103
4	.0625	.18	−.11	.12	−.04	.06	−.02	.17	−.02	.01	−.02	.034
5	.0312	.08	.08	.11	−.09	.11	−.10	.10	−.08	−.06	−.04	.012
6	.0156	.01	.06	−.04	−.05	.13	.07	.14	−.12	−.04	.12	.028
7	.0078	.04	−.01	−.02	−.13	.08	.03	.20	−.08	−.03	.13	.021
8	.0039	.05	.02	.00	−.20	−.03	.01	.19	−.08	−.05	.01	−.006
9	.0020	.08	.06	−.03	−.07	.04	−.07	.22	−.08	−.02	−.01	.010
10	.0010	.02	.10	−.00	.08	.09	−.21	.09	−.06	.01	.07	.021

chap. 5   identification and estimation of arima models

figure 5.1 Sample correlograms for 10 realizations of length $T = 100$ for the process $z_t = .5z_{t-1} + u_t$.

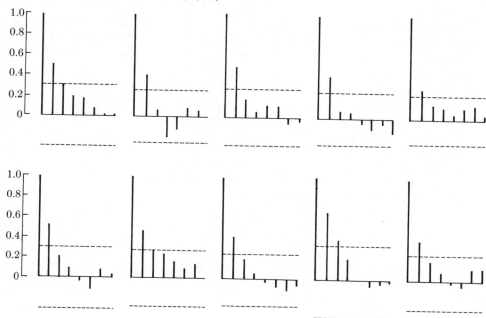

table 5.2 theoretical autocorrelations for the process $z_t = u_t - .5u_{t-1}$ and sample autocorrelations for 10 realizations of $T = 100$

Lag	ρ_j	Sample autocorrelations r_j for 10 independent realizations									Average of r_j over 10 realizations
1	−.40	−.40	−.32	−.36	−.39	−.37	−.30	−.46	−.35	−.56	−.32	−.384
2	.00	.00	−.14	.14	−.01	−.14	−.18	.05	.02	.18	−.10	−.017
3	.00	.01	.02	−.26	.07	.12	.07	−.14	−.04	.04	−.04	−.013
4	.00	−.04	.00	.05	−.05	−.04	−.10	.16	−.06	−.14	.22	−.000
5	.00	−.10	.01	−.04	−.02	.05	.06	.01	.11	.21	−.16	.013
6	.00	.20	.02	.03	.03	−.07	.04	−.15	−.19	−.38	.02	−.045
7	.00	−.03	−.08	.02	−.02	.03	.04	.03	.21	.34	.07	.061
8	.00	.03	.22	.08	.14	.10	−.12	−.02	−.20	−.18	−.08	−.004
9	.00	−.05	−.11	−.08	−.21	.01	−.02	.08	−.03	−.04	−.05	−.050
10	.00	−.01	−.09	.05	.09	−.11	.12	−.04	.06	.15	.04	.028

autocorrelations for the MA (1) process

$$z_t = u_t - .5u_{t-1} \tag{5.1.9}$$

are displayed together with sample autocorrelations for 10 independent artificial realizations of 100 observations. Sample correlograms appear in Fig. 5.2. Note that although $\rho_j = 0$ for $j = 2, 3, \ldots$, the values of r_j are occasionally large at lags greater than 1 as a result of sampling error.

Confronted with the problem of distinguishing what is important from what is not in a sample correlogram, we look for a test of the statistical significance of sample autocorrelations. Bartlett's approximation (5.1.6) for the variance of r_j suggests just such a test. In particular, we note that the variance of r_j for $j > q$ is given by Bartlett's formula *under the hypothesis that the true order of the process is q*. Since the distribution of the r_j for $j > q$ is approximately normal, we may regard a sample autocorrelation larger in absolute value than 1.96 standard deviations; that is,

$$|r_j| > (1.96) \frac{1}{\sqrt{T}} \left(1 + 2 \sum_{i=1}^{q} \rho_i^2 \right)^{1/2} \qquad j > q \tag{5.1.10}$$

as being significantly different from zero at the .05 level. In practice, of course, the ρ_i that enter into the formula are unknown and must be replaced by sample estimates. Thus a standard error for r_j is given by

$$\text{SE}\,(r_j) = \frac{1}{\sqrt{T}} \left(1 + 2 \sum_{i=1}^{q} r_i^2 \right)^{1/2} \qquad j > q \tag{5.1.11}$$

and the rough criterion

$$|r_j| > 2 \frac{1}{\sqrt{T}} \left(1 + 2 \sum_{i=1}^{q} r^2 \right)^{1/2} \qquad j > q \tag{5.1.12}$$

may be used to test whether an r_j at lag greater than q is reasonably considered to be zero.

Some caution is required in applying the test of significance since if we were to look through enough autocorrelation coefficients we would find some (about 5 out of 100) to be "significant." This is illustrated by the sample correlograms of Fig. 5.2, where horizontal lines have been drawn in at ± 2 standard errors [using (5.1.12)]. A few r_j for $j > 1$ are significant among the 10 realizations, although their theoretical counterparts are all zero. The basic philosophical presumption in building ARIMA models (or, for that matter, statistical models generally) is that the final model will be of relatively simple form. In other words, q will be small. Consequently, if our tentative identification is that q is, say, q^*, then one will generally be interested in testing the significance of

figure 5.2 Sample correlograms for 10 realizations of length $T = 100$ for the process $z_t = u_t - .5u_{t-1}$.

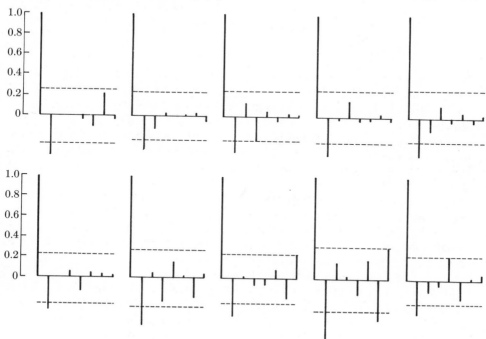

r_{q*+1}. Hence, if r_{q*+1} proves to be significant in a particular instance, we would be inclined to abandon the identification MA $(q*)$ in favor of MA $(q* + 1)$. Thus, for the correlograms of Fig. 5.2, in no case would we have rejected the hypothesis that $q = 1$ in favor of $q = 2$.

5.2 Determining the Appropriate Degree of Differencing

Frequently it will be the case for economic time series that the raw data will exhibit nonstationarity and that it will be the first or second differences which are modeled as a stationary ARMA process. How, then, to determine the appropriate degree of differencing? In particular, how might the sample auto-correlations of the data indicate that differencing is required?

Note that if the series is nonstationary in the sense of being an integrated process, the autocovariances and therefore autocorrelations of the process are simply undefined. However, from any finite set of data *sample* autocorrelations may always be computed. Intuition would suggest that nonstationary series would produce sample autocorrelations that remain large even at long lags. This is because in any realization the series will tend to be on one or the other side of the *sample* mean of the series for many periods. A more technical way of expressing the same idea is as follows. We know that for an ARMA $(1,q)$ process the theoretical autocorrelations for lags greater than q are given by

$$\rho_j = \phi_1 \rho_{j-1} \qquad j = q + 1, \ldots \qquad (5.2.1)$$

Now if ϕ_1 were very close to 1, the ρ_j would decline very slowly with increasing lag. Thus, in sample estimates of the ρ_j, we would expect that characteristic to be mimicked; that is, the sample autocorrelations will damp out very slowly.

How slowly is slow? There is no precise answer that is available from the sample autocorrelations alone. In practice, the context or nature of the data series helps to provide a tentative answer that may be examined further when parameters of the model are estimated. If nonstationarity in the raw data is suspected, then the sample autocorrelations of the first differences are examined for evidence of an appropriate stationary model. Only occasionally in economic data will sample autocorrelations of first differences fail to damp out, in which case sample autocorrelations of *second* differences are examined. A check on our choice of a level of differencing is provided when we come to estimate the parameters of the identified model.

It is very important to keep in mind that we need only identify the *lowest* level of differencing for which a stationary model is apparent. This is because further differences of any stationary series are also stationary and nothing is gained by further differencing. To illustrate, consider the MA (0) process

$$z_t = u_t \qquad (5.2.2)$$

which has zero autocorrelations at all lags. Now, if we examined sample autocorrelations for a realization of this process, we would find, of course, little evidence of autocorrelation; that is, the r_j would probably be small. Now suppose we computed sample autocorrelations of first differences of z_t, that is, of the series

$$w_t = z_t - z_{t-1} = u_t - u_{t-1} \qquad (5.2.3)$$

As the reader may readily verify, the theoretical autocorrelations for (5.2.3) are

$$\rho_1 = -.50$$
$$\rho_j = 0 \qquad j > 1 \qquad (5.2.4)$$

a pattern that would be evidence in sample autocorrelations and that could be suggestive of a first-order–moving-average process. Indeed, the series w_t is a first-order moving average with $\theta_1 = 1$ *but only as an artifact of differencing.* It should be apparent, therefore, that nothing would be gained by working with the w_t rather than the z_t just because the former display some autocorrelation. Superfluous differencing in general merely alters the pattern of autocorrelation evident in a stationary series and only serves to complicate it unnecessarily.

5.3 Example: Expenditures on Producers' Durables

Expenditures on producers' durables (EPD) was referred to in Chap. 4 as an example of a nonstationary series. Looking again at Fig. 4.3, we see that the series displays no affinity for a mean value but rather drifts upward over the sample period. The first differences of the series in Fig. 4.4 do, however, exhibit what appears to be stationary behavior. In order to explore further the need for first differencing and to identify an appropriate ARIMA model for the series, we shall examine the sample autocorrelations of the raw data and its first differences.

These sample statistics are provided by a computer program entitled PDQ, which plots and lists specified differences of the raw data (or of logs of the raw data if desired), computes sample autocorrelations and partial autocorrelations (which we discuss in the next section), and plots the sample correlograms and partial autocorrelations.[1] We need to be familiar with a symbol called the *backshift operator* to be able to read the output from PDQ. This operator, denoted by B, simply shifts the subscript of a time series observation backward in time by one period. Thus

$$Bz_t = z_{t-1}$$
$$Bz_{54} = z_{53} \tag{5.3.1}$$

and so forth. Now if we raise B to a power, we mean that B is applied by the number of times indicated by the power; that is,

$$B^k z_t = \underbrace{BB \cdots Bz_t}_{k}$$

$$= \underbrace{B \cdots Bz_{t-1}}_{k-1}$$

$$\cdots \cdots \cdots \cdots$$

$$= z_{t-k} \tag{5.3.2}$$

for example,

$$B^{12} z_{43} = z_{31} \tag{5.3.3}$$

[1] Program PDQ is described in the Appendix, Sec. A.1.

The first difference of z_t may be indicated by $(1 - B)z_t$, where $(1 - B)$ is referred to as the *difference operator* since

$$(1 - B)z_t = z_t - Bz_t$$
$$= z_t - z_{t-1} \tag{5.3.4}$$

Similarly, the second difference may be indicated by $(1 - B)^2 z_t$ since

$$(1 - B)^2 z_t = (1 - B)(1 - B)z_t$$
$$= (1 - B)(z_t - z_{t-1})$$
$$= (z_t - z_{t-1}) - (z_{t-1} - z_{t-2}) \tag{5.3.5}$$

When we study models for seasonal time series in Chap. 6, we shall have use for the *seasonal difference* $(z_t - z_{t-s})$, where s is the number of periods per seasonal cycle. So if we were analyzing toy sales, which is a highly seasonal series, we would have use for the transformation $(z_t - z_{t-12})$, or, using the backshift operator,

$$(1 - B^{12})z_t = z_t - B^{12}z_t$$
$$= z_t - z_{t-12} \tag{5.3.6}$$

If we were interested in the first differences of the seasonal differences, we would indicate the transformation by $(1 - B)(1 - B^{12})z_t$, which is just

$$(1 - B)(1 - B^{12})z_t = (z_t - z_{t-12}) - B(z_t - z_{t-12})$$
$$= (z_t - z_{t-12}) - (z_{t-1} - z_{t-13}) \tag{5.3.7}$$

If the power zero appears on a backshift operator or difference operator, it simply indicates that the operation is carried out zero times, that is, not at all. Hence we might see $(1 - B)(1 - B^{12})^0 z_t$, which is just $(1 - B)z_t$, the simple first difference of z_t.

We turn now to the PDQ output for EPD for the sample period 1947–01 through 1966–04 (Table 5.3). The number of observations is $T = 80$, and the differences for which autocorrelations are computed are: (1) $(1 - B)^0(1 - B^0)^0 z_t$ or just the raw data z_t and (2) $(1 - B)^1(1 - B^0)^0$ or just the first differences $(1 - B)z_t$. The sample variance of the raw data, an estimate of γ_0 if it exists, is about 94.2 billions of current dollars, and the sample variance of the first differences, an estimate of γ_0 *of the first differences*, is about 1.25 billions of current dollars. The sample autocorrelations are arrayed in rows of 12. At the end of each row is the estimated standard error for each autocorrelation in the row calculated according to Bartlett's formula. For the first row, the standard error is appropriate under the hypothesis $q = 0$, for the second row under the hypothesis $q = 12$, and so forth.

table 5.3 sample autocorrelations and partial autocorrelations for EPD 1947-01 through 1966-04, PDQ output

EXPENDITURES PRODUCERS DURABLES

AUTOCORRELATION AND PARTIAL AUTOCORRELATION FUNCTIONS OF VARIOUS DIFFERENCES
UNLOGGED DATA   T= 80

DIFFERENCE	LAGS	AUTOCORRELATIONS												EST. STD ERROR FOR ROW
$(1-B)^0 (1-B)^0$	1-12	0.93	0.86	0.79	0.73	0.67	0.62	0.58	0.53	0.49	0.45	0.41	0.38	0.11
VAR = 0.942E 02	13-24	0.34	0.31	0.29	0.26	0.24	0.22	0.20	0.18	0.16	0.15	0.13	0.12	0.37
$(1-B)^1 (1-B)^0$	1-12	0.36	0.11	0.03	-0.02	0.01	0.03	0.09	0.01	0.08	0.16	0.08	0.07	0.11
VAR = 0.125E 01	13-24	0.01	0.04	-0.05	-0.01	0.10	-0.06	0.11	0.07	-0.05	-0.12	-0.11	-0.01	0.13

DIFFERENCE	LAGS	PARTIAL AUTOCORRELATIONS												EST. STD ERROR FOR ROW
$(1-B)^0 (1-B)^0$	1-12	0.93	-0.03	-0.03	-0.02	0.01	0.02	-0.01	0.02	0.01	-0.03	-0.01	-0.02	0.11
$(1-B)^1 (1-B)^0$	1-12	0.36	-0.03	-0.03	0.00	-0.03	0.03	0.02	0.08	0.10	0.12	0.12	0.04	0.11

figure 5.3 Sample correlogram for EPD, undifferenced series, 1947-01 through 1966-04, PDQ output.

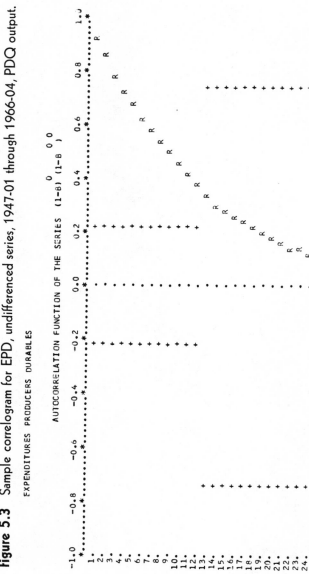

figure 5.4 Sample correlogram of first differences of EPD, 1947-01 through 1966-04, PDQ output.

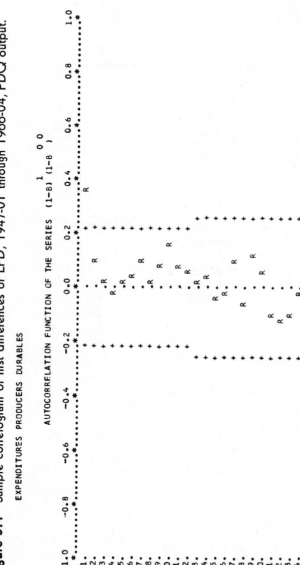

The sample autocorrelations of the raw data decline only very slowly as lag increases, confirming our visual impression of the data as being nonstationary. When we look at the sample autocorrelations of the first differences, however, only the spike at lag 1 period is large relative to its standard error. These results are illustrated by the sample correlograms displayed in Figs. 5.3 and 5.4. The model suggested then is clearly IMA (1,1); that is, the first differences of EPD are well represented by a first-order moving average. Inspection of Fig. 4.3, the plot of the first differences, further suggests that the model will contain a constant since the series of first differences appears to have a positive mean. The model we have arrived at is then

$$w_t = \delta + u_t - \theta_1 u_{t-1} \qquad (5.3.8)$$

or
$$z_t = z_{t-1} + \delta + u_t - \theta_1 u_{t-1} \qquad (5.3.9)$$

Our next objective will be to estimate values of the parameters θ_1, δ, and $\sigma_u{}^2$ from the data at hand.

5.4 Identification of the Order of an Autoregressive Process: The Partial Autocorrelation Function

Identification of the order of a moving-average process from the sample auto-correlations is fairly straightforward by the use of standard errors from Bartlett's formula since testing the hypothesis that q is, say, q^* amounts to testing the significance of r_{q^*+1}. The situation is not nearly as simple for autoregressive processes. At best we might hope to distinguish in the sample autocorrelations the exponential decay pattern of AR (1) from the more complex patterns of higher-order autoregressive processes. But how, for example, could one readily distinguish AR (3) from AR (2)? A set of sample statistics known as *partial autocorrelations* helps in making such distinctions.

Use of partial autocorrelations arises when the specification of a pure auto-regressive model is being considered and the order of the autoregression is in doubt. Now, the Yule–Walker equations for AR (p) are given by

$$
\begin{aligned}
\rho_1 &= \phi_1 \quad\;\; + \phi_2\rho_1 \;\; + \cdots + \phi_p\rho_{p-1} \\
&\cdots \cdots \cdots \cdots \cdots \cdots \cdots \cdots \cdots \cdots \cdots \qquad (5.4.1) \\
\rho_p &= \phi_1\rho_{p-1} + \phi_2\rho_{p-2} \qquad\quad + \phi_p
\end{aligned}
$$

Thus, if we knew p and the values of $\rho_1, \ldots, \rho_p$, we could solve this system of p equations for the p unknowns ϕ_1 through ϕ_p. In practice, however, we are ignorant of the true values of the ρ_i as well as p, which is, of course, the whole problem. Now suppose that we temporarily entertain the hypothesis that $p = 1$. Then an *estimate* of ϕ_1 could be obtained by solution of the Yule–Walker equation for $p = 1$ in which ρ_1 is replaced by the estimate r_1, in particular,

$$r_1 = \hat{\phi}_1 \qquad (5.4.2)$$

where $\hat{\phi}_1$ is the resulting estimate of ϕ_1. Now if ϕ_1 is substantially different from zero, we could conclude that we are dealing with a process of *at least* order 1. To see whether the process is of order 2 or greater, we could solve the Yule–Walker equations for $p = 2$, namely,

$$r_1 = \hat{\phi}_1 \ + \hat{\phi}_2 r_1$$
$$r_2 = \hat{\phi}_1 r_1 + \hat{\phi}_2 \qquad (5.4.3)$$

If the resulting estimate $\hat{\phi}_2$ differs from zero, we would conclude that the process is *at least* of order 2. Now suppose that this procedure is repeated for successively larger values of p. If the true value of p is p^*, then when we solve the system for $p = (p^* + 1)$ the value of $\hat{\phi}_{p*+1}$ will be approximately zero since it is an estimate of ϕ_{p*+1}, which is zero. If we denote by $\hat{\phi}_{jj}$ the value of $\hat{\phi}_j$ implied by solution of the system for $p = j$, then the $\hat{\phi}_{jj}$ are referred to as the *estimated* partial autocorrelations of the process. If the time order of the auto-regression is p^*, then it will be the case that

$$\hat{\phi}_{jj} \approx 0 \qquad j > p^* \qquad (5.4.4)$$

Since the partial autocorrelations are sample statistics and therefore subject to sampling error, we need to have some standard for deciding when $\hat{\phi}_{jj}$ has become "approximately" zero. Under the hypothesis that $p = p^*$, the approximate standard error of $\hat{\phi}_{jj}$ is given by

$$\text{SE } (\hat{\phi}_{jj}) \approx \frac{1}{\sqrt{T}} \qquad j > p\dagger \qquad (5.4.5)$$

Thus we infer that $p = p^*$ if $\hat{\phi}_{p*+1,p*+1}$ is small relative to $1/T^{1/2}$.

If the process generating the data is of pure moving-average form, what pattern would we expect to find in estimated partial autocorrelations? Since an MA process may be written as an AR process of infinite order and the $\hat{\phi}_{jj}$ are rough estimates of the ϕ_j, then the $\hat{\phi}_{jj}$ should decline in magnitude with increasing values of j but not cut off at some distinct lag, as is characteristic of AR processes of finite order.

† See M. H. Quenouille, Approximate Tests of Correlation in Time Series, *Journal of the Royal Statistical Society* **B11**:68 (1949).

5.5 Example: Gross National Product

Gross national product in current dollars was another series referred to in Chap. 4 as illustrating nonstationary behavior. Sample autocorrelations and partial autocorrelations for the raw data and first differences over the sample period 1947–01 through 1966–04 are given in Table 5.4 and are plotted in Figs. 5.5 to 5.7. As expected, autocorrelations of the raw data die off very slowly. In contrast, those of the first differences die off quickly. In particular they decline roughly exponentially, suggesting that a first-order autoregression may be an appropriate model for the first differences. The partial autocorrelations support this conclusion, cutting off abruptly after $p = 1$. Our model should include a constant term since the first differences of GNP most certainly have a positive mean as is quite evident in Fig. 4.1. The tentative model then is of the form

$$w_t = \phi_1 w_{t-1} + \delta + u_t$$

or

$$z_t = z_{t-1} + \phi_1(z_{t-1} - z_{t-2}) + \delta + u_t$$

$$(5.5.1)$$

and we shall be interested in using the data to estimate values of the parameters ϕ_1, δ, and σ_u^2.

5.6 Identification of Mixed Processes

The problem of identifying a mixed model is more complex than that of identifying either pure AR or MA models. To see why, suppose that we have differenced to achieve stationarity and that the resulting data have been generated by a mixed process. What would we expect to be the characteristics of the sample autocorrelations and partial autocorrelations? We know that the first q theoretical autocorrelations are determined by both the moving-average and autoregressive parameters through a relationship which is quite complex even if p and q are small. Autocorrelations for longer lags are given by

$$\rho_j = \phi_1 \rho_{j-1} + \cdots + \phi_1 \rho_{j-p} \qquad j > q \qquad (5.6.1)$$

This suggests that we should be on the lookout for a regular pattern in the autocorrelation past some initial lag assumed to be q. For instance, if we were presented with a sample correlogram that had the appearance of either of the correlograms in Fig. 3.8, we would suspect a mixed model with $p = 1$ and $q = 1$.

We also know that a mixed model, when written in autoregressive form, is of infinite order so that the partial autocorrelations, as rough estimates of those autoregressive coefficients, will die off rather than cut off. Consequently, a mixed model will tend to give rise to a gradual decline in *both* sample autocorrelations and partial autocorrelations.

table 5.4 sample autocorrelations and partial autocorrelations for GNP 1947-01 through 1966-04, PDQ output

GROSS NATIONAL PRODUCT

AUTOCORRELATION AND PARTIAL AUTOCORRELATION FUNCTIONS OF VARIOUS DIFFERENCES
UNLOGGED DATA   T= 80

DIFFERENCE	LAGS						AUTOCORRELATIONS							EST. STD ERROR FOR ROW
$(1-B)^0 (1-B)^0$	1-12	0.95	0.90	0.85	0.81	0.76	0.72	0.68	0.64	0.61	0.57	0.53	0.49	0.11
VAR = 0.207E 05	13-24	0.45	0.42	0.39	0.35	0.32	0.30	0.27	0.24	0.21	0.19	0.16	0.14	0.40
$(1-B)^1 (1-B)^0$	1-12	0.60	0.37	0.13	-0.04	-0.08	0.02	0.09	0.07	0.15	0.15	0.08	0.01	0.11
VAR = 0.351E 02	13-24	-0.03	0.01	0.08	0.13	0.21	0.17	0.38	0.02	-0.09	-0.16	-0.08	-0.07	0.17

DIFFERENCE	LAGS						PARTIAL AUTOCORRELATIONS							EST. STD ERROR FOR ROW
$(1-B)^0 (1-B)^0$	1-12	0.95	-0.02	-0.02	-0.01	0.00	0.01	-0.00	-0.01	-0.01	-0.04	-0.02	-0.03	0.11
$(1-B)^1 (1-B)^0$	1-12	0.60	0.01	-0.14	-0.12	0.05	0.17	0.03	-0.10	0.15	0.06	-0.08	-0.07	0.11

figure 5.5   Sample correlogram for GNP, undifferenced series, 1947-01 through 1966-04, PDQ output.

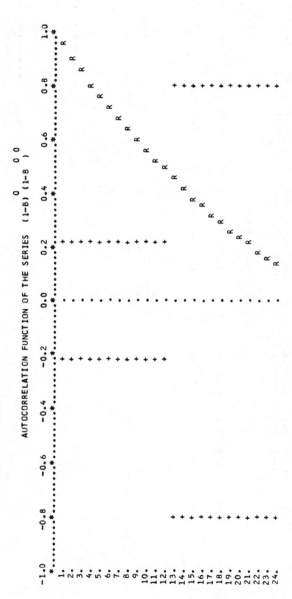

figure 5.6 Sample correlogram of first differences of GNP, 1947-01 through 1966-04, PDQ output.

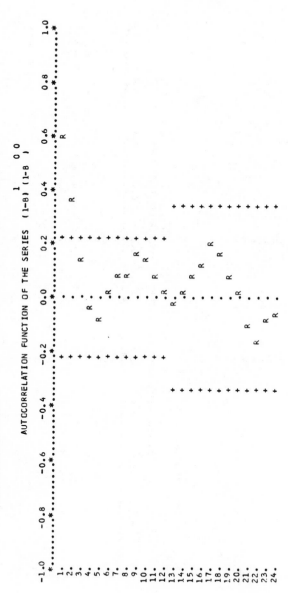

figure 5.7 Plots of sample partial autocorrelations of GNP, 1947-01 through 1966-04, PDQ output.

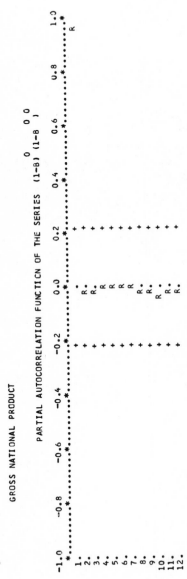

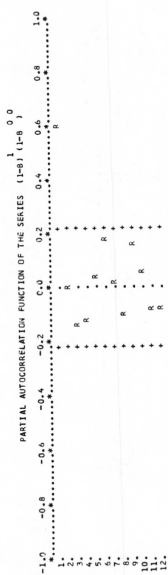

table 5.5 characteristic behavior of autocorrelations and partial autocorrelations for three classes of processes

Class of processes	Autocorrelations	Partial autocorrelations
Moving average	Spikes at lags 1 through q, then cut off	Tail off
Autoregressive	Tail off according to $$\rho_j = \phi_1\rho_{j-1} + \cdots + \phi_p\rho_{j-p}$$	Spikes at lags 1 through p, then cut off
Mixed autoregressive-moving average	Irregular pattern at lags 1 through q, then tail off according to $$\rho_j = \phi_1\rho_{j-1} + \cdots + \phi_p\rho_{j-p}$$	Tail off

As a summary of our discussion of identification, Table 5.5 shows the properties of autocorrelations and partial autocorrelations associated with AR, MA, and mixed processes.

5.7 Preliminary Estimates of Parameters

Having made a tentative model identification for a particular time series, we may then use the sample autocorrelations to obtain preliminary estimates of parameters. These estimates are useful in giving us an indication of how the final model is likely to look as well as providing starting values for the iterative procedure used in computing maximum–likelihood estimates of parameters. The preliminary estimates are obtained by solving for parameter values in the relationships that link parameters and autocorrelations.

The procedure for pure AR processes is straightforward, namely, solution of the p Yule–Walker equations with the r_j inserted in place of ρ_j; that is, we solve the system

$$
\begin{aligned}
r_1 &= \hat{\phi}_1 \quad\quad + \cdots + \hat{\phi}_p r_{p-1} \\
r_p &= \hat{\phi}_1 r_{p-1} + \cdots + \hat{\phi}_p
\end{aligned}
\tag{5.7.1}
$$

which leads to estimates of the p parameters $\phi_1, \ldots, \phi_p$. For example, in the case of the first differences of GNP, we have $p = 1$ and consequently a preliminary estimate of ϕ_1 given by

$$
\hat{\phi}_1 = r_1 = .60
\tag{5.7.2}
$$

The relationship between autocorrelations and parameters is a nonlinear one for MA and mixed processes, and, therefore, the computation of preliminary estimates is less tractable. For MA (1) we have

$$\rho_1 = \frac{-\theta_1}{1 + \theta_1{}^2}$$ (5.7.3)

so an estimate of θ_1 may be obtained from

$$r_1 = \frac{-\hat{\theta}_1}{1 + \hat{\theta}_1{}^2}$$ (5.7.4)

Now (5.7.4) is a quadratic equation in $\hat{\theta}_1$ and has two solutions, namely,

$$\hat{\theta}_1 = -\frac{1}{2r_1} \pm \left[\frac{1}{(2r_1)^2} - 1 \right]^{1/2}$$ (5.7.5)

and each solution is the reciprocal of the other. Thus, alternative estimates might be, say, .2 and 5. Clearly, if one alternative satisfies the invertibility condition $|\theta_1| < 1$, then the other will violate it. Hence the autocorrelation structure is consistent with two generating processes that are empirically indistinguishable. Because of objections to noninvertible processes discussed in Chap. 3 and considerations with regard to maximum-likelihood estimation, the invertible alternative will always be chosen.

For example, in the case of EPD we have a MA (1) model in the first differences, so the value of .36 for r_1 implies estimates of $\hat{\theta}_1$ as follows:

$$\hat{\theta}_1 = -1.39 \pm .96$$
$$= -.43, -2.35$$ (5.7.6)

Then choosing the invertible estimate, we have

$$\hat{\theta}_1 = -.43$$ (5.7.7)

For MA processes of larger order, the q equations

$$r_1 = \frac{-\hat{\theta}_1 + \hat{\theta}_1\hat{\theta}_2 + \cdots + \hat{\theta}_{q-1}\hat{\theta}_q}{1 + \hat{\theta}_1{}^2 + \cdots + \hat{\theta}_q{}^2}$$
$$\cdots \cdots \cdots \cdots \cdots \cdots$$
$$r_q = \frac{-\hat{\theta}_q}{1 + \hat{\theta}_1{}^2 + \cdots + \hat{\theta}_q{}^2}$$ (5.7.8)

may in principle be solved for parameter estimates $\hat{\theta}_1, \ldots, \hat{\theta}_q$. In general, there will be multiple solutions, and the choice of alternative estimates is based on satisfaction of invertibility requirements.

For dealing with mixed processes, a general procedure is as follows. We know that from the equations

$$\rho_{q+1} = \phi_1 \rho_q \quad + \cdots + \phi_p \rho_{q-p+1}$$
$$\cdots \cdots \cdots \cdots \cdots \cdots \cdots \cdots \cdots \qquad (5.7.9)$$
$$\rho_{q+p} = \phi_1 \rho_{q+p-1} + \cdots + \phi_1 \rho_q$$

estimates of $\phi_1, \ldots, \phi_p$ may be obtained if the r_j are inserted in place of the ρ_j. Then from the relationships between $\rho_1, \ldots, \rho_q$, the ϕ's and the θ's, we may solve for $\hat{\theta}_1, \ldots, \hat{\theta}_q$, inserting the r_j in place of the ρ_j and the estimates of the ϕ's already obtained in place of the true values. For example, for ARMA (1,1) we have

$$\hat{\phi}_1 = \frac{r_2}{r_1} \qquad (5.7.10)$$

and hence $\hat{\theta}_1$ given by the solution to

$$r_1 = \frac{(1 - \hat{\theta}_1 \hat{\phi}_1)(\hat{\phi}_1 - \hat{\theta}_1)}{1 + \hat{\theta}_1{}^2 - 2\hat{\phi}_1 \hat{\theta}_1} \qquad (5.7.11)$$

which will again result in alternative values of $\hat{\theta}_1$ from which the invertible one is chosen.

A preliminary estimate of the constant term in an ARIMA model may be obtained readily from the relationship between the mean of the process and the other parameters using the sample mean of the series as an estimate of the mean of the process. For EPD we have the theoretical relationship

$$E(w_t) = \delta + E(u_t) - \theta_1 E(u_{t-1}) = \delta \qquad (5.7.12)$$

Devoting the sample mean of the first differences, which was .51 billion dollars, by $\bar{w}$, we have then

$$\delta = \bar{w} = .51 \qquad (5.7.13)$$

The complete IMA (1,1) model with preliminary parameter estimates is then

$$w_t = .51 + u_t + .43u_{t-1} \qquad (5.7.14)$$
or
$$z_t = z_{t-1} + .5 + u_t + .43u_{t-1} \qquad (5.7.15)$$

For the first differences of GNP we have the theoretical relationship

$$E(w_t) = \frac{\delta}{1 - \phi_1} \qquad (5.7.16)$$

from which we obtain the estimate of δ given by

$$\delta \doteq (1 - \hat{\phi}_1)\bar{w}$$
$$= .40 \times 6.9$$
$$= 2.76 \tag{5.7.17}$$

using our estimate of ϕ_1 and the fact that $\bar{w}$ was 6.9 billion dollars. The complete ARI (1,1) model is then

$$w_t = .60w_{t-1} + 2.76 + u_t \tag{5.7.18}$$

or
$$z_t = z_{t-1} + .60(z_{t-1} - z_{t-2}) + 2.76 + u_t \tag{5.7.19}$$

Although parameter estimates derived from the sample moments of time series are useful for preliminary sketching of a model, such estimates by no means make efficient use of the data in hand. Maximum-likelihood estimates, on the other hand, are generally efficient, at least in large samples, and it is to a discussion of procedures for maximum-likelihood estimation of parameters of ARIMA models that we turn now.

5.8   Maximum-likelihood Estimation of ARIMA Models

Having identified one or more tentative models for a time series, we would like to obtain the *best* or most *efficient* estimates of the parameters before we proceed to actual forecasting. If by efficient we mean an estimate that minimizes the squared difference between the true parameter value and the estimate, then statistical theory is unable to tell us which of the alternative estimates will be efficient in all situations. However, it may be shown that estimates which maximize the *likelihood function* are the efficient estimates if the number of observations is large. An important practical reason for studying maximum-likelihood estimates (MLE) is that there is a computational procedure which will locate these estimates for any ARIMA model we might specify regardless of the data or the particular values of p, d, and q.

The rationale behind MLE is, briefly, as follows. We have in hand a set of observations, say, $z_1, \ldots, z_T$, and an identified model that we suppose has generated those observations. Now, prior to their being generated, the observations were random variables to be drawn from a joint distribution defined by the particular ARIMA model and its unknown parameters $\phi_1, \ldots, \phi_p$; $\theta_1, \ldots, \theta_q$; δ; and σ_u^2. That is, our observations were drawn from a joint distribution $p(\mathbf{w}|\boldsymbol{\phi},\boldsymbol{\theta},\delta,\sigma_u^2)$ where $\mathbf{w}$ simply denotes the sequence or vector of observations on the stationary difference of the z's, $\boldsymbol{\phi}$ the vector of ϕ's, and so forth, and the vertical line means *given*. Having the observations in hand, we might reasonably ask the question "What values of the parameters are *likely* to have given rise to these observations?" A natural measure of likelihood is the function $L(\phi,\theta,\delta,\sigma_u^2|w)$, which is of the same form as the probability density for w. But now the parameters are considered the variables and the observations are given; that function is called the *likelihood function*.

Though little of what we have done thus far in this text has depended on particular distributional assumptions, it is clear that if we are to apply the MLE technique, we must make an assumption about the form of $p(\ )$. The most practical assumption is that the observations come from a joint normal distribution. We begin the actual analysis, however, with the equivalent assumption that the disturbances u_t are normal. The distribution function for a single disturbance u_t is given then by

$$p(u_t|\sigma_u^2) = (2\pi)^{-1/2}(\sigma_u^2)^{-1/2} \exp\left(\frac{-u_t^2}{2\sigma_u^2}\right) \qquad (5.8.1)$$

Since the disturbances are independent their joint distribution is just the product of their marginal distributions; that is,

$$p(u_1, \ldots, u_T|\sigma_u^2) = (2\pi)^{-T/2}(\sigma_u^2)^{-T/2} \exp\left(-\frac{1}{2\sigma_u^2}\sum_{t=1}^{T} u_t^2\right) \qquad (5.8.2)$$

Note that each u_t may be expressed in terms of observations w; parameters ϕ, θ, δ, and σ_u^2; and previous disturbances as

$$u_t = w_t - \phi_1 w_{t-1} - \cdots - \phi_p w_{t-p} - \delta + \theta_1 u_{t-1} + \cdots + \theta_q u_{t-q} \qquad (5.8.3)$$

Expression (5.8.3) may be thought of as a recursive relationship between successive u_t, *given* the parameters and observations on w_t. Consequently, the value of any u_t is computable as a function of the parameters and the observations. We now use (5.8.3) to substitute in (5.8.2), giving the joint density of the w†

$$p(w|\phi,\theta,\delta,\sigma_u^2) = (2\pi)^{-T/2}(\sigma_u^2)^{-T/2}$$

$$\exp\left[-\frac{1}{2\sigma_u^2}\sum_{t=1}^{T} (w_t - \cdots - \phi_p w_{t-p} - \delta - \cdots - \theta_q u_{t-q})^2\right] \qquad (5.8.4)$$

The likelihood function for the parameters *given* the data is therefore

$$L(\phi,\theta,\delta,\sigma_u^2|w) = (2\pi)^{-T/2}(\sigma_u^2)^{-T/2} \exp\left[-\frac{1}{2\sigma_u^2}\sum_{t=1}^{T} \hat{u}(\phi,\theta,\delta)_t^2\right] \qquad (5.8.5)$$

† Because the Jacobian of the transformation is unity.

where by $\hat{u}(\phi,\theta,\delta)_t$ we mean simply the *implied* (or estimated) value of u_t from (5.8.3) as a function of the unknown parameters and observations **w**. Since we are ultimately only interested in relative magnitudes of the likelihood, it suffices to consider the log of the likelihood given by

$$l(\phi,\theta,\delta,\sigma_u{}^2|\mathbf{w}) = -T \ln \sigma_u - \frac{S(\phi,\theta,\delta)}{2\sigma_u{}^2} \tag{5.8.6}$$

where $S(\phi,\theta,\delta)$ is the *sum-of-squares* function

$$S(\phi,\theta,\delta) = \sum_{t=1}^{T} \hat{u}(\phi,\theta,\delta)_t{}^2 \tag{5.8.7}$$

We see that parameters ϕ, θ, and δ enter only into the sum-of-squares part of the likelihood; therefore, to maximize the likelihood we need only *minimize* the sum-of-squares function over values of the parameters. Once MLE of those parameters have been located, it is easily shown that the MLE of $\sigma_u{}^2$ is just

$$\hat{\sigma}_u{}^2 = \frac{S(\hat{\phi},\hat{\theta},\hat{\delta})}{T} \tag{5.8.8}$$

where $\hat{\phi}$, $\hat{\theta}$, and $\hat{\delta}$ simply denote MLE of these parameters.

An example will help to clarify the procedure and will be useful in introducing some refinements. Consider the IMA $(d,1)$ model

$$w_t = u_t - \theta_1 u_{t-1} \tag{5.8.9}$$

where the w_t are the stationary dth differences of the raw data z_t. The sum-of-squares function is

$$\begin{aligned} S(\theta_1) &= \sum_{t=1}^{T} [z_t + \theta_1 \hat{u}(\theta_1)_{t-1}]^2 \\ &= \sum_{t=1}^{T} \hat{u}_t(\theta_1)^2 \end{aligned} \tag{5.8.10}$$

If we are to minimize $S(\theta_1)$ over values of θ_1, we must first see how to evaluate the $\hat{u}(\theta_1)_t$. Let us start with $\hat{u}(\theta_1)_1$, which is

$$\hat{u}(\theta_1)_1 = z_1 + \theta_1 \hat{u}(\theta_1)_0 \tag{5.8.11}$$

It is immediately apparent that there is a problem here because we have no value for $\hat{u}_0$. A practical solution to the difficulty is to *assume* a value of zero for $\hat{u}_0$ because that is its marginal mean. Clearly, if the model had q

moving-average terms, we would set $\hat{u}_0 = \hat{u}_{-1} = \cdots = \hat{u}_{-q+1} = 0$ to start the computations. Using our starting value $\hat{u}_0 = 0$, we have

$$\hat{u}(\theta_1)_1 = z_1 + \theta_1(0)$$
$$\hat{u}(\theta_1)_2 = z_2 + \theta_1\hat{u}(\theta_1)_1$$
$$= z_2 + \theta_1 z_1 \tag{5.8.12}$$
$$\hat{u}(\theta_1)_3 = z_3 + \theta_1\hat{u}(\theta_1)_2$$
$$= z_3 + \theta_1 z_2 + \theta_1{}^2 z_1$$

The $\hat{u}(\theta_1)_t$ now depend only on θ_1 and the observations z so that evaluation of $S(\theta_1)$ is completely operational.

It is now easy to see why we confine our attention to invertible values of moving-average parameters. For any starting value $\hat{u}_0$ in general, we have

$$\hat{u}(\theta_1)_t = z_t + \cdots + \theta_1{}^{t-1} z_1 + \theta_1{}^t \hat{u}_0 \tag{5.8.13}$$

If θ_1 is a fraction (as required by invertibility) and then if t is at all large, our choice of $\hat{u}_0$ will have little effect on the value of $\hat{u}(\theta_1)_t$ (since its weight is $\theta_1{}^t$) and therefore on $S(\theta_1)$. However, if values of θ_1 greater in absolute value than unity were considered, it is clear that our arbitrary choice of $\hat{u}_0$ would *dominate* the value of $S(\theta_1)$.

Having seen how $S(\theta_1)$ may be evaluated operationally, we now turn to the problem of how its minimum may be located. We note first that there is no hope of finding $\hat{\theta}_1$ by setting the first derivative of $S(\theta_1)$ equal to zero since from

$$S(\theta_1) = \sum_{t=1}^{T} (z_t + \theta_1 z_{t-1} + \cdots + \theta_1{}^{t-1} z_1)^2 \tag{5.8.14}$$

it is clear that the equation

$$\frac{\partial S(\theta_1)}{\partial \theta_1} = 0 \tag{5.8.15}$$

would be highly nonlinear in θ_1. This means we are involved in what is generally referred to as *nonlinear estimation*. This may seem distressing at first, but remember that we could always resort to a search for the minimum over a grid of values for θ_1 between -1 and $+1$. Thus, if the data were

$$z_1 = -1.9$$
$$z_2 = 1.6$$
$$z_3 = .1 \tag{5.8.16}$$
$$z_4 = -2.3$$

sec. 5.8   maximum-likelihood estimation of arima models

(an unrealistically short series, just for illustration) we would proceed to evaluate $S(\theta_1)$ at each point on the grid; for example, at $\theta_1 = .5$

$$\hat{u}(.5)_1 = -1.9$$

$$\hat{u}(.5)_2 = 1.6 - .95 = .65 \tag{5.8.17}$$

$$\hat{u}(.5)_3 = .1 + .325 = .425$$

$$\hat{u}(.5)_4 = -2.3 + .2125 = -2.0875$$

and hence

$$S(.5) = (-1.9)^2 + (.65)^2 + (.425)^2 + (-2.0875)^2$$
$$\approx 8.56 \tag{5.8.18}$$

and so forth. After examining the initial results, we might decide to search a finer grid in the neighborhood of the minimum we obtained on the coarse grid. Then, taking the value $S(\hat{\theta}_1)$, we would compute the estimate $\hat{\sigma}_u^2$. If the minimum had happened to be at .5, we would have

$$\hat{\sigma}_u^2 = \frac{8.56}{4} = 2.14 \tag{5.8.19}$$

as the MLE of σ_u^2.

A procedure that is computationally more efficient and is well suited to computer applications is the Gauss–Newton (GN) method. The GN method is based on a linear *approximation* to the model. To see how this is done, note that we may easily evaluate both $\hat{u}(\theta_1)_t$ and $\hat{u}(\theta_1 + \Delta\theta_1)_t$, where $\Delta\theta_1$ is some small change in θ_1. The first derivative of $\hat{u}(\theta_1)$ at the point $\theta_1 = \theta_1^0$ is then approximately

$$\frac{d\hat{u}(\theta_1)_t}{d(\theta_1)} \approx \frac{\hat{u}(\theta_1^0 + \Delta\theta)_t - \hat{u}(\theta_1^0)_t}{\Delta\theta_1} \tag{5.8.20}$$

and may be computed. Now a *linear* approximation to $\hat{u}(\theta_1)_t$ at the point $\theta_1 = \theta_1^0$ is given by

$$\hat{u}(\theta_1)_t \approx \hat{u}(\theta_1^0)_t + (\theta_1 - \theta_1^0)\left[\frac{d\hat{u}(\theta_1)_t}{d\theta_1}\right] \tag{5.8.21}$$

Using this linear approximation for $\hat{u}(\theta_1)_t$, then $S(\theta_1)$ is approximately

$$S(\theta_1) \approx \sum_{t=1}^{T}\left[\hat{u}(\theta_1^0)_t + (\theta_1 - \theta_1^0)\frac{d\hat{u}(\theta_1)_t}{d\theta_1}\right]^2 \tag{5.8.22}$$

The important thing to note is that the approximation to $S(\theta_1)$ is *quadratic* in θ_1; that is, if we were to differentiate (5.8.21) with respect to θ_1 and set the derivative equal to zero, we would have an expression which is *linear* in θ_1; this may be solved for an estimate of θ_1.

We must remember, however, that (5.8.21) is only an approximation which depends on our guess value θ_1^0. Therefore we have probably not minimized

$S(\theta_1)$ exactly. A sensible next step would be to call this first estimate of θ_1, say, $\theta_1^{(1)}$, and repeat or iterate the linearization at $\theta_1 = \theta_1^{(1)}$. It may be shown that if we continue to iterate until the nth estimate of θ_1, $\theta_1^{(n)}$, is close to the $(n+1)$th estimate $\theta_1^{(n+1)}$, we are at a minimum of $S(\theta_1)$ and hence set

$$\hat{\theta}_1 = \theta_1^{(n)} \tag{5.8.23}$$

In principle, a sum-of-squares function may have multiple minima, and we cannot be sure that the GN procedure has led us to the global minimum. In practice, this is not likely to be a serious problem, although graphing of the sum of squares may be useful if there are serious doubts.

Generally the procedure for estimation of ARIMA models is essentially the same as that described in detail for the MA (1) process except that $S(\phi,\theta,\delta)$ may involve several unknown parameters rather than one. Computation of the $u(\phi,\theta,\delta)_t$ is complicated slightly if autoregressive terms are involved since another starting-value problem occurs at the beginning of the series. For example, if we were estimating the ARIMA $(1,d,1)$ model, we would have for $t = 1$

$$\hat{u}(\phi_1,\theta_1)_1 = w_1 - \phi_1 w_0 + \theta_1 \hat{u}_0 \tag{5.8.24}$$

In addition to the fact that we shall need to supply a starting value $\hat{u}_0$, we also have a problem because w_0 is unavailable. One solution is to start the recursive computation of the $\hat{u}$'s at $t = 1$ or in general at $t = p$. Thus, in the present example we may compute

$$\hat{u}(\phi_1,\theta_1)_2 = w_2 - \phi_1 w_1 + \theta_1 \hat{u}_1 \tag{5.8.25}$$

by assuming $\hat{u}_1 = 0$, and so forth. An alternative solution to the starting value problem is the backforecasting procedure suggested by Box and Jenkins. The details do not warrant our attention here; it is sufficient that the reader be aware of just why the starting-value problem arises.[1]

To start the iterative GN procedure, first guess values of each parameter must be supplied. Since we would like to minimize computation and hence the number of iterations it is a good idea to use the preliminary parameter estimates obtained as a by-product of identification as initial values to begin iteration.

5.9 Statistical Inference: Standard Errors for Maximum-likelihood Estimates

Having obtained MLE for our ARIMA model, we would like to have some idea of the precision of those estimates. For instance, if $\hat{\theta}_1 = .1$, can we be

---

[1] The interested reader is referred to G. E. P. Box and G. M. Jenkins, "Time Series Analysis, Forecasting and Control," pp. 212–220, Holden-Day, Inc., San Francisco, 1970.

confident that the time value of θ_1 is not 0 or .5? Could we specify an interval that we are confident includes the true value of θ_1?

It is important to remember that MLE of the parameters are, after all, random variables since they are functions of the data. From statistical theory we know that under fairly general conditions MLE in "large" samples are joint normally distributed with mean value equal to the true parameter values and variance-covariance matrix given by

$$V(\boldsymbol{\beta}) \approx 2\sigma_u{}^2 \begin{bmatrix} \dfrac{\partial^2 S(\boldsymbol{\beta})}{\partial \beta_1{}^2} & \cdots & \dfrac{\partial^2 S(\boldsymbol{\beta})}{\partial \beta_1\,\partial \beta_{p+q+1}} \\ & \ddots & \\ \cdots\cdots\cdots\cdots\cdots\cdots\cdots \\ & \ddots & \\ \cdots & & \dfrac{\partial^2 S(\boldsymbol{\beta})}{\partial \beta_{p+q+1}^2} \end{bmatrix}^{-1} \tag{5.9.1}$$

that is, two times the variance of u_t times the inverse (denoted by the superscript -1) of the matrix of second derivatives of the sum-of-squares function, where we mean by $\boldsymbol{\beta}$ the vector of $p + q + 1$ parameters $\boldsymbol{\phi}$, $\boldsymbol{\theta}$, δ.† The second derivatives are evaluated at the true parameter values. To make a (5.9.1) operational we need to insert the estimate $\hat{\sigma}_u{}^2$ for $\sigma_u{}^2$ and numerical second derivatives of $S(\boldsymbol{\beta})$ evaluated at the point of the MLE values. The actual computation is simplified if the sum-of-squares function is taken to be approximation to $S(\boldsymbol{\beta})$ resulting from the linearization of the $\hat{u}$'s on the last iteration of the GN procedure. Taking square roots of the diagonal elements of the estimated variance-covariance matrix, we have estimated standard deviations of the parameter estimates or standard errors denoted SE $(\hat{\beta}_i)$.

The standard errors allow us to make a number of probability statements about the parameters. Under the hypothesis that $\beta_i = \beta_i^*$, we have that *approximately*

$$\frac{\hat{\beta}_i - \beta_i^*}{\text{SE }(\hat{\beta}_i)} \approx N(0,1) \tag{5.9.2}$$

To test that hypothesis, we compute $(\hat{\beta}_i + \beta_i^*)/\text{SE }(\beta_i)$ and ask the question "What is the probability that a number as large as this in absolute value would be drawn from a standard normal distribution?" We know that the

---

† The inverse of a square matrix is the square matrix which when multiplied by that matrix produces the identity matrix. We shall not be working with matrix inversion, but the interested reader who is unfamiliar with matrix inverses may consult any introductory text on matrix algebra.

chap. 5   identification and estimation of arima models

probability that a standard normal variable lies outside the bounds ± 1.96 is .05, so that if the ratio were, say, 2.26, we would *reject* the *null* hypothesis $\beta_1 = \beta_1^*$ in favor of the *alternative* $\beta_1 \neq \beta_1^*$ at the .05 level. The most common null hypothesis in practice is $\beta_1^* = 0$; in other words, "Is $\hat{\beta}_1$ significant?" The ratio associated with that hypothesis is termed (loosely in the present context) the t ratio.

Similarly, since

$$\text{Prob}\left(-1.96 < \frac{\hat{\beta}_i - \beta_i}{\text{SE}(\hat{\beta}_i)} < +1.96 \right) \approx .95 \qquad (5.9.3)$$

a 95 percent confidence interval for β_i is given by

$$\hat{\beta}_i - 1.96\text{SE}(\hat{\beta}_i) < \beta_i < \hat{\beta}_i + 1.96\text{SE}(\hat{\beta}_i) \qquad (5.9.4)$$

For practical computation we may replace 1.96 with 2 since all probability statements are approximate. The reader who is unfamiliar with the concepts of hypothesis testing and confidence intervals is referred to the Additional Readings at the end of the chapter.

5.10 Examples of Estimation Using Program ESTIMATE

Figure 5.8 presents the output from program ESTIMATE on the model ARI (1,1) for GNP 1947-01 through 1966-04.† The first page describes the problem per control-card input, that is, number of observations, order of differencing, and initial guess values for parameters. After the raw data and differenced data have been listed, the iterations toward ML estimates begin, with the results of each iteration being noted. Iteration is stopped because further reduction in $S(\phi_1, \delta)$ is less than 0.1×10^{-5}. The next page lists *residuals*, which are the $\hat{u}$'s evaluated at ML values of the parameters ϕ_1 and δ. Note that there are more than 78 residuals, the number that would be computed according to the procedure outlined in Sec. 5.8. The residuals preceding the last 78 result from applying the backforecasting technique, permitting us to dispense with the starting-value problem by forecasting presample observations backward in time. That technique may be regarded as a slight refinement, allowing us to extract a bit more information from the data. Final parameter estimates would be very little different if the computationally simpler procedure of Sec. 5.8 were applied.

Finally, we come to the summary of parameter estimates and test statistics. The estimated model is

$$w_t = .62w_{t-1} + 2.69 + u_t$$
$$\hat{\sigma}_u^2 = 22.66 \qquad (5.10.1)$$

† Program ESTIMATE is described in the Appendix, Sec. A.2.

figure 5.8 ESTIMATE output for GNP data model ARI (1,1).

NUMBER OF OBSERVATIONS = 80

INITIAL VALUE(S) OF AUTOREGRESSIVE PARAMETER(S)

   0.6000E 00

INITIAL VALUE OF CONSTANT

   0.2760E 01

MAXIMUM NUMBER OF ITERATIONS = 50

ORDER OF DIFFERENCING = 1

PERIODS PER SEASONAL CYCLE = 0

ORDER OF SEASONAL DIFFERENCING = 0

OPTIONS USED

  NEW RAW SERIES USED
  PLOT RESIDUALS

DATA FROM CARDS

0.224E 03	0.228E 03	0.232E 03	0.242E 03	0.248E 03	0.256E 03	0.263E 03	0.264E 03	0.259E 03	0.255E 03
0.257E 03	0.255E 03	0.266E 03	0.275E 03	0.293E 03	0.305E 03	0.318E 03	0.326E 03	0.333E 03	0.337E 03
0.340E 03	0.339E 03	0.346E 03	0.359E 03	0.364E 03	0.368E 03	0.366E 03	0.361E 03	0.361E 03	0.360E 03
0.365E 03	0.373E 03	0.385E 03	0.394E 03	0.403E 03	0.409E 03	0.411E 03	0.416E 03	0.421E 03	0.430E 03
0.437E 03	0.440E 03	0.446E 03	0.442E 03	0.435E 03	0.438E 03	0.451E 03	0.464E 03	0.474E 03	0.487E 03
0.484E 03	0.491E 03	0.503E 03	0.505E 03	0.504E 03	0.503E 03	0.504E 03	0.515E 03	0.524E 03	0.538E 03
0.548E 03	0.557E 03	0.564E 03	0.572E 03	0.577E 03	0.584E 03	0.595E 03	0.606E 03	0.618E 03	0.628E 03
0.639E 03	0.645E 03	0.663E 03	0.676E 03	0.691E 03	0.710E 03	0.710E 03	0.743E 03	0.756E 03	0.771E 03

MEAN OF SERIES = 0.4432E 03

VARIANCE OF SERIES = 0.2069E 05

GROSS NATIONAL PRODUCT

1-DIFFERENCES OF SERIES   GROSS NATIONAL PRODUCT

0.400E 01	0.103E 02	0.590E 01	0.760E 01	0.690E 01	0.140E 01	-0.540E 01	-0.330E 01	0.190E 01
-0.210E 01	0.110E 02	0.177E 02	0.114E 02	0.135E 02	0.780E 01	0.700E 01	0.410E 01	0.260E 01
-0.400E 00	0.650E 01	0.121E 02	0.330E 01	-0.170E 01	-0.500E 01	-0.999E-01	-0.300E 00	0.430E 01
0.870E 01	0.128E 02	0.310E 01	0.630E 01	0.180E 01	0.560E 01	0.440E 01	0.890E 01	0.740E 01
0.300E 01	-0.430E 01	-0.680E 01	0.360E 01	0.131E 02	0.130E 02	0.960E 01	0.129E 02	-0.290E 01
0.650E 01	0.125E 02	0.170E 01	-0.900E 00	0.300E 00	0.113E 02	0.930E 01	0.135E 02	0.101E 02
0.940E 01	0.720E 01	0.540E 01	0.680E 01	0.105E 02	0.111E 02	0.119E 02	0.103E 02	0.109E 02
0.620E 01	0.177E 02	0.154E 02	0.189E 02	0.195E 02	0.138E 02	0.126E 02	0.148E 02	

MEAN OF SERIES = 0.6925E 01

VARIANCE OF SERIES = 0.3510E 02

NET NUMBER OF OBSERVATIONS = 79

NUMBER OF PARAMETERS = 2

INITIAL SUM OF SQUARES = 0.1746E 04

ITERATION NO.   1

PARAMETER VALUES VIA REGRESSION

     1   2

0.6128E 00   0.2723E 01

SUM OF SQUARES AFTER REGRESSION = 0.1745073E 04

figure 5.8 (continued)

GROSS NATIONAL PRODUCT

ITERATION NO.   2

PARAMETER VALUES VIA REGRESSION

        1   2

0.6165E 00 0.2694E 01

                                SUM OF SQUARES AFTER REGRESSION =   0.1745030E 04

ITERATION NO.   3

PARAMETER VALUES VIA REGRESSION

        1   2

0.6167E 00 0.2692E 01

                                SUM OF SQUARES AFTER REGRESSION =   0.1745030E 04

ITERATION STOPS - RELATIVE CHANGE IN SUM OF SQUARES LESS THAN 0.1000E-05

RESIDUALS: LAST 79 FROM SERIES
PREVIOUS VALUES FROM BACK FORECASTS

0.0	0.0	0.0	0.0	0.0	0.0	0.0	0.0	0.0	0.0
0.0	0.0	0.0	0.0	0.0	0.0	0.0	0.0	0.0	0.0
0.0	0.0	0.0	0.0	0.0	0.0	0.0	0.0	0.0	0.0
0.0	0.0	0.0	0.0	0.0	0.0	0.0	0.0	0.0	0.0
0.0	0.0	0.0	0.0	0.0	0.0	0.0	0.0	0.0	0.0
0.0	0.0	0.0	0.0	0.0	0.0	0.0	0.0	0.0	0.0
0.0	0.0	0.0	0.0	0.0	0.0	0.0	0.0	0.0	0.0
0.0	0.0	0.0	0.0	0.0	0.0	0.0	0.0	0.0	0.0
0.0	0.0	0.0	0.0	0.0	0.0	0.0	0.0	0.0	0.0
-0.2766E-04	-0.4482E-04	-0.7248E-04	-0.1183E-03	-0.9537E-06	-0.2861E-05	-0.4768E-05	-0.6676E-05	-0.1049E-04	-0.1717E-04
-0.3492E-02	-0.5664E-02	-0.9186E-02	-0.1490E-01	-0.1926E-03	-0.3119E-03	-0.5054E-03	-0.8192E-03	-0.1328E-02	-0.2154E-02
-0.4392E 00	-0.7122E 00	-0.1155E 01	-0.1873E 01	-0.2415E-01	-0.3917E-01	-0.6352E-01	-0.1030E 00	-0.1670E 00	-0.2709E 00
-0.8955E 01	-0.2662E 01	-0.1243E 01	-0.5963E 01	-0.9585E 00	-0.5018E 01	-0.3144E 01	-0.1270E 01	-0.4785E 00	-0.5547E 01
-0.5017E 00	-0.2908E 01	-0.2620E 01	-0.4695E 01	0.9603E 01	-0.7529E-01	0.9211E 01	-0.2207E 01	0.3778E 01	-0.3217E 01
0.2917E 00	-0.2930E 00	0.1793E 01	0.3356E 01	0.4055E 01	0.5400E 01	-0.3654E 01	-0.3400E 01	-0.6427E 01	-0.6643E 01
-0.1745E 01	0.3495E 01	-0.7804E 00	-0.4255E 01	0.4743E 01	-0.2385E 01	0.3516E 01	-0.1387E 01	-0.4777E 01	0.1798E 01
-0.1108E 01	0.4288E 01	-0.1355E 01	0.5596E 01	0.1858E 01	-0.1144E 02	-0.6532E 01	0.5101E 01	0.8188E 01	0.2230E 01
-0.3602E 00	0.5073E 01	-0.9170E 00	0.4800E 00	0.5800E 01	-0.8700E 01	-0.4240E 01	-0.3284E 01	-0.1837E 01	0.8423E 01
0.2363E 01	0.2698E 01	0.1866E 01	-0.3214E 01	-0.1289E 00	0.4683E 00	-0.1979E 01	0.7783E 00	0.3615E 01	0.1933E 01
0.1398E 01	0.4338E 01		0.1118E 02	-0.7067E 00	0.4753E 01	0.6712E 01	0.5153E 01	-0.9171E 00	

figure 5.8 (continued)

GROSS NATIONAL PRODUCT

VARIANCE OF RESIDUALS (BACK FORECAST RESIDUALS INCLUDED) = 0.2266E 02 , 77 DEGREES OF FREEDOM

VARIANCE OF RESIDUALS (BACK FORECAST RESIDUALS EXCLUDED) = 0.2263E 02 , 77 DEGREES OF FREEDOM

AUTOREGRESSIVE PARAMETERS

0.616669E 00

CONSTANT TERM

0.269183E 01

95% CONFIDENCE LIMITS (+ & - TWO STD. ERRORS)

1	2
0.7989E 00	0.4313E 01
0.4344E 00	0.1070E 01

STANDARD ERROR FOR EACH PARAMETER (ON LINEAR HYPOTHESIS)

1	2
0.9113E-01	0.8107E 00

T-STATISTIC FOR EACH PARAMETER   77 DEGREES OF FREEDOM

1	2
0.6767E 01	0.3321E 01

GROSS NATIONAL PRODUCT

CORRELATION MATRIX OF PARAMETERS

            1   2

1   1.0000

2   -0.7619   1.0000

AUTOCORRELATIONS OF RESIDUALS   T = 79

                                 AUTOCORRELATIONS
LAGS   EST. S. E
 1-12   -0.01   0.09 -0.03 -0.13 -0.13   0.05   0.09 -0.05   0.11   0.11   0.01 -0.02   0.11
13-24   -0.07 -0.02   0.04 -0.00   0.17   0.08 -0.00   0.06 -0.05 -0.17   0.06 -0.05   0.12
25-36   -0.04   0.03   0.08   0.02 -0.01 -0.19   0.07   0.04   0.12 -0.02   0.13

CHI-SQUARE TEST OF AUTOCORRELATIONS

    Q(12) =   6.4   10 DEGREES OF FREEDOM

    Q(24) = 12.9   22 DEGREES OF FREEDOM

    Q(36) = 18.6   34 DEGREES OF FREEDOM

CHI-SQUARE VALUES FROM TABLE

    CHI-SQUARE = 30.8   10% LEVEL OF SIGNIFICANCE   22 DEGREES OF FREEDOM

    CHI-SQUARE = 33.9   5% LEVEL OF SIGNIFICANCE   22 DEGREES OF FREEDOM

figure 5.8 (continued)

GROSS NATIONAL PRODUCT

CROSS CORRELATIONS OF RESIDUALS AND DIFFERENCED SERIES

CROSS CORRELATION ZERO LAG = 0.79

CROSS CORRELATIONS U(T),W(T+K)

LAGS												
1-12	0.47	0.36	0.20	0.01	-0.12	-0.04	0.05	-0.04	0.07	0.12	0.09	0.03
13-24	-0.04	-0.04	0.00	0.00	0.13	0.14	0.08	0.10	0.01	-0.13	-0.05	-0.07
25-36	-0.07	-0.01	0.07	0.04	0.03	0.04	-0.14	-0.14	-0.04	-0.01	0.07	0.04

CROSS CORRELATIONS U(T+K),W(T)

LAGS												
1-12	-0.00	0.01	-0.10	-0.13	-0.04	0.11	0.10	0.05	0.14	0.08	-0.01	-0.03
13-24	-0.03	0.04	0.09	0.10	0.17	0.05	-0.02	-0.02	-0.12	-0.12	0.03	-0.03
25-36	0.01	0.06	0.05	-0.01	-0.05	-0.10	-0.15	0.00	0.10	0.07	0.06	-0.06

which is quite close to that given in (5.7.19) on the basis of preliminary estimates. Note that an estimate of the variance of disturbances may be computed either with or without the presample residuals included in the sum of squares. Using the standard errors .09 and .81 for $\hat{\phi}_1$ and $\hat{\delta}$, respectively, we see that individual 95 percent confidence intervals are $(.80 > \phi_1 > .43)$ and $(4.3 > \delta > 1.1)$. The t statistics are large on both parameters, and so we may reject the null hypothesis $\phi_1 = 0$, that is, that there is no serial correlation in quarter-to-quarter changes. If we were interested in testing the hypothesis that there is no drift or nonzero mean change in the series, we would examine the hypothesis $\delta = 0$ and reject it on the basis of the t statistic. How could we test the hypothesis that the first difference series is nonstationary? If the value of ϕ_1 were unity, the first differences would be nonstationary, and so to test that hypothesis we form the ratio

$$\frac{\hat{\phi}_1 - 1}{.09} = -4.2 \qquad (5.10.2)$$

Now the probability that $\hat{\phi}_1$ would be as small as .62 if it were true that $\phi_1 = 1$ is less than .0001, and the hypothesis is strongly rejected in favor of $\phi_1 < 1$.

At the bottom of the same page is the estimated correlation matrix of the parameter estimates. The correlation between $\hat{\phi}_1$ and $\hat{\delta}$ is estimated by taking their estimated covariance from matrix (5.9.1) and dividing by the product of their standard errors. In this example the correlation is estimated to be $-.76$; that is, a large value of $\hat{\phi}_1$ in a given sample will tend to be associated with a small value of $\hat{\delta}$. In other words, if we overestimate the serial dependence between successive differences, we shall tend to underestimate the drift in the level of the raw series. The remainder of the output of program ESTIMATE deals with *diagnostic checks* on the model and will be discussed in the next section.

Figure 5.9 presents ESTIMATE output on the IMA (1,1) model identified for EPD. Iterative minimization of the sum of squares leads to the model

$$w_t = .52 + v_t + .35v_{t-1}$$
$$\hat{\sigma}_v{}^2 = 1.12 \qquad (5.10.3)$$

which is again quite close to our preliminary model (5.7.14) for this series. We note that the hypothesis of zero correlation in the differences, that is, the hypothesis $\theta_1 = 0$ is readily rejected. The hypothesis that there is no drift in the series, that is, $\delta = 0$, may be rejected.

5.11 Diagnostic Checks

Once an identified model has been estimated, we would like to check on the adequacy of that model for the data at hand. If our model is ARI (1,d), we

figure 5.9 ESTIMATE output for EPD data model IMA (1,1).

EXPENDITURES ON PRODUCERS' DURABLES

NUMBER OF OBSERVATIONS = 80

INITIAL VALUE(S) OF MOVING AVERAGE PARAMETER(S)

-0.4300E 00

INITIAL VALUE OF CONSTANT

0.5100E 00

MAXIMUM NUMBER OF ITERATIONS = 50

ORDER OF DIFFERENCING = 1

PERIODS PER SEASONAL CYCLE = 0

ORDER OF SEASONAL DIFFERENCING = 0

OPTIONS USED

NEW RAW SERIES USED
PLOT RESIDUALS

DATA FROM CARDS

0.155E 02	0.156E 02	0.167E 02	0.180E 02	0.174E 02	0.179E 02	0.188E 02	0.176E 02	0.170E 02
0.161E 02	0.159E 02	0.179E 02	0.203E 02	0.204E 02	0.202E 02	0.205E 02	0.209E 02	0.209E 02
0.211E 02	0.182E 02	0.201E 02	0.214E 02	0.213E 02	0.219E 02	0.213E 02	0.204E 02	0.204E 02
0.207E 02	0.209E 02	0.230E 02	0.249E 02	0.265E 02	0.256E 02	0.261E 02	0.270E 02	0.272E 02
0.281E 02	0.291E 02	0.283E 02	0.257E 02	0.245E 02	0.244E 02	0.255E 02	0.270E 02	0.287E 02
0.291E 02	0.296E 02	0.312E 02	0.306E 02	0.298E 02	0.276E 02	0.277E 02	0.290E 02	0.303E 02
0.310E 02	0.321E 02	0.335E 02	0.332E 02	0.338E 02	0.355E 02	0.368E 02	0.379E 02	0.390E 02
0.410E 02	0.437E 02	0.444E 02	0.466E 02	0.483E 02	0.502E 02	0.521E 02	0.540E 02	0.560E 02

MEAN OF SERIES = 0.2745E 02

VARIANCE OF SERIES = 0.9423E 02

EXPENDITURES ON PRODUCERS' DURABLES

1-DIFFERENCES OF SERIES

EXPENDITURES ON PRODUCERS' DURABLES

0.200E 00	-0.100E 00	0.110E 01	0.130E 01	-0.600E 00	0.500E 00	0.900E 00	-0.120E 01	-0.600E 00	-0.900E 00
-0.400E 00	0.200E 00	0.200E 01	0.240E 01	0.100E 01	-0.200E 00	0.300E 00	0.400E 00	0.0	0.200E 00
0.300E 00	-0.320E 00	0.190E 01	0.130E 01	-0.100E 01	0.600E 00	-0.600E 00	-0.900E 00	0.0	0.300E 00
0.0	0.200E 00	0.210E 01	0.190E 01	0.160E 01	-0.900E 00	0.500E 00	0.900E 00	0.200E 00	0.900E 00
-0.100E 00	0.110E 01	-0.800E 00	-0.260E 01	0.120E 01	-0.100E 01	0.110E 01	0.150E 01	0.170E 01	0.400E 00
-0.100E 00	0.600E 00	0.160E 01	-0.600E 00	-0.800E 00	-0.220E 01	0.100E 01	0.130E 01	0.130E 01	0.700E 00
0.110E 01	0.140E 01	-0.300E 00	-0.300E 00	-0.600E 00	0.170E 01	0.130E 01	0.110E 01	0.110E 01	0.200E 01
0.600E 00	0.210E 01	0.700E 00	0.220E 01	0.170E 01	0.190E 01	0.190E 01	0.190E 01	0.200E 01	0.200E 01

MEAN OF SERIES = 0.5127E 00

VARIANCE OF SERIES = 0.1250E 01

NET NUMBER OF OBSERVATIONS = 79

NUMBER OF PARAMETERS = 2

INITIAL SUM OF SQUARES = 0.8735E 02

ITERATION NO. 1

PARAMETER VALUES VIA REGRESSION

1	2
-0.3519E 00	0.5172E 00

SUM OF SQUARES AFTER REGRESSION = 0.8655022E 02

ITERATION NO. 2

PARAMETER VALUES VIA REGRESSION

1	2
-0.3468E 00	0.5172E 00

SUM OF SQUARES AFTER REGRESSION = 0.8654820E 02

figure 5.9 (continued)

EXPENDITURES ON PRODUCERS' DURABLES

ITERATION NO.   3

PARAMETER VALUES VIA REGRESSION

   1   2

-0.3474E 00 0.5172E 00

SUM OF SQUARES AFTER REGRESSION =   0.8654813E 02

ITERATION STOPS - RELATIVE CHANGE IN SUM OF SQUARES LESS THAN   0.1000E-05

RESIDUALS: LAST   79 FROM SERIES
PREVIOUS VALUES FROM BACK FORECASTS

0.0	0.0	0.0	0.0	0.0	0.0	0.0	0.0	0.0	0.0
0.0	0.0	0.0	0.0	0.0	0.0	0.0	0.0	0.0	0.0
0.0	0.0	0.0	0.0	0.0	0.0	0.0	0.0	0.0	0.0
0.0	0.0	0.0	0.0	0.0	0.0	0.0	0.0	0.0	0.0
0.0	0.0	0.0	0.0	0.0	0.0	0.0	0.0	0.0	0.0
0.0	0.0	0.0	0.0	0.0	0.0	0.0	0.0	0.0	0.0
0.0	0.0	0.0	0.0	0.0	0.0	0.0	0.0	0.0	0.0
0.0	0.0	0.0	0.0	0.0	0.0	0.0	0.0	0.0	0.0
0.0	0.0	0.0	0.0	0.0	0.0	0.0	0.0	0.0	0.0
0.0	0.0	0.0	0.0	0.0	0.0	0.0	0.0	0.0	0.0
0.0	0.0	-0.2775E-01	-0.3076E 00	-0.5104E 00	0.76010 00	0.51875 00	-0.1297E 01	0.4336E 00	0.2321E 00
-0.1798E 01	-0.4925E 00	-0.1246E 01	-0.4843E 00	-0.1490E 00	0.1535E 01	0.1350E 01	-0.8861E 00	-0.4093F 00	-0.7500E-01
-0.9117E-01	-0.4855E 00	-0.1485E 00	-0.1656E 00	-0.3660E 01	0.2654E 01	-0.1395F 00	-0.5688F 00	0.2804E 00	-0.1215E 01
-0.9952E 00	-0.1714E 00	-0.1577E 00	-0.4624E 00	-0.1566E 00	0.1637E 01	0.3130F 01	0.3000E 00	-0.1695E 01	0.5718F 00

EXPENDITURES ON PRODUCERS' DURABLES

```
0.1841E 00  -0.3812E 00   0.5152E 00  -0.7962E 00   0.8594E 00  -0.1616E 01  -0.2556E 01  -0.8292E 00  -0.3291E 00   0.6971E 00
0.7406E 00   0.9255E 00  -0.4388E 00   0.2442E 00   0.9979E 00  -0.1464E 01  -0.3086E 00  -0.2436E 01   0.4293E 00
0.6336E 00   0.5626E 00  -0.1269E-01   0.5872E 00   0.6788E 00  -0.1053E 01  -0.1513E 00   0.1353E 00   0.1136E 01   0.3881E 00
0.4479E 00   0.4272E 00   0.1334E 01  -0.3809E 00   0.1715E 01  -0.4131E 00   0.1826E 00   0.5482E 00   0.1192E 01   0.5685E 00
0.1046E 01   0.1119E 01
```

VARIANCE OF RESIDUALS(BACK FORECAST RESIDUALS INCLUDED) =   0.1124E 01 ,   77 DEGREES OF FREEDOM

VARIANCE OF RESIDUALS(BACK FORECAST RESIDUALS EXCLUDED) =   0.1124E 01 ,   77 DEGREES OF FREEDOM

MOVING AVERAGE PARAMETERS

-0.347449E 00

CONSTANT TERM

0.517225E 00

95% CONFIDENCE LIMITS (+ & - TWO STD. ERRORS)

```
        1            2
-0.1331E 00   0.8375E 00
-0.5618E 00   0.1969E 00
```

STANDARD ERROR FOR EACH PARAMETER (ON LINEAR HYPOTHESIS)

```
        1            2
 0.1072E 00   0.1601E 00
```

figure 5.9 (continued)

EXPENDITURES ON PRODUCERS' DURABLES

T-STATISTIC FOR EACH PARAMETER   77 DEGREES OF FREEDOM

	1	2
	-0.3242E 01	0.3230E 01

CORRELATION MATRIX OF PARAMETERS

	1	2
1	1.0000	
2	-0.0069	1.0000

AUTOCORRELATIONS OF RESIDUALS   T = 79

LAGS						AUTOCORRELATIONS						EST. S. E.
1-12	0.03	0.10	0.01	-0.02	0.02	0.00	0.10	-0.02	0.04	0.16	0.01	0.08	0.11
13-24	-0.03	0.08	-0.05	-0.05	0.17	-0.16	0.15	0.05	-0.09	-0.06	-0.10	0.02	0.12
25-36	-0.05	0.01	-0.00	0.05	0.04	-0.10	-0.17	-0.02	-0.08	0.11	0.08	0.06	0.13

CHI-SQUARE TEST OF AUTOCORRELATIONS

Q(12) =   4.4   10 DEGREES OF FREEDOM

Q(24) = 13.4   22 DEGREES OF FREEDOM

Q(36) = 19.4   34 DEGREES OF FREEDOM

CHI-SQUARE VALUES FROM TABLE

CHI-SQUARE = 30.8   10% LEVEL OF SIGNIFICANCE   22 DEGREES OF FREEDOM

CHI-SQUARE = 33.9   5% LEVEL OF SIGNIFICANCE   22 DEGREES OF FREEDOM

EXPENDITURES ON PRODUCERS' DURABLES

CROSS CORRELATIONS OF RESIDUALS AND DIFFERENCED SERIES

CROSS CORRELATION ZERO LAG = 0.95

CROSS CORRELATIONS U(T),W(T+K)

LAGS												
1-12	0.35	0.10	0.04	-0.02	0.01	0.00	0.10	0.00	0.03	0.15	0.06	0.08
13-24	-0.01	0.06	-0.03	-0.07	0.15	-0.10	0.09	0.10	-0.07	-0.08	-0.11	0.00
25-36	-0.04	0.00	-0.00	0.04	0.05	-0.08	-0.20	-0.08	-0.09	0.08	0.12	0.09

CROSS CORRELATIONS U(T+K),W(T)

LAGS												
1-12	0.06	0.10	0.00	-0.01	0.02	0.04	0.09	-0.01	0.09	0.15	0.03	0.07
13-24	-0.01	0.05	-0.07	0.01	0.11	-0.10	0.16	0.02	-0.10	-0.08	-0.08	0.01
25-36	-0.04	0.01	0.02	0.06	0.00	-0.15	-0.16	-0.05	-0.04	0.13	0.10	0.05

may wonder whether ARI $(2,d)$ might be the more appropriate model. Should a moving-average term be added to the model to make it an ARIMA $(1,d,1)$ model? The most obvious check on such hypotheses is by *overfitting* and testing the hypothesis that the added parameter is equal to zero. In the case of GNP, adding an autoregressive parameter gives us the model ARI $(2,1)$. The value of $\hat{\phi}_2$ is about .03 and not significant, but $\hat{\phi}_1$ and $\hat{\delta}$ are close to their previous values and significant. Similarly, estimating the model ARIMA $(1,1,1)$ yields $\hat{\theta}_1 = .03$, which is not significant.

What about expanding the model in both the autoregressive and moving-average directions? A serious pitfall called *parameter redundancy* awaits. Suppose that the correct model is the one estimated. Then it is true that

$$w_t - .62w_{t-1} = \delta + u_t \qquad (5.11.1)$$

and of course

$$w_{t-1} - .62w_{t-2} = \delta + u_{t-1} \qquad (5.11.2)$$

Subtracting (5.11.2) from (5.11.1), we obtain

$$w_t = 1.62w_{t-1} - .62w_{t-2} + u_t - u_{t-1} \qquad (5.11.3)$$

which appears to be an ARIMA $(2,1,1)$ model. In fact, estimating a model of that form results very close to (5.11.3). Does that mean that we should abandon (5.11.1) in favor of (5.11.3)? Certainly not, since they are in fact the *same* model; (5.11.1) implies (5.11.3)! For that matter, any multiple of (5.11.2) subtracted from (5.11.1) will yield a model consistent with the data, although it is simply the same model in different form. One must therefore be careful in practice to be sure that the simplest adequate model is being used and to be on the lookout for such redundancies when experimenting with overfitting.

Estimates of the variance of disturbances provide another tool for discriminating among alternative models for a given series. The criterion of minimum sum of squares may equivalently be thought of as the criterion of minimum variance of residuals since for the MLE of $\sigma_u{}^2$ we have $\hat{\sigma}_u{}^2 = S(\phi,\theta,\delta)/T$. Now generally the addition of any parameter to a model may be expected to reduce $S(\ )$ and $\hat{\sigma}_u{}^2$ since the additional parameter offers one additional *degree of freedom* along which to reduce them. Consequently, to penalize a model for its use of parameters or degrees of freedom, one may compute estimates of $\sigma_u{}^2$ by dividing $S(\ )$ by the number of observations *less* the number of ϕ's, θ's, and δ (0 or 1) used by the model, that is, the net remaining degrees of freedom. Thus, when a parameter is added for overfitting, the value of $\hat{\sigma}_u{}^2$ provides a "corrected" measure improvement in terms of residual variance. In ESTIMATE output for GNP (Fig. 5.8), estimates of disturbance variance are accompanied by a note that the number of degrees of freedom is 77, the number of observations on the first differences of the series (79) less the number of parameters used (2), and similarly for EPD in Fig. 5.9.

One way of viewing the process of modeling time series is as an attempt to find a transformation that reduces the observed data to random noise. If we have succeeded in this, we would expect to find that the residuals $\hat{u}_t$ have the properties of random numbers—in particular are not serially correlated. It is clear then that we would want to examine the sample autocorrelations of the residuals as a diagnostic check. Autocorrelation, if evident in the residuals, may help to suggest the direction in which the model should be modified. For example, a large value of r_1 might indicate that a first-order moving average ought to be added to the model. How can we determine whether sample autocorrelation is "critical" for a particular model? Standard errors computed from Bartlett's formula provide some guidance, although they may considerably *understate* the standard deviation of sample autocorrelations at low lags. This is essentially because even if the model we have identified is the correct one, the computed residuals are only estimates of the underlying disturbances, which we cannot observe. Box and Pierce have suggested a statistic that not only disposes of this problem but offers a test on the smallness of a whole set of sample autocorrelations for lags 1 through K. This is the Q statistic, given by

$$Q = T \sum_{j=1|}^{K} r_j^2 \tag{5.11.4}$$

which is approximately chi-square distributed with $(K - p - q)$ degrees of freedom.[1] Program ESTIMATE output presents Q's for $K = 12$, 24, and 36 lags and critical values for $K = 24$. For both GNP and EPD $Q(24)$ is small relative to critical values.

An important property of the theoretical disturbances is that they are correlated in general with the current value of w_t and *future* values of w_t but not *past* values. As an additional check in the model, corresponding sample correlations between *residuals* and the w_t are displayed in ESTIMATE output. For both GNP and EPD they support the models estimated. Finally, it is often useful to simply inspect a plot of the residuals for evidence of model inadequacy. For example, departures from homogeneity in a series with positive drift would be indicated by a general spreading of the residual scatter as the sample period progressed and the level of the series rose.

---

[1] See G. E. P. Box and D. A. Pierce, Distribution of Residual Autocorrelations in Autoregressive Moving Average Time Series Models, *Journal of the American Statistical Association,* **64** (1970).

5.12 Additional Examples: Tool Sales Series A and B and the Unemployment Rate

The tool sales series plotted in Figs. 2.1 and 2.2 and the unemployment rate series plotted in Fig. 2.3 provide additional examples for the identification, estimation, and diagnostic checking of ARIMA models. Tool sales series A gives us an example of a very simple stationary model, series B an unusual nonstationary model, and the unemployment rate a stationary model of mixed form.

tool sales series A

Table 5.6 presents PDQ output for tool sales series A, and Figs. 5.10 and 5.11 show plots of autocorrelations and partial autocorrelations of the undifferenced data. Autocorrelations of the undifferenced data decline roughly exponentially, suggesting an AR (1) model. Partial autocorrelations cut off after lag 1, reinforcing the choice of AR (1). Preliminary estimates of parameters ϕ_1 and δ are as follows:

$$\hat{\phi}_1 = r_1 = .77 \tag{5.12.1}$$

$$\hat{\delta} = (1 - \hat{\phi}_1)\bar{z}$$

$$= 154 \tag{5.12.2}$$

From Fig. 5.12 the estimated model is seen to be

$$z_t = .770z_{t-1} + 152 + u_t$$

$$\hat{\sigma}_u{}^2 = 7451 \tag{5.12.3}$$

Referring to the appropriate t statistic, we see that the hypothesis $\phi_1 = 1$, that is, the series is nonstationary, may be rejected. Diagnostic checks based on the autocorrelations of residuals, the Q statistics, and cross correlations between the residuals and the data support the AR (1) model.

tool sales series B

PDQ output for tool sales series B (Table 5.7 and Figs. 5.13 and 5.14) reveals quite a different picture for the companion series. Autocorrelations of the raw data fail to die off; those of the first differences, however, display a rather interesting pattern. In particular, at odd lags little autocorrelation is apparent, but at even lags autocorrelation is strong and alternates in sign. Partial autocorrelations cut off after lag 2, suggesting that the stochastic structure of this series may be accounted for by a second-order autoregression in the first differences.

table 5.6 PDQ output for tool sales series A

TOOL SALES SERIES "A"

AUTOCORRELATION AND PARTIAL AUTOCORRELATION FUNCTIONS OF VARIOUS DIFFERENCES
UNLOGGED DATA
T= 80

AUTOCORRELATIONS

DIFFERENCE	LAGS													EST. STD ERROR FOR ROW
$(1-B)^0(1-B)^0$ VAR = 0.177E 05	1-12	0.77	0.55	0.41	0.34	0.20	0.13	0.10	0.12	0.12	0.11	0.15	0.24	0.11
	13-24	0.22	0.15	0.13	0.14	0.08	-0.02	-0.10	-0.10	-0.08	-0.07	-0.10	-0.07	0.21
	25-36	-0.10	-0.11	-0.12	-0.09	-0.14	-0.21	-0.25	-0.22	-0.24	-0.24	-0.21	-0.17	0.22
$(1-B)^1(1-B)^0$ VAR = 0.829E 04	1-12	-0.04	-0.16	-0.14	0.14	-0.15	-0.10	-0.07	0.02	0.04	-0.13	-0.08	0.21	0.11
	13-24	0.08	-0.10	-0.05	0.16	0.08	-0.05	-0.14	-0.03	0.00	0.07	-0.10	0.12	0.13
	25-36	-0.05	-0.02	-0.09	0.15	0.01	-0.05	-0.13	0.14	-0.03	-0.07	-0.02	0.17	0.14

PARTIAL AUTOCORRELATIONS

DIFFERENCE	LAGS													EST. STD ERROR FOR ROW
$(1-B)^0(1-B)^0$	1-12	0.77	-0.09	0.04	0.07	-0.20	0.09	0.03	0.05	0.06	-0.07	0.19	0.13	0.11
$(1-B)^1(1-B)^0$	1-12	-0.04	-0.16	-0.15	0.10	-0.19	-0.10	-0.11	-0.10	0.01	-0.20	-0.14	0.13	0.11

figure 5.10 Sample correlogram for tool sales series A, PDQ output.

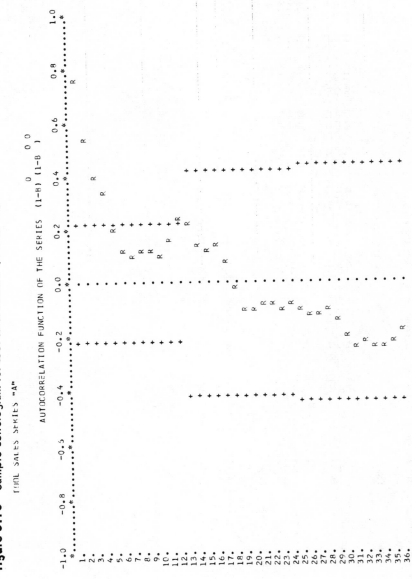

figure 5.11 Plot of sample partial autocorrelations of tool sales series A, PDQ output.

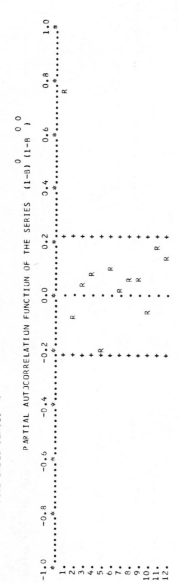

figure 5.12 ESTIMATE output for tool sales series A model AR (1).

TOOL SALES SERIES "A"

VARIANCE OF RESIDUALS(BACK FORECAST RESIDUALS INCLUDED) = 0.7451E 04 , 78 DEGREES OF FREEDOM

VARIANCE OF RESIDUALS(BACK FORECAST RESIDUALS EXCLUDED) = 0.7430E 04 , 78 DEGREES OF FREEDOM

AUTOREGRESSIVE PARAMETERS

0.7700011E 00

CONSTANT TERM

0.151952E 03

95% CONFIDENCE LIMITS (+ & - TWO STD. ERRORS)

	1	2
	0.9134E 00	0.2489E 03
	0.6267E 00	0.5499E 02

STANDARD ERROR FOR EACH PARAMETER (ON LINEAR HYPOTHESIS)

	1	2
	0.7168E-01	0.4848E 02

T-STATISTIC FOR EACH PARAMETER   78 DEGREES OF FREEDOM

	1	2
	0.1074E 02	0.3134E 01

TOOL SALES SERIES "A"

CORRELATION MATRIX OF PARAMETERS

	1	2
1	1.0000	
2	-0.9815	1.0000

AUTOCORRELATIONS OF RESIDUALS   T = 80

LAGS			AUTOCORRELATIONS									EST. S. E.
1-12	0.07	-0.07	0.17	-0.10	-0.07	-0.05	0.03	0.06	-0.10	-0.05	0.22	0.11
13-24	0.10	-0.08	0.16	0.08	-0.04	-0.14	-0.05	-0.00	0.05	-0.10	0.09	0.13
25-36	-0.05	-0.03	-0.10	0.12	-0.02	-0.08	-0.16	0.08	-0.06	-0.09	-0.05	0.12	0.13

CHI-SQUARE TEST OF AUTOCORRELATIONS

Q(12) = 10.1   10 DEGREES OF FREEDOM

Q(24) = 17.8   22 DEGREES OF FREEDOM

Q(36) = 25.4   34 DEGREES OF FREEDOM

CHI-SQUARE VALUES FROM TABLE

CHI-SQUARE = 30.8   10% LEVEL OF SIGNIFICANCE   22 DEGREES OF FREEDOM

CHI-SQUARE = 33.9   5% LEVEL OF SIGNIFICANCE   22 DEGREES OF FREEDOM

figure 5.12 (continued)

TOOL SALES SERIES "A"

CROSS CORRELATIONS OF RESIDUALS AND DIFFERENCED SERIES

CROSS CORRELATION ZERO LAG = 0.64

CROSS CORRELATIONS U(T),W(T+K)

LAGS												
1-12	0.53	0.36	0.24	0.29	0.16	0.07	0.02	0.04	0.07	-0.02	-0.05	0.11
13-24	0.15	0.07	0.02	0.12	0.15	0.08	-0.03	-0.05	-0.04	0.01	-0.06	0.01
25-36	-0.02	-0.03	-0.09	0.01	0.00	-0.05	-0.14	-0.06	-0.08	-0.13	-0.13	-0.02

CROSS CORRELATIONS U(T+K),W(T)

LAGS												
1-12	-0.00	-0.06	-0.03	0.03	-0.10	-0.04	-0.00	0.05	0.05	0.01	0.11	0.19
13-24	0.04	-0.04	-0.01	0.07	-0.06	-0.13	-0.13	-0.05	-0.01	-0.01	-0.07	-0.00
25-36	-0.07	-0.06	-0.06	0.00	-0.12	-0.15	-0.14	-0.04	-0.11	-0.09	-0.05	-0.02

table 5.7 PDQ output for tool sales series B

TOOL SALES SERIES "B"

AUTOCORRELATION AND PARTIAL AUTOCORRELATION FUNCTIONS OF VARIOUS DIFFERENCES
UNLOGGED DATA   T= 80

DIFFERENCE	LAGS	AUTOCORRELATIONS												EST. STD ERROR FOR ROW
$(1-B)^0 (1-B)^0$	1-12	0.92	0.86	0.85	0.83	0.77	0.73	0.71	0.70	0.64	0.60	0.58	0.57	0.11
VAR = 0.675E 05	13-24	0.52	0.45	0.42	0.39	0.34	0.27	0.23	0.21	0.17	0.12	0.09	0.07	0.41
	25-36	0.03	-0.01	-0.03	-0.05	-0.10	-0.15	-0.19	-0.20	-0.23	-0.26	-0.28	-0.29	0.45
$(1-B)^1 (1-B)^0$	1-12	-0.09	-0.46	0.04	0.31	-0.06	-0.32	-0.02	0.35	-0.06	-0.28	0.04	0.29	0.11
VAR = 0.953E 04	13-24	0.07	-0.27	-0.02	0.16	0.18	-0.27	-0.14	0.19	0.07	-0.18	-0.04	0.19	0.17
	25-36	0.04	-0.18	-0.05	0.25	0.03	-0.17	-0.14	0.14	0.07	-0.06	-0.16	0.12	0.20

DIFFERENCE	LAGS	PARTIAL AUTOCORRELATIONS												EST. STD ERROR FOR ROW
$(1-B)^0 (1-B)^0$	1-12	0.92	0.06	0.33	0.04	-0.20	0.01	0.08	0.06	-0.17	0.02	-0.01	0.06	0.11
$(1-B)^1 (1-B)^0$	1-12	-0.09	-0.47	-0.07	0.12	-0.02	-0.19	-0.16	0.13	-0.05	-0.07	-0.06	0.07	0.11

figure 5.13 Sample correlogram for first differences of tool sales series B, PDQ output.

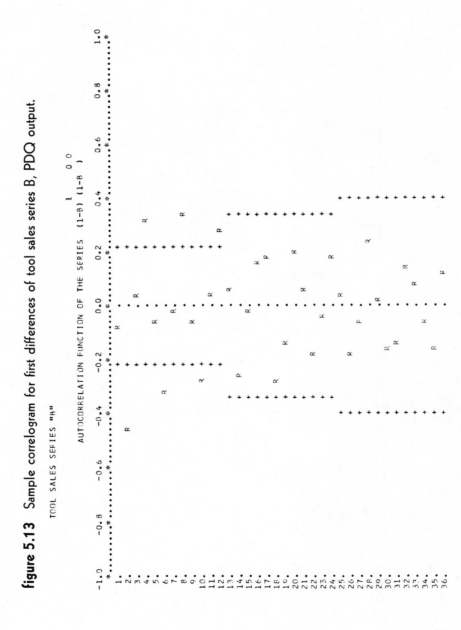

figure 5.14 Plot of sample partial autocorrelations for first differences of tool sales series B, PDQ output.

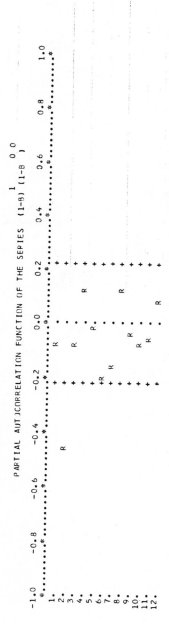

Preliminary estimates of ϕ_1 and ϕ_2 are given by solution of the Yule–Walker equations

$$-.09 = \hat{\phi}_1 - .09\hat{\phi}_2$$
$$-.46 = -.09\hat{\phi}_1 + \hat{\phi}_2$$

(5.12.4)

yielding

$$\phi_1 = -.036$$
$$\phi_2 = -.59$$

(5.12.5)

from which we obtain $\quad \hat{\delta} = (1 - \hat{\phi}_1 - \hat{\phi}_2)\bar{w} = 8.5$ (5.12.6)

The estimated model (see Fig. 5.15) is

$$w_t = -.123w_{t-1} - .484w_{t-2} + 9.24 + u_t$$
$$\hat{\sigma}_u{}^2 = 7620$$

(5.12.7)

where w_t denotes the first differences of the raw data. Note from its t statistic that ϕ_1 is not significantly different from zero. For practical purposes, then, the value of w_t is determined only by the value of w_{t-2} and the disturbance u_t, which explains the peculiar shape of the autocorrelation function. The fact that δ is not significant implies that we *cannot* reject the hypothesis that the series has no drift, in spite of its apparent historical trend. Diagnostic checks from ESTIMATE support the ARI (2,1) specification for this series.

the unemployment rate

Quarterly observations on the unemployment rate 1948–01 through 1966–04 display the sample autocorrelation structure presented in Table 5.8 and Figs. 5.16 and 5.17. Autocorrelations of the undifferenced data die off quickly. The large value of r_1 (.91) relative to the rapid rate of decay of the autocorrelations rules out AR (1). Considering then AR processes of higher order as a possibility, we note that the partial autocorrelations cut off after lag 2. An AR (2) model would have preliminary parameter estimates given by

$$.91 = \phi_1 + .91\phi_2$$
$$.70 = .91\phi_1 + \phi_2$$

(5.12.8)

thus

$$\hat{\phi}_1 = 1.47$$
$$\hat{\phi}_2 = -.62$$

(5.12.9)

and for the constant term

$$\hat{\delta} = (1 - 1.47 + .62)\bar{z}$$
$$= .70$$

(5.12.10)

chap 5   identification and estimation of arima models

figure 5.15 ESTIMATE output for tool sales series B model ARI (2,1).

TOOL SALES SERIES "B"

VARIANCE OF RESIDUALS(BACK FORECAST RESIDUALS INCLUDED) =   0.7620E 04 ,   76 DEGREES OF FREEDOM

VARIANCE OF RESIDUALS(BACK FORECAST RESIDUALS EXCLUDED) =   0.7612E 04 ,   76 DEGREES OF FREEDOM

AUTOREGRESSIVE PARAMETERS

-0.123072E 00 -0.483887E 00

CONSTANT TERM

0.923622E 01

95% CONFIDENCE LIMITS (+ & - TWO STD. ERRORS)

        1   2   3
 0.7897E-01 -0.2791E 00 0.2912E 02
-0.3251E 00 -0.6887E 00 -0.1065E 02

STANDARD ERROR FOR EACH PARAMETER (ON LINEAR HYPOTHESIS)

        1   2   3
 0.1010E 00 0.1024E 00 0.9942E 01

T-STATISTIC FOR EACH PARAMETER   76 DEGREES OF FREEDOM

        1   2   3
-0.1218E 01 -0.4725E 01 0.9290E 00

figure 5.15 (continued)

TOOL SALES SERIES "B"

CORRELATION MATRIX OF PARAMETERS

	1	2	3
1	1.0000		
2	0.0727	1.0000	
3	-0.0512	-0.0698	1.0000

AUTOCORRELATIONS OF RESIDUALS   T = 79

AUTOCORRELATIONS

LAGS													EST. S. E
1-12	-0.03	0.05	-0.05	-0.01	-0.09	-0.15	-0.10	0.17	-0.05	-0.09	0.09	0.14	0.11
13-24	0.12	-0.14	0.10	-0.03	0.16	-0.21	-0.08	0.04	-0.01	-0.04	0.01	0.09	0.12
25-36	-0.01	-0.01	-0.06	0.18	-0.07	-0.07	-0.16	0.06	-0.05	0.04	-0.09	0.03	0.14

CHI-SQUARE TEST OF AUTOCORRELATIONS

Q(12) =   9.0   9 DEGREES OF FREEDOM

Q(24) = 19.4   21 DEGREES OF FREEDOM

Q(36) = 26.4   33 DEGREES OF FREEDOM

CHI-SQUARE VALUES FROM TABLE

CHI-SQUARE = 29.6   10% LEVEL OF SIGNIFICANCE   21 DEGREES OF FREEDOM

CHI-SQUARE = 32.7   5% LEVEL OF SIGNIFICANCE   21 DEGREES OF FREEDOM

figure 5.15 (continued)

TOOL SALES SERIES "B"

CROSS CORRELATIONS OF RESIDUALS AND DIFFERENCED SERIES

CROSS CORRELATION ZERO LAG = 0.88

CROSS CORRELATIONS U(T),W(T+K)

LAGS												
1-12	-0.14	-0.34	0.05	0.16	-0.13	-0.18	-0.01	0.23	-0.08	-0.16	0.12	0.19
13-24	0.03	-0.22	0.10	0.06	0.10	-0.22	-0.09	0.13	0.03	-0.10	0.00	0.12
25-36	-0.02	-0.08	-0.03	0.19	-0.07	-0.13	-0.10	0.13	-0.01	-0.03	-0.08	0.05

CROSS CORRELATIONS U(T+K),W(T)

LAGS												
1-12	0.00	0.00	-0.06	0.11	0.01	-0.23	-0.11	0.23	-0.02	-0.17	-0.01	0.18
13-24	0.13	-0.15	-0.02	0.05	0.21	-0.21	-0.09	0.08	0.02	-0.09	-0.03	0.11
25-36	0.05	-0.09	-0.09	0.19	0.03	-0.07	-0.16	0.05	0.03	0.01	-0.15	0.09

table 5.8 PDQ output for unemployment rate 1948-01 through 1966-04

UNEMPLOYMENT RATE QUARTERLY: 1948-01 THRU 1966-04

AUTOCORRELATION AND PARTIAL AUTOCORRELATION FUNCTIONS OF VARIOUS DIFFERENCES
UNLOGGED DATA   T= 76

AUTOCORRELATIONS

DIFFERENCE	LAGS													EST. STD ERROR FOR ROW
$(1-B)^0 (1-R)^0$	1-12	0.91	0.70	0.47	0.27	0.14	0.08	0.05	0.06	0.07	0.08	0.07	0.05	0.11
VAR = 0.136E 01	13-24	0.05	0.05	0.09	0.13	0.14	0.11	0.05	-0.04	-0.13	-0.20	-0.25	-0.27	0.24
	25-36	-0.27	-0.25	-0.25	-0.28	-0.30	-0.32	-0.31	-0.26	-0.17	-0.09	-0.04	-0.04	0.25
$(1-B)^1 (1-R)^0$	1-12	0.65	0.19	-0.18	-0.37	-0.32	-0.18	-0.11	-0.09	0.01	0.05	0.03	-0.08	0.12
VAR = 0.231E 00	13-24	-0.11	-0.15	-0.05	0.15	0.25	0.24	0.13	0.02	-0.09	-0.11	-0.10	-0.12	0.19
	25-36	-0.07	0.07	0.13	0.02	-0.07	-0.21	-0.24	-0.13	0.05	0.20	0.26	0.20	0.20

PARTIAL AUTOCORRELATIONS

DIFFERENCE	LAGS													EST. STD ERROR FOR ROW
$(1-B)^0 (1-B)^0$	1-12	0.91	-0.65	0.07	0.10	0.14	-0.08	-0.05	0.08	0.06	-0.12	-0.01	0.08	0.11
$(1-B)^1 (1-B)^0$	1-12	0.65	-0.41	-0.19	-0.11	0.06	-0.09	-0.18	-0.08	0.19	-0.16	-0.13	-0.22	0.12

figure 5.16 Sample correlogram for unemployment rate 1948-01 through 1966-04, PDQ output.

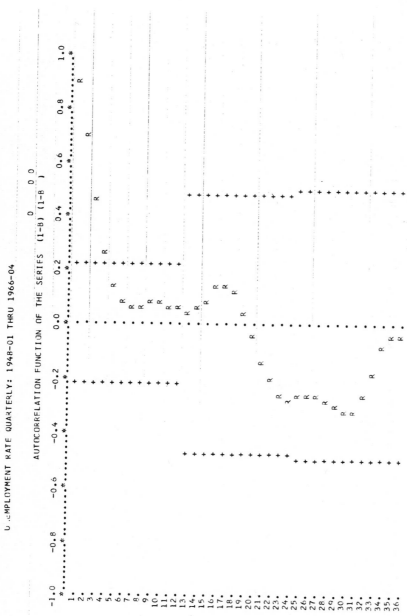

figure 5.17 Sample partial autocorrelations for unemployment rate 1948-01 through 1966-04, PDQ output.

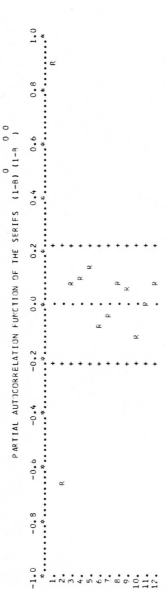

UNEMPLOYMENT RATE QUARTERLY: 1948-01 THRU 1966-04

PARTIAL AUTOCORRELATION FUNCTION OF THE SERIES $(1-B)^0 (1-B)^0$

figure 5.18 ESTIMATE output for unemployment rate model AR (2).

UNEMPLOYMENT RATE QUARTERLY: 1948-01 THRU 1966-04

VARIANCE OF RESIDUALS(BACK FORECAST RESIDUALS INCLUDED) = 0.1090E 00 , 73 DEGREES OF FREEDOM

VARIANCE OF RESIDUALS(BACK FORECAST RESIDUALS EXCLUDED) = 0.1082E 00 , 73 DEGREES OF FREEDOM

AUTOREGRESSIVE PARAMETERS

0.158038E 01 -0.724930E 00

CONSTANT TERM

0.668289E 00

95% CONFIDENCE LIMITS (+ & - TWO STD. ERRORS)

1	2	3
0.1732E 01	-0.5689E 00	0.9819E 00
0.1429E 01	-0.8810E 00	0.3546E 00

STANDARD ERROR FOR EACH PARAMETER (ON LINEAR HYPOTHESIS)

1	2	3
0.7575E-01	0.7804E-01	0.1568E 00

T-STATISTIC FOR EACH PARAMETER 73 DEGREES OF FREEDOM

1	2	3
0.2086E 02	-0.9290E 01	0.4261E 01

figure 5.18 (continued)

UNEMPLOYMENT RATE QUARTERLY: 1948-01 THRU 1966-04

CORRELATION MATRIX OF PARAMETERS

	1	2	3
1	1.0000		
2	-0.9103	1.0000	
3	-0.1414	-0.2690	1.0000

AUTOCORRELATIONS OF RESIDUALS   T = 76

	AUTOCORRELATIONS											
LAGS												
1-12	0.18	-0.03	-0.08	-0.15	0.05	0.22	0.15	-0.08	0.12	0.09	0.13	-0.11
13-24	0.07	-0.16	-0.16	0.14	0.11	0.08	-0.05	-0.02	-0.16	-0.06	-0.00	-0.14
25-36	-0.19	0.08	0.06	-0.08	0.01	-0.19	-0.22	-0.13	-0.03	0.02	0.05	0.07

CHI-SQUARE TEST OF AUTOCORRELATIONS

Q(12) = 14.6   9 DEGREES OF FREEDOM

Q(24) = 25.7   21 DEGREES OF FREEDOM

Q(36) = 37.8   33 DEGREES OF FREEDOM

CHI-SQUARE VALUES FROM TABLE

CHI-SQUARE = 29.6   10% LEVEL OF SIGNIFICANCE   21 DEGREES OF FREEDOM

CHI-SQUARE = 32.7   5% LEVEL OF SIGNIFICANCE   21 DEGREES OF FREEDOM

EST. S. E
0.11
0.13
0.15

CROSS CORRELATIONS OF RESIDUALS AND DIFFERENCED SERIES

CROSS CORRELATION ZERO LAG = 0.28

CROSS CORRELATIONS U(T),W(T+K)

LAGS												
1-12	0.48	0.55	0.51	0.35	0.20	0.12	0.09	0.03	0.02	0.04	0.08	0.06
13-24	0.07	0.02	-0.07	-0.06	-0.03	0.02	0.05	0.05	-0.00	-0.06	-0.09	-0.13
25-36	-0.18	-0.17	-0.12	-0.11	-0.07	-0.06	-0.13	-0.18	-0.23	-0.22	-0.15	-0.04

CROSS CORRELATIONS U(T+K),W(T)

LAGS												
1-12	-0.01	-0.01	0.06	0.13	0.20	0.18	0.12	0.09	0.07	0.02	-0.02	-0.01
13-24	0.03	0.06	0.12	0.11	0.00	-0.07	-0.11	-0.14	-0.14	-0.12	-0.12	-0.10
25-36	-0.06	-0.09	-0.16	-0.21	-0.20	-0.16	-0.08	-0.01	-0.01	-0.04	-0.10	-0.15

figure 5.19 ESTIMATE output for unemployment rate model ARMA (2,1).

```
VARIANCE OF RESIDUALS(BACK FORECAST RESIDUALS INCLUDED) =    0.1047E 00 ,    72 DEGREES OF FREEDOM

VARIANCE OF RESIDUALS(BACK FORECAST RESIDUALS EXCLUDED) =    0.1040E 00 ,    72 DEGREES OF FREEDOM


AUTOREGRESSIVE PARAMETERS

   0.146275E 01  -0.616525E 00

MOVING AVERAGE PARAMETERS

  -0.285073E 00

CONSTANT TERM

   0.707852E 00

95% CONFIDENCE LIMITS (+ & - TWO STD. ERRORS)

         1              2              3              4

   0.1695E 01  -0.3852E 00   0.4878E-02   0.1098E 01
   0.1231E 01  -0.8478E 00  -0.5750E 00   0.3174E 00


STANDARD ERROR FOR EACH PARAMETER (ON LINEAR HYPOTHESIS)

         1              2              3              4

   0.1159E 00   0.1156E 00   0.1450E 00   0.1952E 00
```

UNEMPLOYMENT RATE QUARTERLY: 1948-01 THRU 1966-04

T-STATISTIC FOR EACH PARAMETER   72 DEGREES OF FREEDOM

1	2	3	4
0.1262E 02	-0.5332E 01	-0.1966E 01	0.3625E 01

CORRELATION MATRIX OF PARAMETERS

	1	2	3	4
1	1.0000			
2	-0.9381	1.0000		
3	0.6243	-0.6042	1.0000	
4	-0.1803	-0.1614	-0.0606	1.0000

AUTOCORRELATIONS OF RESIDUALS   T = 76

LAGS	AUTOCORRELATIONS												EST. S. E
1-12	0.01	0.06	-0.03	-0.14	0.03	0.14	0.12	-0.13	0.14	0.01	0.16	-0.17	0.11
13-24	0.13	-0.14	-0.14	0.16	0.05	0.09	-0.07	0.03	-0.16	-0.04	-0.00	-0.11	0.13
25-36	-0.18	0.09	0.04	-0.11	0.05	-0.18	-0.16	-0.10	-0.01	0.02	0.03	0.07	0.14

CHI-SQUARE TEST OF AUTOCORRELATIONS

Q(12) = 11.3   8 DEGREES OF FREEDOM
Q(24) = 21.7   20 DEGREES OF FREEDOM
Q(36) = 31.7   32 DEGREES OF FREEDOM

CHI-SQUARE VALUES FROM TABLE

CHI-SQUARE = 28.4   10% LEVEL OF SIGNIFICANCE   20 DEGREES OF FREEDOM
CHI-SQUARE = 31.4   5% LEVEL OF SIGNIFICANCE   20 DEGREES OF FREEDOM

figure 5.19 (continued)

UNEMPLOYMENT RATE QUARTERLY: 1948-01 THRU 1966-04

CROSS CORRELATIONS OF RESIDUALS AND DIFFERENCED SERIES

CROSS CORRELATION ZERO LAG = 0.26

CROSS CORRELATIONS U(T),W(T+K)

LAGS												
1-12	0.46	0.52	0.49	0.34	0.19	0.11	0.09	0.03	0.02	0.02	0.07	0.04
13-24	0.05	0.02	-0.36	-0.05	-0.02	0.04	0.06	0.07	0.01	-0.04	-0.07	-0.10
25-36	-0.15	-0.15	-0.09	-0.10	-0.07	-0.06	-0.13	-0.17	-0.20	-0.19	-0.13	-0.03

CROSS CORRELATIONS U(T+K),W(T)

LAGS												
1-12	-0.01	-0.01	0.01	0.06	0.12	0.11	0.07	0.06	0.06	0.01	-0.01	-0.01
13-24	-0.03	0.05	-0.11	0.09	-0.01	-0.07	-0.11	-0.14	-0.14	-0.13	-0.13	-0.11
25-36	-0.06	-0.09	-0.15	-0.19	-0.17	-0.14	-0.06	-0.00	-0.00	-0.03	-0.08	-0.12

Program ESTIMATE output in Fig. 5.18 indicates the fitted model

$$z_t = 1.580z_{t-1} - .725z_{t-2} + .668 + u_t$$
$$\hat{\sigma}_u{}^2 = .109 \tag{5.12.11}$$

Note that $Q(12)$ is significant at the 10 percent level, casting some doubt on the adequacy of the AR (2) model. Examining the autocorrelations of the residuals for some clue to a remedy, note that r_1 is quite large, suggesting extension of the model to ARMA (2,1).

Parameter estimates for the extended model appear in Fig. 5.19. The model is now

$$z_t = 1.463z_{t-1} - .616z_{t-2} + .708 + u_t + .285u_{t-1}$$
$$\hat{\sigma}_u{}^2 = .1047 \tag{5.12.12}$$

with Q statistics well within critical bounds and r_1 of the residuals reduced to .01. The unemployment rate data are *seasonally adjusted* and as is typical of such data, a certain amount of *negative seasonality* is revealed by some negative correlation in the residuals at lags 4 and 5 (see also the results for GNP, Fig. 5.8). Nevertheless, it would seem that the ARMA (2,1) model accounts well for the stochastic structure of the series. As we shall see in Chap. 8, this model performs very well against the Federal Reserve Board-MIT-Penn econometric model in predicting the unemployment rate.

Exercises

5.1 The following is a sequence of 11 random variables drawn independently from the $N(0,1)$ distribution:

$$
\begin{array}{r}
-.6704 \\
-1.2069 \\
-2.0158 \\
-.7139 \\
-.5883 \\
1.1354 \\
.7638 \\
.9620 \\
.6221 \\
.1968 \\
-1.4729
\end{array}
$$

(a) Glancing at the sequence, does it look random to you? Why not?
(b) For the random numbers, what is the theoretical value of ρ_1 and ρ_2? Compute their sample values r_1 and r_2 in this sequence.
(c) Use the sequence to construct a realization of the process

$$z_t = 1.2 + u_t - .7u_{t-1} \qquad t = 1, \ldots , 10$$

exercises

(d)   For the z_t you have constructed, what are the *theoretical* values of

$$E(z_t)$$
$$\gamma_0, \gamma_1, \gamma_2, \gamma_{15}$$
$$\rho_0, \rho_1, \rho_2, \rho_{15}$$

(e)   For the z_t you have constructed, *estimate* from the sample

$$E(z_t)$$
$$\gamma_0, \gamma_1, \gamma_2$$
$$\rho_0, \rho_1, \rho_2$$

(f)   How would you characterize the difference between theoretical parameter values and the particular estimates of them obtained from this sample?

Note: For the computer-inclined, you may use the random-number generator to create your sequence of u_t and use the computer to answer the questions.

5.2   Monthly usage of a computer system in hours was (read down columns):

243	308	257
230	346	275
291	268	328
246	331	228

Compute r_1, r_2, r_3, r_4, and plot the sample correlogram.

5.3   The following data were generated by the MA (1) process:

$$z_t = u_t - \theta_1 u_{t-1}$$
$$u_t \approx N(0, \sigma_u{}^2)$$

t	z_t
1	$-.859$
2	$.953$
3	-1.373
4	$.758$
5	$-.730$
6	$.990$
7	$-.042$
8	$-.887$
9	$.876$
10	-1.444

(a)   Evaluate $S(\theta_1)$ for $\theta_1 = .1, .5, .9$ conditional on $u_0 = 0$.
(b)   Sketch the sum-of-squares function using the points you have computed in (a).
(c)   Provide an estimate of $\sigma_u{}^2$ based on the sum-of-squares evaluated at your best $\hat{\theta}$.

chap. 5   identification and estimation of arima models

5.4   For the AR (1) model

$$z_t = \phi_1 z_{t-1} + u_t$$
$$u_t \approx N(0, \sigma_u^2)$$

(a)   Write down $S(\phi_1) = \hat{u}(\phi_1)_2^2 + \cdots + \hat{u}(\phi_1)_{10}^2$ in terms of ϕ_1 and the observations only, using the identities

$$\hat{u}(\phi_1)_2 = z_2 - \phi_1 z_1$$
$$\cdots \cdots \cdots \cdots$$
$$\hat{u}(\phi_1)_{10} = z_{10} - \phi_1 z_9$$

What is the largest power of ϕ_1 appearing in $S(\phi_1)$?

(b)   Differentiate $S(\phi_1)$ with respect to ϕ_1, equate the derivative to zero, and solve for $\hat{\phi}_1$ in terms of the z's.

(c)   For the following observations compute the MLE of ϕ_1.

t	z_t
1	$-.63$
2	$.49$
3	$.67$
4	1.34
5	-1.16
6	-1.62
7	$.30$
8	$-.24$
9	$.40$
10	$.92$

(d)   Compute residuals $\hat{u}(\hat{\phi}_1)_2, \ldots, \hat{u}(\hat{\phi}_1)_{10}$, and evaluate $S(\hat{\phi}_1)$.

(e)   What is the MLE of σ_u^2? (Since z_1 is used up as a "starting value" in the computation of residuals, you may regard the effective number of observations as 9.)

Additional Readings

Box, G. E. P., and G. M. Jenkins: "Time Series Analysis, Forecasting and Control," Holden-Day, Inc., San Francisco, 1970. The classical reference on the use of sample autocorrelations for identification of time series models; see chap. 6. Maximum-likelihood estimation of ARIMA models is developed in detail in chap. 7, including the "backforecasting" technique. Diagnostic checks are discussed in chap. 8.

Freeman, H.: "Introduction to Statistical Inference," Addison-Wesley Publishing Company, Inc., Reading, Mass., 1963. The basic concepts of hypothesis testing and confidence intervals are developed in chaps. 28 and 29.

Hogg, R. V., and A. T. Craig: "Introduction to Mathematical Statistics," 3d ed., The Macmillan Company, New York, 1970. For an alternative reference on hypothesis testing and confidence intervals, see chap. 3, pp. 57–59, and chaps. 6 and 9.

Nelson, C. R.: "The Term Structure of Interest Rates," Basic Books, Inc., New York, 1972. Chapter 5 serves as a case study in the application of the identification and estimation procedures to 1-year bond yields. The diagnostic checks utilized there emphasize overfitting as a check on model identification.

6
Forecasting
ARIMA
Processes

When we introduced the concept of stochastic processes as models for time series in Chap. 2 it was with the ultimate objective of using the models to infer from the past history of a series its likely course in the future. More precisely, we want to derive from a model the conditional distribution of future observations given the past observations that it implies. This final step in the model-building process is what we refer to loosely as *forecasting*.

It should be noted that in practice the model in hand is never the hypothetical "true" process generating the data we have observed. Rather, it is an approximation to the generating process and is subject to errors in both identification and estimation. Thus, although we shall discuss forecasting as if we knew the generating process, it is clear that our success in practice will depend in part on the adequacy of our empirical model and therefore on success in the preceding stages of identification and estimation.

6.1 Minimum Mean-square-error Forecasts

It would seem natural to begin our discussion of the conditional distribution of future observations with the mean of that distribution, that is, the conditional expectation of each future observation. There is an additional motivation for beginning with the conditional expectation since in many operational contexts it is desirable to be able to quote a point forecast, a single number, and the conditional expectation has the desirable property of being the *minimum mean-square-error forecast*. That is, if the model is correct, there is no other extrapolative forecast which will produce errors whose squares have smaller expected value. Although we have not yet discussed how conditional expectations are computed, this general result is easily demonstrated as follows. We denote by $\hat{z}_t(l)$ the expectation of z_{t+l}, given the history of the series up to time t and that history $(\ldots, z_{t-1}, z_t)$ by H_t. Let F be any other forecast of z_{t+l}; then the expected or mean square of the error for F (conditional on information H_t) is

$$E[(z_{t+l} - F)^2 | H_t] = E\{[z_{t+l} - (\hat{z}_t(l) + g)]^2 | H_t\} \quad (6.1.1)$$

where g is the discrepancy between F and the conditional expectation forecast $\hat{z}_t(l)$. Now (6.1.1) reduces to

$$E[(z_{t+l} - F)^2 | H_t] = E[(z_{t+l} - \hat{z}_t(l))^2 | H_t] + 2gE[z_{t+l} - \hat{z}_t(l) | H_t] + g^2$$
$$= E\{[z_{t+l} - \hat{z}_t(l)]^2 | H_t\} + g^2 \quad (6.1.2)$$

which is just the mean-square-error for the conditional expectation forecast *plus* an amount g^2 that must be positive if F differs from $\hat{z}_t(l)$. To minimize squared error then, we set $g = 0$ and conclude that $\hat{z}_t(l)$ is the minimum square error forecast.

6.2   Computation of Conditional Expectation Forecasts

one-step-ahead forecasts

Consider the possibility of computing the conditional expectation forecast directly from the difference-equation form of the process. In particular, suppose that we are at time t, knowing H_t, and wish to forecast one step ahead, that is, compute $\hat{z}_t(1)$, which is the conditional expectation $E(z_{t+1} | H_t)$. Now z_{t+1}, when it is observed next period, will be given by

$$z_{t+1} = \Phi_1 z_t + \cdots + \Phi_{p+d} z_{t-(p+d)+1}$$
$$+ \delta + u_{t+1} - \theta_1 u_t - \cdots - \theta_q u_{t-q+1} \quad (6.2.1)$$

where the coefficients Φ_i are determined by ϕ_i and the value of d. Since all variables with time subscripts through period t have been realized (are no longer random) and $E(u_{t+1} | H_t)$ is zero, $\hat{z}_t(1)$ is just given by

$$\hat{z}_t(1) = E(z_{t+1} | H_t) = \Phi_1 z_t + \cdots + \Phi_{p+d} z_{t-(p+d)+1}$$
$$+ \delta - \theta_1 u_t - \cdots - \theta_q u_{t-q+1} \quad (6.2.2)$$

The prospects for numerical evaluation of $\hat{z}_t(1)$ from (6.2.2) do not appear particularly encouraging at first blush since, after all, the disturbances included in the equation are unobserved. They may, however, be computed just by keeping track of past forecasts. This is because a given disturbance, say, u_{t-i}, is just the error in forecasting z_{t-i} made in period $t - i - 1$. In other words, the disturbances are just the succession of one-step-ahead forecast errors. To see this, note that if z_{t-i} is expressed in difference-equation form (6.2.1) and $\hat{z}_{t-i-1}(1)$ is written in the form (6.2.2), then we have directly

$$z_{t-i} - \hat{z}_{t-i-1}(1) = u_{t-i} \qquad i = 0, 1, 2, \ldots \qquad (6.2.3)$$

Therefore, as long as we have kept track of our previous one-step-ahead errors, expression (6.2.2) is a completely operational formula for computation of forecasts.

For example, consider the problem of computing forecasts for a MA (2) model. From (6.2.2) we know that the one-step-ahead forecast $\hat{z}_t(1)$ is given by

$$\hat{z}_t(1) = \delta - \theta_1 u_t - \theta_2 u_{t-1} \qquad (6.2.4)$$

To be able to evaluate that expression we need values for u_t and u_{t-1}. Now our previous one-step-ahead forecast was $\hat{z}_{t-1}(1)$, and the error made by that forecast was

$$[z_t - \hat{z}_{t-1}(1)] = (\delta + u_t - \theta_1 u_{t-1} - \theta_2 u_{t-2}) - (\delta - \theta_1 u_{t-1} - \theta_2 u_{t-2})$$
$$= u_t \qquad (6.2.5)$$

Similarly, u_{t-1} is given by the error we made in period $(t - 1)$, namely, $[z_{t-1} - \hat{z}_{t-2}(1)]$. Provided that we recorded those past errors and have them available then to evaluate $\hat{z}_t(1)$ numerically, we simply compute

$$\hat{z}_t(1) = \delta - \theta_1[z_t - \hat{z}_{t-1}(1)] - \theta_2[z_{t-1} - \hat{z}_{t-2}(1)] \qquad (6.2.6)$$

A moment's thought will indicate that there is a *starting-value* problem in forecast computation since there must have been a first forecast, at which time there were no past errors available to use in the formula. To compute the first forecast, clearly some assumption must be made about the values of prior disturbances. The most intuitively appealing procedure is to set them at their marginal expected values of zero. Of course, these initial disturbances were not in fact zero, and so the first and subsequent forecasts will be distorted by some amount because of this approximation. Fortunately, this amount becomes smaller the further we get away from the period in which the first forecast was made provided we have chosen the invertible values for the moving-average parameters. Consequently, in practice we should begin forecast computation at the beginning of our data series to have available the longest possible sequence of past errors for computation of the forecasts of real interest.

To illustrate, consider forecasting a MA (1) process that has no constant. If our data consists of $z_1, \ldots, z_T$, then we compute first

$$\hat{z}_0(1) = -\theta_1 u_0 \qquad (6.2.7)$$

Now we need to assign a value to u_0, say, $\hat{u}_0$, since the actual u_0 is unobserved. Then we have the sequence of one-step-ahead forecasts

$$
\begin{aligned}
\hat{z}_0(1) &= -\theta_1 \hat{u}_0 \\
\hat{z}_1(1) &= -\theta_1 \hat{u}_1 \\
&= -\theta_1 [z_1 - \hat{z}_0(1)] \\
&= -\theta_1 z_1 + \theta_1^2 \hat{u}_0 \\
\hat{z}_2(1) &= -\theta_1 \hat{u}_2 \\
&= -\theta_1 [z_2 - \hat{z}_1(1)] \qquad\qquad (6.2.8)\\
&= -\theta_1 z_2 - \theta_1^2 z_1 + \theta_1^3 \hat{u}_0 \\
&\cdots\cdots\cdots\cdots\cdots\cdots\cdots \\
\hat{z}_T(1) &= -\theta_1 \hat{u}_T \\
&= -\theta_1 [z_T - \hat{z}_{T-1}(1)] \\
&= -\theta_1 z_T - \theta_1^2 z_{T-1} - \cdots - \theta_1^T z_1 + \theta_1^{T+1} \hat{u}_0
\end{aligned}
$$

Now $\hat{u}_0$ may be thought of as consisting of two parts: the actual and unknown value u_0 and the discrepancy $(\hat{u}_0 - u_0)$ between our guess and the actual value; hence

$$\theta_1^{T+1} \hat{u}_0 = \theta_1^{T+1} u_0 + \theta_1^{T+1} (\hat{u}_0 - u_0) \qquad (6.2.9)$$

If θ_1 satisfies the invertibility requirement $|\theta_1| < 1$, then the term $\theta_1^{T+1}(\hat{u}_0 - u_0)$ is smaller the larger T is. Consequently, we want to make T as large as possible; that is, we should build up our sequence of forecasts from the beginning of the data series even though ultimately we may only be interested in the value of $\hat{z}_T(1)$. The motivation for setting $\hat{u}_0$ at zero is that zero is the unconditional expectation of u_0, and we want $(\hat{u}_0 - u_0)$ to be as small as possible.

multistep-ahead forecasts

Having solved the problem of computing one-step-ahead forecasts, we may readily proceed to computation of forecasts of any horizon. In particular, for l steps ahead we have directly

$$
\begin{aligned}
\hat{z}_t(l) = E(z_{t+l}|H_t) = \Phi_1 E(z_{t+l-1}|H_t) + \cdots + \Phi_{p+d} E(z_{t+l-(p+d)}|H_t) \\
+ \delta - \theta_l u_t - \cdots - \theta_q u_{t-(q-l)} \qquad (6.2.10)
\end{aligned}
$$

since all future disturbances have expectation zero and where the terms in past disturbances disappear entirely if $l > q$. Since the conditional expectations required are simply forecasts of shorter horizon, it is apparent that forecasts are computed efficiently by proceeding in a recursive fashion for $l = 1, 2, \ldots,$ and so forth, to the longest horizon desired. The sequence of computations is then

$$
\begin{aligned}
\hat{z}_t(1) &= \Phi_1 z_t + \cdots + \Phi_{p+d} z_{t-(p+d)+1} + \delta - \theta_1 u_t - \cdots - \theta_q u_{t-q+1} \\
\hat{z}_t(2) &= \Phi_1 \hat{z}_t(1) + \Phi_2 z_t + \cdots + \Phi_{p+d} z_{t-(p+d)+2} \\
&\qquad\qquad + \delta - \theta_2 u_t - \cdots - \theta_q u_{t-q+2}
\end{aligned}
\tag{6.2.11}
$$

. . . .

and for $l > q$

$$
\hat{z}_t(l) = \Phi_1 \hat{z}_t(l-1) + \cdots + \Phi_{p+d} \hat{z}_t[l-(p+d)] + \delta \qquad l > q \quad (6.2.12)
$$

where $\hat{z}_t(l-i)$ is understood to be the actual observation z_{t+l-i} if $i \geq l$. Note that the moving-average part of the process enters into only forecasts of horizons 1 through q, establishing initial values for the difference equation (6.2.12) that determines the forecasts for successively longer horizons.

limiting properties of forecast profiles for stationary models

Intuition suggests that for any stationary process the profile of forecasts should approach the mean of the process as a limit since the further we look into the future the influence of past history in the determination of the realization we are trying to predict will be less. This may be confirmed by considering that from the random-shock form for a stationary process the forecast $\hat{z}_t(l)$ is seen to be

$$
\begin{aligned}
\hat{z}_t(l) &= E(z_{t+l}|H_t) = E(\mu + u_{t+l} + \Psi_1 u_{t+l-1} + \cdots |H_t) \\
&= \mu + \Psi_l u_t + \Psi_{l+1} u_{t-1} + \cdots
\end{aligned}
\tag{6.2.13}
$$

since future disturbances have expectation zero. The limit of $\hat{z}_t(l)$ is given then by

$$
\lim_{l \to \infty} \hat{z}(l) = \mu + \lim_{l \to \infty} (\Psi_l u_t + \Psi_{l+1} u_{t-1} + \cdots) \tag{6.2.14}
$$

However, since the sum $\Sigma_{i=0}^{\infty} \Psi_i$ converges and the realized disturbances are bounded in magnitude, we have

$$
\lim_{l \to \infty} (\Psi_l u_t + \Psi_{l+1} u_{t-1} + \cdots) = 0 \tag{6.2.15}
$$

and therefore

$$
\lim_{l \to \infty} \hat{z}_t(l) = \mu \tag{6.2.16}
$$

The forecast profile must, then, approach the mean of the process as forecast horizon becomes large.

6.3 Examples of Forecast Profiles for Stationary Processes

A few examples will help to clarify the computational procedure as well as to illustrate the properties of forecast profiles for some of the processes, both stationary and nonstationary, often encountered in practice.

Consider first the AR (1) for which forecasts are given by the simple relations

$$\hat{z}_t(1) = \phi_1 z_t + \delta$$
$$\hat{z}_t(l) = \phi_1 \hat{z}_t(l-1) + \delta \qquad l > 1 \tag{6.3.1}$$

Note that previous errors play no part in the computations since the process has no moving-average terms. The forecast profile implied by (6.3.1) is always a geometric decay from the last observation to the mean of the process. To see why this is so, write future observation z_{t+l} in random-shock form

$$z_{t+l} = \mu + u_{t+l} + \phi_1 u_{t+l-1} + \phi_1^2 u_{t+l-2} + \cdots \tag{6.3.2}$$

where μ is the mean of the process $\delta/(1 - \phi_1)$. The profile of forecasts is given then by

$$\hat{z}_t(l) = \mu + \phi_1^l u_t + \phi_1^{l+1} u_{t-1} + \cdots$$
$$= \mu + \phi_1^l (u_t + \phi_1 u_{t-1} + \phi_1^2 u_{t-2} + \cdots) \qquad l \geq 1 \tag{6.3.3}$$

Now the expression in parentheses in the second line of (6.3.3) is just $(z_t - \mu)$, the deviation of the last observed value from the mean of the process. The forecast profile then becomes

$$\hat{z}_t(l) = \mu + \phi_1^l (z_t - \mu) \tag{6.3.4}$$

In other words, the forecasts for successively longer horizons deviate from the mean of the process by an amount that decays at rate ϕ_1 as horizon increases.

For an MA (1) process we have

$$\hat{z}_t(1) = \delta - \theta_1 u_t$$
$$\hat{z}_t(l) = \delta \qquad l > 1 \tag{6.3.5}$$

We see that the forecast profile for any MA (1) process will always consist of a one-step-ahead forecast determined by the most recent disturbance and then simply the mean of the process. Recalling that MA (1) has nonzero auto-correlation only at lag 1, that is, has a memory of only one period, the forecast profile is consistent with intuition. It should be immediately apparent from the result for MA (1) that the forecast profile for any MA (q) process will consist of values at $l = 1, \ldots, q$, which are determined by past disturbances and then just the mean of the process δ for all horizons longer than q. This is the forecasting implication of the fact that, in general, moving-average processes have a memory of only q periods.

The simplest stationary mixed process, ARMA (1,1), gives rise to forecasts

$$\hat{z}_t(1) = \phi_1 z_t + \delta - \theta_1 u_t$$
$$\hat{z}_t(l) = \phi_1 \hat{z}_t(l - 1) + \delta \qquad l > 1 \tag{6.3.6}$$

Thus the current disturbance helps to determine only the one-step-ahead forecast, which in turn serves as the starting point from which the forecast profile decays geometrically to the mean of the process, as in the case of AR (1). The general result for ARMA (1,q) is readily demonstrated. Past disturbances will enter into computation of forecasts through horizon q periods after which successive forecasts are given by

$$\hat{z}_t(l) = \phi_1 \hat{z}_t(l - 1) + \delta \qquad l > q \tag{6.3.7}$$

producing a geometric decay to the mean of the process from the value of $\hat{z}_t(q)$.

6.4 Examples of Forecast Profiles for Nonstationary Processes

Forecasts for the simple nonstationary process ARI (1,1) are given directly by (6.2.12); thus

$$\hat{z}_t(1) = (1 + \phi_1)z_t \qquad\quad - \phi_1 z_{t-1} \qquad + \delta$$
$$\hat{z}_t(2) = (1 + \phi_1)\hat{z}_t(1) \qquad - \phi_1 z_t \qquad + \delta$$
$$\cdots\cdots\cdots\cdots\cdots\cdots\cdots\cdots\cdots\cdots\cdots\cdots \tag{6.4.1}$$
$$\hat{z}_t(l) = (1 + \phi_1)\hat{z}_t(l - 1) - \phi_1 \hat{z}_t(l - 2) + \delta \qquad l > 2$$

Although it is clear that these forecasts are readily computed, the general structure of forecast profiles for such processes is more readily apparent if we note that the conditional expectation $\hat{z}_t(l)$ must be the sum of expected changes.

$$\hat{z}_t(l) = z_t + \hat{w}_t(1) + \cdots + \hat{w}_t(l) \tag{6.4.2}$$

where the $\hat{w}_t(\ )$ are conditional expectation *forecasts of the first differences* These forecasts of the first differences are generated by

$$w_t = \phi_1 w_{t-1} + \delta + u_t \tag{6.4.3}$$

From what we now know about the forecast profile of a stationary AR (1) process, such as the w_t's, we may easily infer the characteristics of the forecast profile for the z_t's.

In particular, if w_t is above the mean of the first differences, then the forecasted *changes* will decrease geometrically to that mean. Consequently, the forecast profile of the *levels* rises at a *decreasing* rate and that rate approaches $\delta/(1 - \phi_1)$, the mean of the first difference process. In economic contexts we usually have $\delta \geq 0$, that is, positive drift or none at all. Consequently, the forecast profile approaches a straight line that has positive slope equal to $\delta/(1 - \phi_1)$. Suppose now that w_t were below the mean change, say, negative. In that case the forecast profile for the differences will approach the mean exponentially from below. Thus the one-step-ahead forecast might be negative, the two-step-ahead slightly positive, and so forth, producing for the levels a profile that predicts a decrease and then increases, gradually approaching the rate of $\delta/(1 - \phi_1)$. Note that in this latter example the model predicts a *turning point*, that is, a change in direction. It is important to remember that the forecast profile for any ARI (1,1) process *always* approaches a straight line with slope $\delta/(1 - \phi_1)$.

To illustrate the forecast profile for ARI (1,1), we return to the model for quarterly GNP developed in Chap. 5 from data for the quarters 1947-01 through 1966-04. In terms of first differences the model may be written as

$$w_t = .62w_{t-1} + 2.69 \tag{6.4.4}$$

implying that the mean of the first difference process is

$$\mu = \frac{.2.69}{1 - .62} = 7.1 \tag{6.4.5}$$

Thus forecasts of the differences will decay geometrically from the current value w_t to the mean of 7.1 billion dollars. For example, suppose the model had been available in 1949–01 when a recession was in progress, and the value of w_9 (the ninth observation on the differences) was -5.4 billion dollars. The forecasted *changes* for the subsequent four quarters were then

$$
\begin{aligned}
\hat{w}_9(1) &= \quad .62w_9 \quad + 2.69 \\
&= -.64 \\
\hat{w}_9(2) &= \quad .62\hat{w}_9(1) + 2.69 \\
&= \quad 2.30 \\
\hat{w}_9(3) &= \quad .62\hat{w}_9(2) + 2.69 \\
&= \quad 4.00 \\
\hat{w}_9(4) &= \quad .62\hat{w}_9(3) + 2.69 \\
&= \quad 5.17
\end{aligned}
\tag{6.4.6}
$$

thus beginning with a forecast of continued decline in GNP for the next quarter and then a turning point followed by expansion at an increasing rate. The profile of forecasted levels of GNP is then given by

$$\hat{z}_9(1) = z_9 + \hat{w}_9(1)$$
$$= 258.5 + (-.64)$$
$$= 257.9$$

$$\hat{z}_9(2) = \hat{z}_9(1) + \hat{w}_9(2)$$
$$= 257.9 + 2.30$$
$$= 260.2 \qquad\qquad (6.4.7)$$

$$\hat{z}_9(3) = \hat{z}_9(2) + \hat{w}_9(3)$$
$$= 260.2 + 4.00$$
$$= 264.2$$

$$\hat{z}_9(4) = \hat{z}_9(3) + \hat{w}_9(4)$$
$$= 264.2 + 5.17$$
$$= 269.4$$

which reflect an initial forecasted decrease and then a forecasted increasing rate of expansion. Figure 6.1 presents a section of output from program FORECAST, which computes forecasts for any ARIMA model and parameter values specified by the user.[1] Forecasted levels of GNP from original data 1949-01, observation 9, appear alongside subsequent realized values as do forecast errors and confidence limits, which will be discussed in Sec. 6.6. The same results are presented graphically in Fig. 6.2.

The GNP model was, of course, actually estimated through 1966-04, and therefore the forecast profile for origin date 1966-04, observation 80, is of particular interest. Program FORECAST output for that origin date is included in Fig. 6.1, and the profile is plotted against subsequent actuals for the following four quarters in Fig. 6.3.

The IMA (1,1) process was studied in some detail in Chap. 4, where we indicated that the one-step-ahead forecast was an EWMA of past observations, that is, an exponential smoothing forecast. To review briefly, we noted that the inverted form of IMA (1,1) is

$$z_t = (1 - \theta_1)z_{t-1} + \theta_1(1 - \theta_1)z_{t-2} + \cdots + u_t \qquad (6.4.8)$$

Hence $\quad \hat{z}_t(1) = E(z_{t+1}|H_t) = (1 - \theta_1)z_{t-1} + \theta_1(1 - \theta_1)z_{t-2} + \cdots \quad (6.4.9)$

which is the EWMA forecast. An alternative way of expressing $\hat{z}_t(1)$ and the one used for computation in practice is implied by the difference-equation

---

[1] Program FORECAST is described in the Appendix, Sec. A.3.

figure 6.1 Program FORECAST output for GNP model ARI (1,1), origin dates 1949-01 and 1966-04.

FORECASTS FOR MODEL 1 OF 1 TENTATIVE MODELS FOR SERIES GROSS NATIONAL PRODUCT

STARTING AT ORIGIN DATE 2, FORECASTS ARE COMPUTED UP TO 4 STEPS AHEAD.

FOR THIS MODEL

```
DEGREE OF DIFFERENCING = 1
SPAN OF SEASONAL DIFFERENCING = 0
DEGREE OF SEASONAL DIFFERENCING = 0
NUMBER OF AUTOREGRESSIVE PARAMETERS = 1
NUMBER OF SEASONAL AUTOREGRESSIVE PARAMETERS = 0
NUMBER OF MOVING AVERAGE PARAMETERS = 0
NUMBER OF SEASONAL MOVING AVERAGE PARAMETERS = 0
```

WITH PARAMETER VALUES

AUTOREGRESSIVE PARAMETER(S)

```
1
0.616700
```

CONSTANT = 2.691799

STEPS AHEAD	STD. ERROR IN FORECASTING	PSI WEIGHTS
1	0.478357E 01	0.16167E 01
2	0.909345E 01	0.19970E 01
3	0.131889E 02	0.22316E 01
4	0.169676E 02	0.23762E 01

ORIGIN	OBSERVATION	LOWER CONF. LIMIT	FORECAST	UPPER CONF. LIMIT	ACTUAL	ERROR
9						
	10	0.249486E 03	0.257861E 03	0.267237E 03	0.255200E 03	-0.261133E 01
	11	0.242336E 03	0.260159E 03	0.277982E 03	0.257100E 03	-0.305884E 01
	12	0.238415E 03	0.264267E 03	0.290117E 03	0.255000E 03	-0.926660E 01
	13	0.236235E 03	0.269491E 03	0.302748E 03	0.266000E 03	-0.349121E 01
80						
	81	0.773142E 03	0.782518E 03	0.791894E 03	0.774200E 03	-0.831836E 01
	82	0.774675E 03	0.792498E 03	0.810321E 03	0.783500E 03	-0.899780E 01
	83	0.775493E 03	0.801343E 03	0.827193E 03	0.800400E 03	-0.943359E 00
	84	0.776233E 03	0.809490E 03	0.842746E 03	0.816100E 03	0.661035E 01

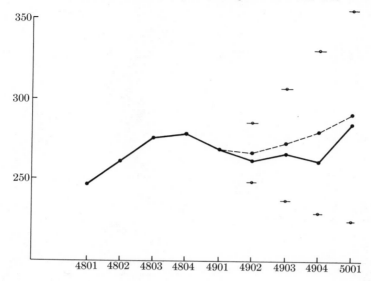

figure 6.2 Forecast profile and confidence limits for GNP model ARI (1,1) from origin date 1949-01.

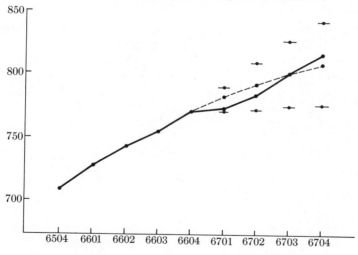

figure 6.3 Forecast profile and confidence limits for GNP model ARI (1,1) from origin date 1966-04.

figure 6.4 Program FORECAST output for EPD model IMA (1,1), origin dates 1952-04 and 1966-04.

FORECASTS FOR MODEL 1 OF 1 TENTATIVE MODELS FOR SERIES EXPENDITURES ON PRODUCERS' DURABLES

STARTING AT ORIGIN DATE 1, FORECASTS ARE COMPUTED UP TO 4 STEPS AHEAD.

FOR THIS MODEL

DEGREE OF DIFFERENCING = 1
SPAN OF SEASONAL DIFFERENCING = 0
DEGREE OF SEASONAL DIFFERENCING = 0
NUMBER OF AUTOREGRESSIVE PARAMETERS = 0
NUMBER OF SEASONAL AUTOREGRESSIVE PARAMETERS = 0
NUMBER OF MOVING AVERAGE PARAMETERS = 1
NUMBER OF SEASONAL MOVING AVERAGE PARAMETERS = 0

WITH PARAMETER VALUES

MOVING AVERAGE PARAMETER(S)

1
-0.347400

CONSTANT = 0.517200

STEPS AHEAD	STD. ERROR IN FORECASTING	PSI WEIGHTS
1	0.106019E 01	0.13474E 01
2	0.177894E 01	0.13474E 01
3	0.228151E 01	0.13474E 01
4	0.269182E 01	0.13474E 01

FORECASTS FOR MODEL 1 OF 1 TENTATIVE MODELS FOR SERIES EXPENDITURES ON PRODUCERS' DURABLES

STARTING AT ORIGIN DATE 1, FORECASTS ARE COMPUTED UP TO 4 STEPS AHEAD.

ORIGIN	OBSERVATION	LOWER CONF. LIMIT	FORECAST	UPPER CONF. LIMIT	ACTUAL	ERROR
24						
	25	0.194612E 02	0.215392E 02	0.236172E 02	0.214000E 02	-0.139236E 00
	26	0.185697E 02	0.220564E 02	0.255432E 02	0.213000E 02	-0.756439E 00
	27	0.181019E 02	0.225736E 02	0.270454E 02	0.219000E 02	-0.673630E 00
	28	0.178148E 02	0.230908E 02	0.283668E 02	0.213000E 02	-0.179083E 01
80						
	81	0.543280E 02	0.569060E 02	0.589840E 02	0.542000E 02	-0.270604E 01
	82	0.539365E 02	0.574232E 02	0.609100E 02	0.558000E 02	-0.162325E 01
	83	0.534687E 02	0.579404E 02	0.624122E 02	0.557000E 02	-0.224043E 01
	84	0.531817E 02	0.584576E 02	0.637336E 02	0.572000E 02	-0.125763E 01

form of the process, which yields

$$\hat{z}_t(1) = z_t - \theta_1 u_t \tag{6.4.10}$$

and for longer horizons $\quad \hat{z}_t(l) = \hat{z}_t(l-1) \qquad l > 1 \tag{6.4.11}$

or equivalently $\quad\quad\quad \hat{z}_t(l) = \hat{z}_t(1) \qquad\quad l > 1 \tag{6.4.12}$

From (6.4.12), we see that forecasts of all horizons are given by the EWMA and, furthermore, that the forecast profile for IMA (1,1) is a horizontal line at the value, or *level*, as it was referred to in Chap. 4, given by $\hat{z}_t(1)$.

If a constant is present in the process, we have a slightly different but still very simple picture. The forecasts are given by

$$\begin{aligned} \hat{z}_t(1) &= z_t + \delta - \theta_1 u_t \\ \hat{z}_t(l) &= \hat{z}_t(l-1) + \delta \\ &= \hat{z}_t(1) + (l-1)\delta \qquad l > 1 \end{aligned} \tag{6.4.13}$$

Consequently, the forecast profile is just a straight line with slope δ that originates at value $\hat{z}_t(1)$ at time $(t+1)$.

We take as an illustration of forecasting IMA (1,1) the model obtained in Chap. 5 for the EPD series, namely,

$$w_t = .52 + u_t + .35u_{t-1} \tag{6.4.14}$$

figure 6.5 Forecast profile and confidence limits for EPD model IMA (1,1) from origin date 1952-04.

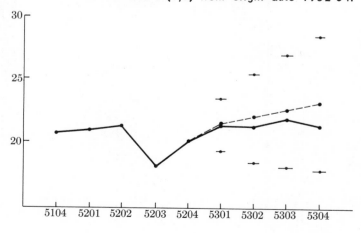

chap. 6   forecasting arima processes

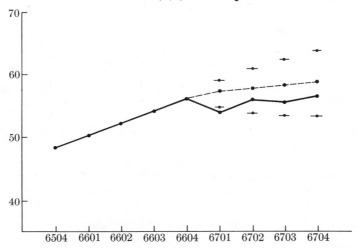

figure 6.6 Forecast profile and confidence limits for EPD model IMA (1,1) from origin date 1966-04.

or
$$z_t = z_{t-1} + .58 + u_t + .35u_{t-1} \qquad (6.4.15)$$

The forecast profile for EPD is given by

$$\hat{z}_t(1) = z_t + .52 + .35u_t$$
$$\hat{z}_t(l) = \hat{z}_t(1) + (l-1).52 \qquad (6.4.16)$$

which is simply a straight line with slope (.52) originating with the value $\hat{z}_t(1)$ at time $(t + 1)$. Program FORECAST output for origin dates 1952-04 and 1966-04, the end of the sample period, appear in Fig. 6.4. The profiles through four quarters ahead are plotted in Figs. 6.5 and 6.6, respectively. The characteristic shape of the IMA (1,1) profile is particularly apparent in Fig. 6.5 for origin date 1952-04.

6.5 Adaptive Forecasting

In many operational settings where forecasting is done on an on-going basis, it is convenient if forecasts can be updated from period to period without performing computations that require a computer. Fortunately, forecasts for any ARIMA process are readily and simply updated, and all the data required consist of the set of forecasts for the previous period and the current one-step-ahead forecast error. This updating is referred to as *adaptive forecasting*.

To see how adaptive forecasting may be carried out, note that any ARIMA process may be written in random-shock form as

$$z_{t+l} = \mu + u_{t+l} + \Psi_1 u_{t+l-1} + \Psi_2 u_{t+l-2} + \cdots \qquad (6.5.1)$$

Now our forecast of z_{t+l} at time t may be expressed, according to (6.5.1), as

$$\hat{z}_t(l) = \mu + \Psi_l u_t + \Psi_{l+1} u_{t-1} + \cdots \tag{6.5.2}$$

whereas correspondingly the forecast we had made in period $(t-1)$ for z_{t+l} was

$$\hat{z}_{t-1}(l+1) = \mu + \Psi_{l+1} u_{t-1} + \Psi_{l+2} u_{t-2} + \cdots \tag{6.5.3}$$

The difference between $\hat{z}_t(l)$ and $\hat{z}_{t-1}(l+1)$ is the *revision* in our forecast of z_{t+l} and is given by subtracting (6.5.3) from (6.5.2). Thus the revision is simply

$$\hat{z}_t(l) - \hat{z}_{t-1}(l+1) = \Psi_l u_t \tag{6.5.4}$$

We know, however, that u_t is the current one-step-ahead forecast error since it is the difference between z_t and $\hat{z}_{t-1}(1)$ [readily confirmed by using the random-shock form of z_t to evaluate $\hat{z}_{t-1}(1)$]. Consequently, the operational version of (6.5.4) is

$$\hat{z}_t(l) - \hat{z}_{t-1}(l+1) = \Psi_l[z_t - \hat{z}_{t-1}(1)] \tag{6.5.5}$$

The practicality of adaptive forecasting is apparent from the fact that application of (6.5.5) requires only that we keep track of our last set of forecasts and make note of our current one-step-ahead error. In principle, we need not retain any past data, although in practice we would do so since we might want to check the adequacy of our empirical model from time to time and reestimate parameters as we add observations to our data set. It is interesting to think about why the constant term μ in the random-shock form of the process does not appear in our final expression for forecast revision. Intuitively this is because the constant may be anticipated from the beginning and is not subject to revision as is the forecast of a random variable.

The origin of the term *adaptive forecasting* is now clear since (6.5.5) essentially says that we adapt our forecasts in accordance with each error as it occurs. Another term often used for adaptive forecasting is *error learning* since the revision of forecasts is quite literally a procedure for learning from errors.

To take some simple examples, we have for AR (1)

$$\hat{z}_t(l) - \hat{z}_{t-1}(l+1) = \phi_1{}^l[z_t - \hat{z}_{t-1}(1)] \qquad l = 1, 2, \ldots \tag{6.5.6}$$

which reflects the fact that the current error provides less information the further we look into the future. For MA (1) we have

$$\begin{aligned}
\hat{z}_t(1) - \hat{z}_{t-1}(2) &= \theta_1[z_t - \hat{z}_{t-i}(1)] \\
\hat{z}_t(l) - \hat{z}_{t-1}(l+1) &= 0 \qquad l > 1
\end{aligned} \tag{6.5.7}$$

which reflects the fact that forecasts of horizons greater than one period are simply the mean of the process and hence not in need of revision.

Finally, consider the familiar IMA (1,1) process. From (4.4.3) we have that $\Psi_i = (1 - \theta_1)$ and hence

$$\hat{z}_t(l) - \hat{z}_{t-1}(l+1) = (1 - \theta_1)[z_t - \hat{z}_{t-1}(1)] \tag{6.5.8}$$

Because the forecast profile for this process is always a straight line of constant slope δ, forecasts of all horizons must be revised by the same amount, as (6.5.8) indicates. Also note that (6.5.8) is the same expression we obtained in Chap. 4 [see (4.5.7)] for updating of the *level*, or EWMA, forecast of the IMA (1,1) process, which we now know to be equivalent to the conditional expectation forecast for that process.

Program FORECAST computes the error-learning coefficients, the Ψ_i, for any ARIMA model of interest. Weights for the ARI (1,1) GNP model and the IMA (1,1) model are given in Figs. 6.1 and 6.4.

6.6 The Dispersion of Forecast Errors: Variance, Standard Deviation, and Confidence Intervals

Thus far we have considered in detail only the expected value of future observations in series generated by ARIMA processes, although in many situations having a measure of the dispersion of forecast error or confidence limits may be as or more important than being able to quote a point forecast.

Such information is readily obtained for forecasts of ARIMA processes if we consider the fact that from expression (6.5.1) for the random-shock form of the process and expression (6.5.2) for the forecast $\hat{z}_t(l)$, the l-step-ahead forecast error $[z_{t+l} - \hat{z}_t(l)]$, denoted $e_t(l)$, is given by

$$e_t(l) = u_t + \Psi_1 u_{t-1} + \cdots + \Psi_{l-1} u_{t+1} \tag{6.6.1}$$

The error has expectation zero since each future disturbance has expectation zero and has variance

$$V[e_t(l)] = \sigma_u^2(1 + \Psi_1^2 + \cdots + \Psi_{l-1}^2) \tag{6.6.2}$$

and hence standard deviation

$$SD [e_t(l)] = \sigma_u(1 + \Psi_1^2 + \cdots + \Psi_{l-1}^2)^{1/2} \tag{6.6.3}$$

Thus measures of dispersion are readily computed from parameters σ_u^2 and the Ψ_i. Using *estimates* of σ_u^2 and the weights Ψ_i computed from estimates of the ϕ's and θ's, program FORECAST provides standard errors for forecast errors in accordance with (6.6.3), as in Figs. 6.1 and 6.4.

In the case that the u_t are normal, then we have described the whole distribution of future errors and hence future observations.[1] In that case, the results are

$$e_t(l) \approx N\{0, V[e_t(l)]\} \tag{6.6.4}$$

or equivalently

$$(z_{t+l}|H_t) \approx N\{\hat{z}_t(l), V[e_t(l)]\} \tag{6.6.5}$$

Probability statements about future observations may then be made simply by consulting a normal probability table. It follows, for example, that z_{t+l} will fall in the interval $\hat{z}_t(l) \pm 1.96\text{SD}\,[e_t(l)]$ with probability .95. Such confidence limits are listed in the program FORECAST output for GNP and EPD in Figs. 6.1 and 6.4. Similarly, we could state that the probability that z_{t+l} will be less than $\{\hat{z}_t(l) - 1.96\text{SD}\,[e_t(l)]\}$ is only .025. When forecast profiles are displayed graphically it is often useful to bracket them with confidence intervals as we have in Figs. 6.2, 6.3, 6.5, and 6.6.

A general observation about the distribution of forecast errors is that for stationary processes the variance of errors approaches the variance of the process as a limit since

$$\lim_{l \to \infty} V[e_t(l)] = \lim_{l \to \infty} [\sigma_u^2(1 + \Psi_1^2 + \cdots + \Psi_{l-1}^2)] = V(z_t) \tag{6.6.6}$$

This result may be visualized graphically in terms of confidence bounds around a forecast profile that become parallel lines as forecast horizon becomes large. For example, in the case of AR (1), we have

$$V[e_t(l)] = \sigma_u^2(1 + \phi_1 + \cdots + \phi_1^{l-1}) \tag{6.6.7}$$

which approaches $\sigma_u^2/(1 - \phi_1^2)$, the variance of the process, as l becomes large. For MA (1) we have

$$\begin{aligned} V[e_t(1)] &= \sigma_u^2 \\ V[e_t(l)] &= \sigma_u^2(1 + \theta_1^2) \quad l > 1 \end{aligned} \tag{6.6.8}$$

and hence the variance of errors two or more steps ahead is just the variance of the process. In summary, these results tell us that if we look far enough into the future, all we really know about a stationary process are its unconditional mean and variance; that is, the conditional distribution approaches the unconditional or marginal distribution.

---

[1] Forecast errors will not (strictly speaking) be normal in practice even if the theoretical disturbances u_t are normal since our forecasts are computed using estimates of the parameters of the process rather than their true values. Presumably, if our model is suitable to the data and has been estimated over a substantial number of observations, the normal assumption for forecast errors will suffice for practical computation.

The situation for nonstationary processes is illustrated by IMA (1,1) for which

$$V[e_t(l)] = \sigma_u{}^2[1 + (l-1)(1-\theta_1)^2] \tag{6.6.9}$$

which clearly increases without limit as l get large, a general property shared with all nonstationary processes. The confidence limits surrounding a forecast profile will become wider without bound. Loosely speaking, if we look far enough into the future, we know practically nothing of the probable whereabouts of the series if it is nonstationary.

Some other general properties of forecast errors are also of interest. Uncertainty, in the sense of the variance of forecast errors or the width of confidence intervals, must increase with horizon since from (6.6.2)

$$V[e_t(l)] \geq V[e_t(l-1)] \tag{6.6.10}$$

In other words, we can never know more as we look further into the future. In addition, it is clear that the sequence of errors of given horizon, that is, the time series $[. . . ,e_{t-1}(l),e_t(l),e_{t+1}(l), . . .]$, is a stochastic process and from (6.6.1) is recognized to be simply a moving-average process of order $(l-1)$ *regardless of the form of the process being forecast.* We know then the correlogram of the errors for horizon l will consist of spikes at lags $k = 1, . . . , l-1$ only. Thus, one-step-ahead errors are uncorrelated, two-step-ahead errors are correlated only in successive periods, and so forth. If correlation in the errors persisted for more than $(l-1)$ periods, then they could not possibly have arisen from minimum mean-square-error forecasts because that serial correlation could be used to predict future errors and thus reduce mean square error. For example, if one-step-ahead errors were correlated, then we could use the correlation to predict the next error and adjust our forecast accordingly.

6.7 Forecasting after Transformation to Logs

In Sec. 4.2 we were concerned with the problem of modeling nonhomogeneous series for which the magnitude of fluctuations is positively related to the level of the series in such a way that percentage changes *are* spatially homogeneous. We saw that if we worked with the natural logs of the levels, the resulting transformation gave us a spatially homogeneous series because log changes are approximately percentage changes. If we proceed to model the transformed series on an ARIMA process, then the forecasts generated by the model will of course be forecasts of the *log* of future observations. Offhand it would not seem that we would be very interested in seeing forecasts of the logs of the series. After a moment's thought, however, it is apparent that one might want to quote forecasts of log changes if forecasts of percentage changes are of interest. For example, suppose that the log of sales in thousands of dollars this month is 5.217 and our ARIMA forecasts 5.194 for next month. The forecasted log change is then $-.023$ or a drop in sales of 2.3 percent. Furthermore, if we quote a confidence interval of 5.217 of $\pm.017$, then we are effectively quoting a confidence interval of 1.7 percent on our forecast of -2.3 percent change in sales.

It is tempting to suggest that to quote a forecast in dollars we need only take the antilog of our forecast. Would such a forecast be a conditional expectation of sales implied by our model? The answer is readily seen to be "no" since, denoting the raw series by z'_t and $\ln (z'_t)$ by z_t, the proposed forecast would be $\exp [E(z_{t+1}|H_t])$, and generally it is *not* true that this is the condition of z'_{t+1}; that is,

$$\exp [E(z_{t+1}|H_t)] \neq E[(\exp z_{t+1})|H_t] \tag{6.7.1}$$

Rather, because of the convexity of the exponential function, it is the case that

$$\exp [E(z_{t+1}|H_t)] \leq E[(\exp z_{t+1})|H_t] \tag{6.7.2}$$

If the log series is normal; then the exact relationship is

$$\begin{aligned} E[(\exp z_{t+1})|H_t] &= \exp [E(z_{t+1}|H_t) + \tfrac{1}{2}V(z_{t+1}|H_t)] \\ &= \exp [E(z_{t+1}|H_t)] \exp [\tfrac{1}{2}V(z_{t+1}|H_t)] \\ &> \exp [E(z_{t+1}|H_t)] \end{aligned} \tag{6.7.3}$$

Expression (6.7.3) arises from the fact that if z_t is normal, then the raw series z'_t is log-normal. It is useful before presenting further results to digress briefly to discuss the log-normal distribution.

the log-normal distribution

Let Y be a random variable with distribution $N(\mu,\sigma^2)$ and X a random variable related to Y by $X =$ antilog (Y) or

$$X = e^Y \tag{6.7.4}$$

The density function for X is then the log-normal density function given by

$$\begin{aligned} p(X) &= \frac{1}{X\sigma \sqrt{2\pi}} \exp\left[-\frac{1}{2\sigma^2} (\ln X - \mu)^2 \right] \qquad & X > 0 \\ &= 0 & X \leq 0 \end{aligned} \tag{6.7.5}$$

since X takes on only positive values and at $X = 0$ $p(X) = 0$. The mode of the distribution is at $X = e^{\mu-\sigma^2}$ and the median at $X = e^\mu$. The moments about the origin are given by

$$m_j = e^{j\mu+1/2j^2\sigma^2} \qquad j = 1, 2, \ldots \tag{6.7.6}$$

from which the mean is

$$E(X) = m_1 = e^{\mu + 1/2\sigma^2} \tag{6.7.7}$$

and the variance is

$$V(X) = m_2 - m_1{}^2 = e^{2\mu + \sigma^2} e^{\sigma^2} - 1 \tag{6.7.8}$$

The standard normal and corresponding log-normal frequency curves are illustrated in Fig. 6.7. Note the relative positions of the mode, median, and mean for the log-normal. Also illustrated in Fig. 6.7 are log-normal curves for various values of μ and σ^2.†

A property of the log-normal distribution that is very convenient for our purposes is as follows. Since Y is normal, then the probability that Y is less than $\mu - k\sigma$ depends only on k, for example, $P(Y < \mu - 1.96\sigma) = .025$. In view of the relation between Y and X, it must then be that the probability that $X < e^{\mu - k\sigma}$ is just the probability that $Y < \mu - k\sigma$ and depends only on k. The situation is of course identical for the probability that $X > e^{\mu - k\sigma}$. Consequently, if confidence limits on a realization of Y are $\mu \pm k\sigma$, then the same level of confidence may be quoted with regard to Y in the interval $e^{\mu \pm k\sigma}$.

application to forecasting

These results are directly applicable to forecasting where the log of the raw series is represented as a normal ARIMA process, in which case at time t the random variable z_{t+l} has the conditional distribution

$$z_{t+l} \approx N\{\hat{z}_t(l), V[e_t(l)]\} \tag{6.7.9}$$

given history H_t. Consequently, the conditional expectation forecast of $z'_{t+l} = \exp(z_{t+l})$ is given by

$$\hat{z}'_t(l) = \exp\{\hat{z}_t(l) + \tfrac{1}{2}V[e_t(l)]\} \tag{6.7.10}$$

and the variance of z'_{t+l} conditional on H_t, or equivalently the variance of the forecast error $e'_t(l) = [z'_{t+l} - \hat{z}'_t(l)]$, by

$$V(z'_{t+l}|H_t) = V[e'_t(l)] = \exp\{2\hat{z}_t(l) + V[e_t(l)]\}\{\exp(V[e_t(l)]) - 1\} \tag{6.7.11}$$

Furthermore. if $\hat{z}_t(1) \pm k\mathrm{SD}[e_t(l)]$ constitutes an α percent confidence interval on z_{t+l}, then $\exp(\hat{z}_t(l) \pm k\mathrm{SD}[e_t(l)]$ constitutes an α percent confidence interval for z'_{t+1}. Note that the confidence interval for z'_{t+l} is not symmetric about $\hat{z}'_t(l)$ although the confidence interval for z_{t+l} is symmetric.

†From Aitchison and Brown, "The Lognormal Distribution" (listed in the Additional Readings at end of the chapter).

figure 6.7 The log-normal density function. (a) Frequency curves of the normal and log-normal distributions; (b) frequency curves of the log-normal distribution for three values of μ.

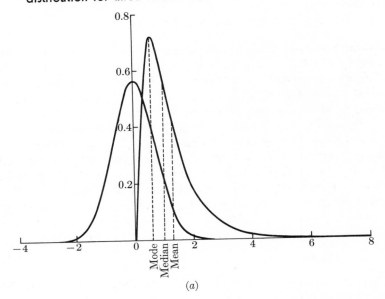

(a)

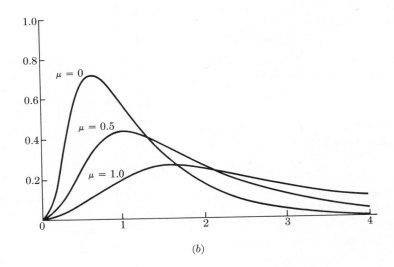

(b)

figure 6.7 (continued) (c) frequency curves of the log-normal distribution for three values of σ^2.

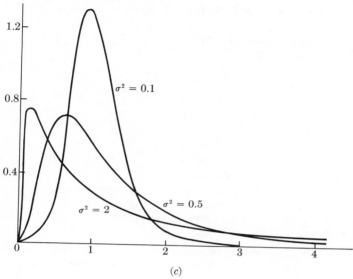

(c)

Exercises

6.1 Monthly sales (in millions of dollars) of an after-shave lotion of a certain firm are well represented by the model

$$z_t = .33z_{t-1} + 1.5 + u_t$$
$$\sigma_u^2 = .9$$

This month's sales are

$$z_{100} = \$3.0 \text{ million}$$

(a) Compute $\hat{z}_{100}(l)$ for $l = 1, 2, \ldots, 1$ million.
(b) Compute $V[e_{100}(l)]$ for $l = 1, 2, \ldots, 1$ million.
(c) Provide 95 percent confidence limits for $l = 1, 2, \ldots, 1$ million under the assumption that u_t is normal.
(d) Provide an adaptive forecasting rule for $l = 1, 2, \ldots, 1$ million.
(e) Confirm that your forecast $\hat{z}_{100}(1)$ satisfies the adaptive forecasting rule given previous forecasts

$$\hat{z}_{99}(1) = 2.4 \quad \hat{z}_{99}(2) = 2.3$$

6.2 Consider the problem of forecasting the volume of new orders for a certain grade of aluminum where new orders are generated by the process

$$z_t = 3 + u_t + .5u_{t-1} - .25u_{t-2}$$
$$\sigma_u^2 = 4$$

exercises

(a) Provide the expression for $\hat{z}_t(l)$, $l = 1, 2, 3, 100$.

(b) Evaluate $V[e_t(l)]$, $l = 1, 2, 3, 100$.

(c) Provide confidence limits of ± 1.96 standard deviations for $[z_{t+l} - \hat{z}_t(l)]$, $l = 1, 2, 3, 100$.

(d) Obtain the coefficients k_l in the adaptive forecasting expression
$$\hat{z}_t(l) - z_{t-1}(l + 1) = k_l[z_t - \hat{z}_{t-1}(1)]$$

(e) Given the data

t	z_t
1	3.25
2	4.75
3	2.25
4	1.75

compute $\hat{z}_4(l)$, $l = 1, 2, 3, 100$ by building up the necessary sequence of previous one-step-ahead forecasting errors from the beginning of the series.

(f) For the forecasts computed in (e), provide confidence intervals of ± 1.96 standard deviations.

6.3 Verify that for any ARMA (1,q) process forecasts, $\hat{z}_t(1)$, . . . , $\hat{z}_t(q)$ depend on the moving-average part of the model, whereas forecasts for horizons $q + 1$, $q + 2$, . . . are simply given by
$$\hat{z}_t(l) = \phi_1\hat{z}_t(l - 1) + \delta \quad l > q$$

6.4 Monthly registrations of new automobiles in the United States may be regarded as homogeneous in logs rather than raw levels (see Chap. 7). This month the log of unit sales in thousands is 6.593, and our forecast for next month is 6.648. The 95 percent confidence interval for this forecast is 6.648 ± .06.

(a) Express the forecast as a forecast of percentage change.

(b) Quote a confidence interval on this percentage-change forecast.

(c) Provide a conditional expectation forecast of the level of unit sales.

(d) Quote a confidence interval for automobile sales next month.

6.5 In Chap. 5, Sec. 5.12, models for tool sales series A and B and the unemployment rate were developed. Comment on the forecasting properties of the models, giving numerical examples of forecast computation with standard errors for one- and two-step-ahead forecasts. Set up numerical relationships for adaptive revision of forecasts.

Additional Readings

Aitchison, J., and J. A. C. Brown: "The Lognormal Distribution," Cambridge University Press, London, 1963. The basic properties of the log-normal distribution are presented in chap. 2.

Box, G. E. P., and G. M. Jenkins: "Time Series Analysis, Forecasting and Control," Holden-Day, Inc., San Francisco, 1970. Forecasting of ARIMA processes is

chap. 6 forecasting arima processes

discussed in chap. 5. Also of interest is app. A7.3, pp. 267–269, dealing with the effect of parameter estimation errors on the variance of forecast errors. The effect of estimation errors is shown to be of the order T^{-1}.

Nelson, C. R.: "The Term Structure of Interest Rates," Basic Books, Inc., New York, 1972. The last section of chap. 5 discusses computation conditional expectation forecasts for two tentative models of annual 1-year bond yields. The models are AR (2) and IMA (1,1).

7
Models
for
Seasonal
Time Series

Seasonality is one of the most pervasive phenomena of economic life. Seasonality means a *tendency* to repeat a pattern of behavior over a seasonal period, generally one year. Seasonal series are therefore characterized by a display of strong serial correlation at the *seasonal lag*, that is, the lag corresponding to the number of observations per seasonal period, usually at multiples of that lag. Among the numerous examples of seasonal series are: the price of fresh produce, revenues to a taxing authority, automobile sales, airline travel, and hospital utilization.

Many of the reported statistical series on economic activity are published in *seasonally adjusted* form. Seasonal adjustment refers to any smoothing procedure applied to raw data that is designed to destroy the correlation at seasonal lags. Although we do not intend to present a review of these procedures in this text, it suffices to say that the procedures in general use are essentially of an ad hoc nature. Nevertheless, adjusted data may be very useful for certain purposes, particularly when the data in question are meant to convey information about general economic conditions. For example, the GNP series used as an illustration in earlier chapters is a seasonally adjusted series; in fact, its components (consumer spending, investment expenditures, and so forth) are adjusted prior to aggregation. Thus, if we were to forecast a decline of $2 billion in GNP in the first quarter of next year, we would really be predicting a worsening of business conditions in that quarter apart from any systematic tendency for actual business activity to be slow during first quarters generally.

For many purposes, however, seasonally adjusted data are of little interest; rather, our objective is to forecast the raw, unadjusted seasonal series itself. This is almost always the situation in the case of firm- or market-level data. For example, if our objective is production planning, a forecast of seasonally adjusted sales would clearly be of little interest. Consequently, there is an important role in operational forecasting for models of seasonal series.

Many of the models that have been suggested incorporate seasonal variation in a deterministic way. For example, a seasonal series might be modeled as a periodic function of time plus a random component. Alternatively, *dummy variables* could be introduced to reflect additive effects associated with particular months or quarters. Unfortunately, economic time series rarely exhibit these kinds of deterministic seasonality. Rather, the pattern and intensity of seasonal variation undergoes constant change. For example, the series of monthly automobile registrations in the United States pictured in Fig. 7.2 is highly seasonal. A brief inspection of the figure will reveal, however, little hope of representing that seasonality in a deterministic framework since the seasonal pattern shifts considerably as the sample period progresses. Winters has suggested an adaptive scheme for forecasting seasonal series in which both the level and the seasonal factor in each time period are revised in accordance with a smoothing formula.[1] His method may be regarded as a conceptual extension of simple exponential smoothing, having the advantages of adaptation but still lacking a basis in statistical theory. We consider instead a particular class of linear stochastic processes that display seasonal behavior as the basis for models of seasonal time series.

7.1 The Seasonal Moving-average Process

Consider a moving-average process that has the following peculiar specifications: (1) if s is the number of observations per seasonal period, then the order of the moving-average process is an integer multiple of s, and (2) the only non-zero coefficients are those with subscripts that are an integer multiple of s. Such a process would have the following appearance:

$$z_t = u_t - \theta_s u_{t-s} - \cdots - \theta_{Qs} u_{t-Qs} \tag{7.1.1}$$

[1] Peter R. Winters, Forecasting Sales by Exponentially Weighted Moving Averages, *Management Science*, 6(3):324–342 (April 1960); also in Holt et al., "Planning Production, Inventories, and Work Force," chap. 14, Prentice-Hall, Inc., Englewood Cliffs, N.J., 1960.

where Q is the largest multiple of s, that is, the order of the process is Qs. To distinguish the seasonal process from more mundane MA processes, we adopt the notation

$$\Delta_j = \theta_{js} \qquad (7.1.2)$$

so that (7.1.1) becomes

$$z_t = u_t - \Delta_1 u_{t-s} - \cdots - \Delta_Q u_{t-Qs} \qquad (7.1.3)$$

referred to as a seasonal MA process of order Q.

It should be clear at this point why we refer to (7.1.3) as a seasonal MA process since the autocorrelation function for the process will be nonzero only at lags s, $2s$, . . . , Qs; in particular,

$$\rho_s = \frac{-\Delta_1 + \Delta_1 \Delta_2 + \cdots + \Delta_{Q-1} \Delta_Q}{1 + \Delta_1{}^2 + \cdots + \Delta_Q{}^2}$$

$$\cdots \cdots \cdots \cdots \cdots \cdots \cdots \cdots \cdots \qquad (7.1.4)$$

$$\rho_{Qs} = \frac{-\Delta_Q}{1 + \Delta_1{}^2 + \cdots + \Delta_Q{}^2}$$

corresponding to a correlogram with spikes at lags s, $2s$, . . . , and Qs only.

For example, let $Q = 1$, $s = 12$, and $\Delta_1 = -.8$. Then we have

$$z_t = u_t + .8u_{t-12} \qquad (7.1.5)$$

The nonzero autocovariances are

$$\gamma_0 = \sigma_u{}^2(1.64)$$
$$\gamma_{12} = \sigma_u{}^2(.8) \qquad (7.1.6)$$

and the only nonzero autocorrelation is

$$\rho_{12} = .49 \qquad (7.1.7)$$

The correlogram is plotted in Fig. 7.1.

It is important to understand that the autocorrelation function implies that a given observation is correlated *only* with the observations following and preceding by 12 periods. In effect, then, the observations at each January constitute a time series that is completely independent of the series of February or July observations. Furthermore, the seasonal correlation that is present is effective only over the span of one seasonal period. In general, for a seasonal MA process of order Q the correlation persists only for Q seasonal periods. Although few seasonal series encountered in practice display seasonal correlation which cuts off in that manner, we shall nevertheless find that the seasonal

chap. 7   models for seasonal time series

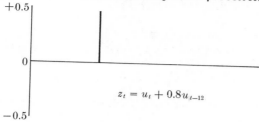

$$z_t = u_t + 0.8u_{t-12}$$

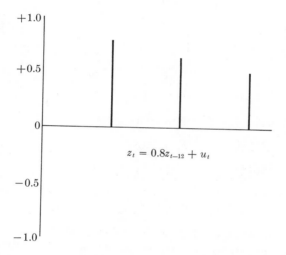

$$z_t = 0.8z_{t-12} + u_t$$

MA process is an important building block for a more general model of seasonal series.

7.2 The Seasonal Autoregressive Process

The natural autoregressive counterpart to the seasonal MA process would be an AR process of the form

$$z_t = \phi_s z_{t-s} + \cdots + \phi_{Ps} z_{t-Ps} + u_t \qquad (7.2.1)$$

where P is the largest multiple of s present in the model. Again it is convenient to provide special notation for the season model, and so if we let

$$\phi_{js} = \Gamma_j \qquad (7.2.2)$$

then the model becomes

$$z_t = \Gamma_1 z_{t-s} + \cdots + \Gamma_P z_{t-Ps} + u_t \qquad (7.2.3)$$

referred to as a seasonal AR process of order P.

The seasonal nature of such processes becomes apparent when we consider the case $P = 1$; that is,

$$z_t = \Gamma_1 z_{t-s} + u_t \qquad (7.2.4)$$

The autocovariances are nonzero *only* at lags that are integer multiples of s; thus,

$$\gamma_0 = \frac{\sigma_u{}^2}{1 - \Gamma_1{}^2}$$

$$\gamma_s = \Gamma_1 \gamma_0$$

$$\gamma_{2s} = \Gamma_1{}^2 \gamma_0 \qquad (7.2.5)$$

$$\cdots \cdots$$

$$\gamma_{js} = \Gamma_1{}^j \gamma_0$$

and hence the only nonzero autocorrelations are

$$\rho_{js} = \Gamma_1{}^j \qquad j = 0, 1, 2, 3, \ldots \qquad (7.2.6)$$

For example, letting $\Gamma_1 = .8$ and $s = 12$, we have

$$\rho_{j(12)} = (.8)^j \qquad j = 0, 1, 2, 3, \ldots \qquad (7.2.7)$$

The correlogram corresponding to (7.2.7) is plotted in Fig. 7.1.

It is important to understand how the first-order seasonal AR process is different from the first-order seasonal MA processes and how they are similar. First, correlation at the seasonal lags persists indefinitely, although with declining intensity in the AR case, but it cuts off after one seasonal period in the MA case. On the other hand, the processes are similar in that for both the series of January observations is a time series which is independent of the series of February observations, and so forth.

Leaving this second point aside for the moment, let us note that the persistence of seasonal autocorrelation characteristic of the AR process more closely resembles the kind of seasonality we observe in economic time series. Since the persistence of seasonal correlation at long lags depends on the value of Γ_1, we can say that highly regular seasonal behavior, such as that of monthly toy sales, must be associated with values of Γ_1 approaching 1. In the limiting case, process (7.2.4) becomes just

$$z_t - z_{t-s} = u_t \qquad (7.2.8)$$

that is, the *seasonal differences* $z_t - z_{t-s}$ of the observed series are random. Note that z_t is then a nonstationary process since

$$z_t = u_t + u_{t-s} + u_{t-2s} + \cdots \qquad (7.2.9)$$

for which no mean is defined. Although our seasonal models will generally be more complex than (7.2.8), this reasoning suggests that seasonal differencing will play an important role in those models.

7.3 The Seasonal Integrated Autoregressive–Moving-average Model

The logical generalization of the seasonal AR and MA processes is, of course, a mixed model incorporating both. Such a model would be of the form

$$z_t = \Gamma_1 z_{t-s} + \cdots + \Gamma_P z_{t-sP} + u_t - \Delta_1 u_{t-s} - \cdots - \Delta_Q u_{t-sQ} \qquad (7.3.1)$$

Generalizing further, we consider the possibility that a seasonal series may be nonstationary and that the seasonal differences of the series are generated by a stationary seasonal process. Denoting the seasonal differences of z_t by x_t, then

$$x_t = z_t - z_{t-s} \qquad (7.3.2)$$

and the integrated model is

$$x_t = \Gamma_1 x_{t-s} + \cdots + \Gamma_P x_{t-sP} + u_t - \Delta_1 u_{t-s} - \cdots - \Delta_Q u_{t-sQ} \qquad (7.3.3)$$

It is useful for future purposes to see how the model may be expressed more compactly using the backshift operator B. Rewriting (7.3.3), we have

$$(1 - \Gamma_1 B^s - \cdots - \Gamma_P B^{sP})(1 - B^s)^1 z_t = (1 - \Delta_1 B^s - \cdots - \Delta_Q B^{sQ}) u_t \qquad (7.3.4)$$

since $x_t = (1 - B^s)^1 z_t$. Allowing more generally for a stationary model in the Dth seasonal differences, the model becomes

$$(1 - \Gamma_1 B^s - \cdots - \Gamma_P B^{sP})(1 - B^s)^D z_t = (1 + \Delta_1 B^s - \cdots - \Delta_Q B^{sQ}) u_t \qquad (7.3.5)$$

It is apparent that the autocorrelation structure of the seasonal ARMA process is precisely analogous to that of nonseasonal ARMA processes with nonzero correlation occurring only at the lags s, $2s$, and so forth. Stationarity conditions on the parameters Γ_i must be the same as those on the ϕ_i of a non-seasonal model and similarly for the invertibility conditions on the Δ_i. Thus, if $P = 1$, we have the stationarity condition $|\Gamma_1| < 1$.

The property of model (7.3.5), which remains seriously deficient for purposes of describing economic data, is that of the independence of successive observations; that is, there is no interaction between observations at other than multiples of seasonal lag. This consideration motivates the multiplicative model presented in the next section.

7.4 The General Multiplicative Seasonal Model

Box and Jenkins have proposed that correlation between observations within seasonal periods may be introduced by supposing that the noise input to the seasonal ARIMA is serially correlated rather than independent. In particular, they suggest that z_t be generated by the seasonal model

$$(1 - \Gamma_1 B^s - \cdots - \Gamma_P B^{sP})(1 - B^s)^D z_t = (1 - \Delta_1 B^s - \cdots - \Delta_Q B^{sQ}) \epsilon_t$$
(7.4.1)

where the noise input ϵ_t is generated by an ARIMA process of the usual form, namely,

$$(1 - \phi_1 B - \cdots - \phi_P B^p)(1 - B)^d \epsilon_t = (1 - \theta_1 B - \cdots - \theta_q B^q) u_t \quad (7.4.2)$$

Solving (7.4.2) for ϵ_t and substituting in (7.4.1), we have the general multiplicative seasonal model

$$(1 - \Gamma_1 B^s - \cdots - \Gamma_P B^{sP})(1 - \phi_1 B - \cdots - \phi_p B^p)(1 - B^s)^D (1 - B)^d z_t$$
$$= (1 - \Delta_1 B^s - \cdots - \Delta_Q B^{sQ})(1 - \theta_1 B - \cdots - \theta_q B^q) u_t + \delta \quad (7.4.3)$$

where the constant δ has been added to accommodate the possibility that the stationary series $(1 - B^s)^D (1 - B)^d z_t$ may have a nonzero mean. The degree of seasonal differencing D and that of consecutive differencing d will in economic contexts usually be either 0 or 1 as required to achieve stationarity in the differenced series. The seasonal model is multiplicative in the sense that the observed data result from the successive *filtering* of the random-noise series u_t through the nonseasonal filter (7.4.2) and then the seasonal filter (7.4.1).

seasonal adjustment: an alternative view

Model (7.4.3) is in direct contrast with the traditional concept of seasonality, which conceived of the observed series as the *sum* of two components, one being the seasonal component s_t, which has mean zero, and the other a nonseasonal "trend-cycle" component c_t.† The resulting components model is then

$$z_t = s_t + c_t \quad (7.4.4)$$

---

† The components model has a long history in time series analysis, beginning with meteorological studies in the early nineteenth century where readings on temperature or barometric pressure were supposed to consist of unobserved periodic components. The basic concept of additive decomposition was extended to economic data, for example, to clearinghouse statistics by Charles Babbage (1858) and later to financial data by Jevons (1884). The most visible manifestation of the concept in postwar economics is undoubtedly the general acceptance of seasonal adjustment procedures and the implicit assumption of almost all econometric research that it is the adjusted series which are the appropriate testing ground for economic theory.

where s_t and c_t are, in turn, stochastic processes of some specified form. The components model provides the conceptual basis for seasonal adjustment, namely, that a series ought to be decomposable into a seasonal component and a seasonally adjusted series, which is the residual after the seasonal is subtracted from the raw data. A moment's thought will convince the reader that such a procedure is meaningless if seasonality is actually of a multiplicative nature. The multiplicative model suggests, however, an alternative and non-additive decomposition of seasonal series.

We note that because of the multiplicative nature of (7.4.3) z_t may be thought of as being generated by the seasonal model (7.4.1), to which the nonseasonal series ϵ_t is the input, or alternatively and equivalently as being generated by the nonseasonal model

$$(1 - \phi_1 B - \cdots - \phi_p B^p)(1 - B)^d z_t = (1 - \theta_1 B - \cdots - \theta_q B^q)v_t \quad (7.4.5)$$

where v_t is a *seasonal* input generated according to

$$(1 - \Gamma_1 B^s - \cdots - \Gamma_P B^{sP})(1 - B^s)^D v_t = (1 - \Delta_1 B^s - \cdots - B^{sQ})u_t$$
$$(7.4.6)$$

In this context, then, the series v_t may be thought of as the seasonal series associated with z_t and ϵ_t as the nonseasonal series or seasonally adjusted series associated with z_t. Note, however, that the two series do not sum to z_t; therefore they are not additive components.

autocorrelation structure of the multiplicative seasonal process

The autocorrelation structure of the stationary process $(1 - B^s)^D(1 - B)^d z_t$ may be generally very complex. Nevertheless, it is worthwhile to make some general observations and work out a few examples.

First of all, if we combine the polynomials in B on both sides of the model, it is seen to be essentially an ARMA process of orders $sP + p$ and $sQ + q$. Many of the coefficients appearing in the expanded model will, however, be zero, resulting in certain simplifications in the autocorrelation structure. Nevertheless, all the results for mixed models discussed in Chap. 3 must also apply to the expanded model.

An example that will arise later as a model for monthly automobile registrations is

$$(1 - B^{12})(1 - B)z_t = (1 - \Delta_1 B^{12})(1 - \theta_1 B - \theta_2 B^2)u_t \quad (7.4.7)$$

which in expanded form is

$$y_t = (1 - \theta_1 B - \theta_2 B^2 - \Delta_1 B^{12} + \Delta_1 \theta_1 B^{13} + \Delta_1 \theta_2 B^{14})u_t \quad (7.4.7a)$$

where y_t denotes the stationary series $(1 - B^{12})(1 - B)z_t$. Allowing the backshift operators to act on u_t, we have

$$y_t = u_t - \theta_1 u_{t-1} - \theta_2 u_{t-2} - \Delta_1 u_{t-12} + \Delta_1 \theta_1 u_{t-13} - \Delta_1 \theta_2 u_{t-14} \quad (7.4.8)$$

which for analytical purposes is simply a MA (14) process where only the first, second, twelfth, thirteenth, and fourteenth coefficients are nonzero.

The autocovariances of y_t are straightforward:

$$\begin{aligned}
\gamma_0 &= (1 + \theta_1^2 + \theta_2^2)(1 + \Delta_1^2)\sigma_u^2 \\
\gamma_1 &= -\theta_1(1 - \theta_2)(1 + \Delta_1^2)\sigma_u^2 \\
\gamma_2 &= -\theta_2(1 + \Delta_1^2)\sigma_u^2 \\
\gamma_{10} &= \theta_2 \Delta_1 \sigma_u^2 \\
\gamma_{11} &= \theta_1 \Delta_1 (1 - \theta_2)\sigma_u^2 \\
\gamma_{12} &= -\Delta_1 (1 + \theta_1^2 + \theta_2^2)\sigma_u^2 \\
\gamma_{13} &= \theta_1 \Delta_1 (1 - \theta_2)\sigma_u^2 = \gamma_{11} \\
\gamma_{14} &= \theta_2 \Delta_1 \sigma^2 = \gamma_{10}
\end{aligned} \quad (7.4.9)$$

and all other γ_j are zero. Thus the correlogram of this process will display spikes at lags 1, 2, 10, 11, 12, 13, 14, with the latter five spikes being symmetric around ρ_{12}.

As a second example, consider the seasonal model

$$(1 - \Gamma_1 B^{12})y_t = (1 - \theta_1 B)u_t \quad (7.4.10)$$

Computation of autocovariances is again straightforward and yields

$$\begin{aligned}
\gamma_0 &= \frac{(1 + \theta_1^2)\sigma_u^2}{1 - \Gamma_1^2} \\
\gamma_1 &= \frac{-\theta_1 \sigma_u^2}{1 - \Gamma_1^2} \\
\gamma_2 &= \cdots = \gamma_{10} = 0
\end{aligned} \quad (7.4.11)$$

Then, using the general result (3.5.29) for ARMA processes, we have

$$\gamma_j = \Gamma_1 \gamma_{j-12} \qquad j > 1 \quad (7.4.12)$$

Hence

$$\begin{aligned}
\gamma_{11} &= \Gamma_1 \gamma_{-1} = \Gamma_1 \gamma_1 = \frac{-\Gamma_1 \theta_1 \sigma_u^2}{1 - \Gamma_1^2} \\
\gamma_{12} &= \Gamma_1 \gamma_0 = \frac{\Gamma_1(1 + \theta_1^2)\sigma_u^2}{1 - \Gamma_1^2} \\
\gamma_{13} &= \frac{-\Gamma_1 \theta_1 \sigma_u^2}{1 - \Gamma_1^2} = \gamma_{11}
\end{aligned} \quad (7.4.13)$$

and generally for s observations per seasonal period

$$\gamma_{ks-1} = \frac{-\Gamma_1{}^k\theta_1\sigma_u{}^2}{1 - \Gamma_1{}^2}$$

$$\gamma_{ks} = \frac{\Gamma_1{}^k(1 + \theta_1{}^2)\sigma_u{}^2}{1 - \Gamma_1{}^2} \qquad (7.4.14)$$

$$\gamma_{ks+1} = \gamma_{ks-1} \qquad k = 0, 1, 2, \ldots$$

and all other autocovariances are zero. The correlogram of this process would then display groups of three symmetric spikes around lags 0, s, $2s$, and so forth, with the size of the spikes declining geometrically according to Γ_1.

7.5 Identification, Estimation, and Forecasting of the Multiplicative Seasonal Model: The Example of Monthly Automobile Registrations

The approach to identification, estimation, and forecasting of seasonal models is in principle no different from the corresponding procedures for nonseasonal series since the seasonal models are simply ARIMA models of special form. Nevertheless, it is the particular structure of seasonal models that is the key to their identification, particularly to identification of the most parsimonious model appropriate to the data. Perhaps the most useful way to review these topics as they apply to seasonal models is in the context of a particular data set. The illustrative series is monthly registration of new automobiles reported by the state licensing bureaus in the United States, 1947 through 1968.[1]

identification

The monthly automobile registration data, 264 observations over 22 years, are plotted in Fig. 7.2. The seasonal nature of the series is readily apparent in the annual slump in registrations during model changeover in late summer and the surge of registrations with the introduction of new models. Also evident is an increase in the variability of the series as its general level rises through the sample period, suggesting that the natural logs rather than the raw series may display greater spatial homogeneity. Indeed, the log series also plotted in Fig. 7.2 does display greater homogeneity through the sample period. Evidence for the log transformation is reinforced by examination of the first differences of the raw and logged series in Fig. 7.3. Note the distinct spreading of the raw first differences as the sample period progresses and the level of the series rises and the relative stability of the log differences.

[1] The source of the data is the *Survey of Current Business*.

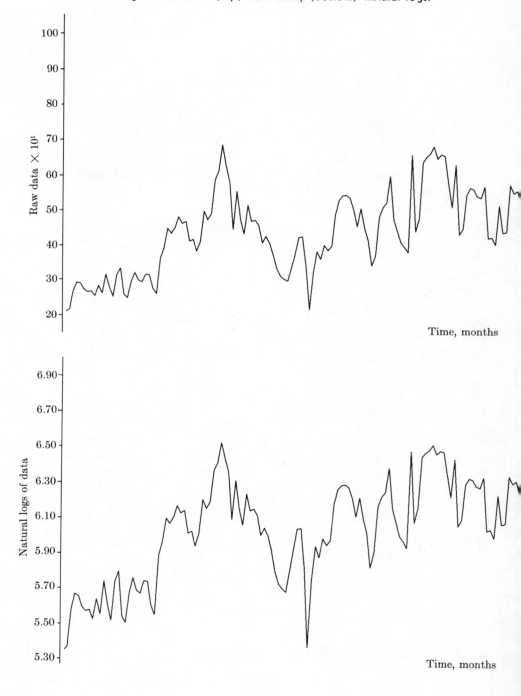

figure 7.2 Plots of raw data and natural logs of automobile registrations, 1947-01 through 1968-12. (top) Raw data; (bottom) natural logs.

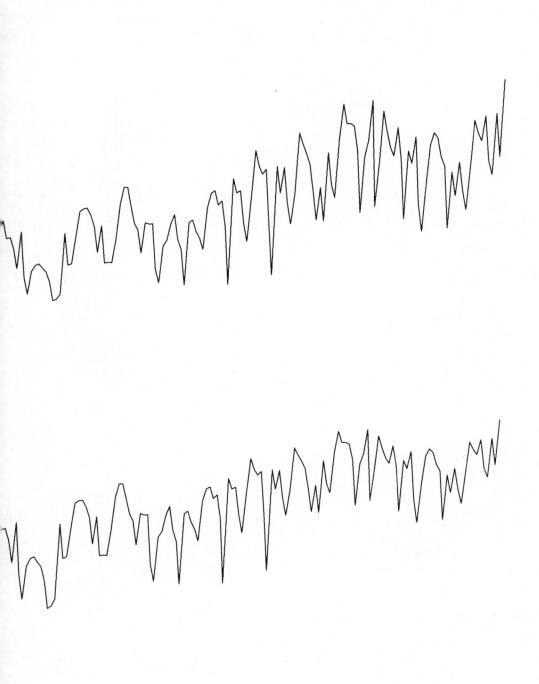

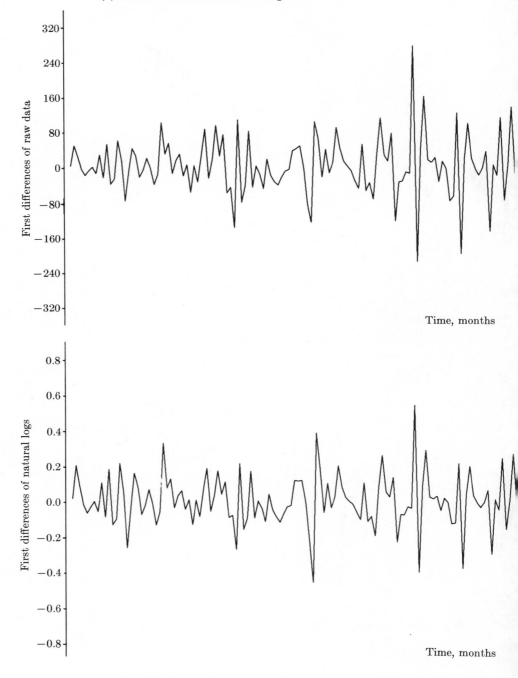

figure 7.3 Plots of first differences of raw data and natural logs of monthly registrations, 1947-01 through 1968-12. (*a*) First differences of raw data; (*b*) first differences of natural logs.

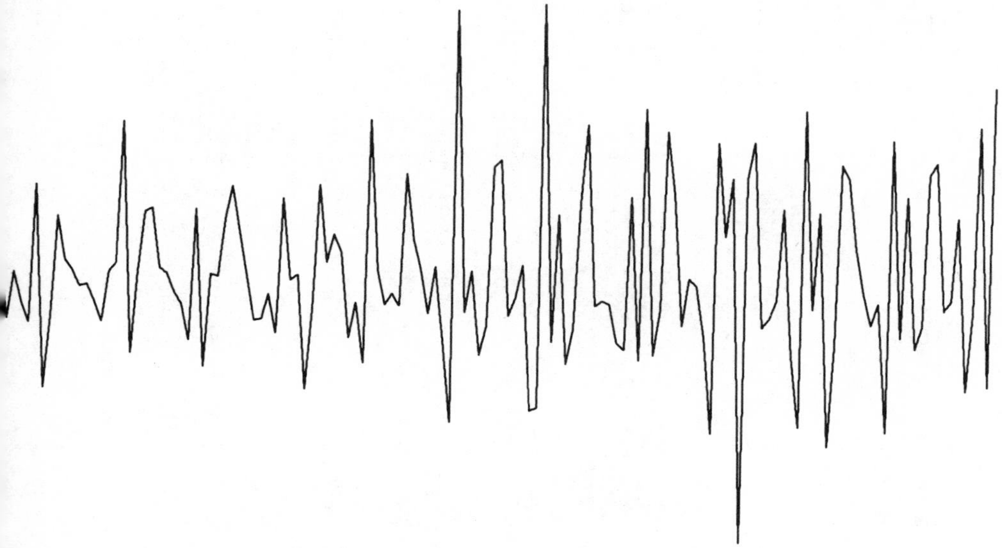

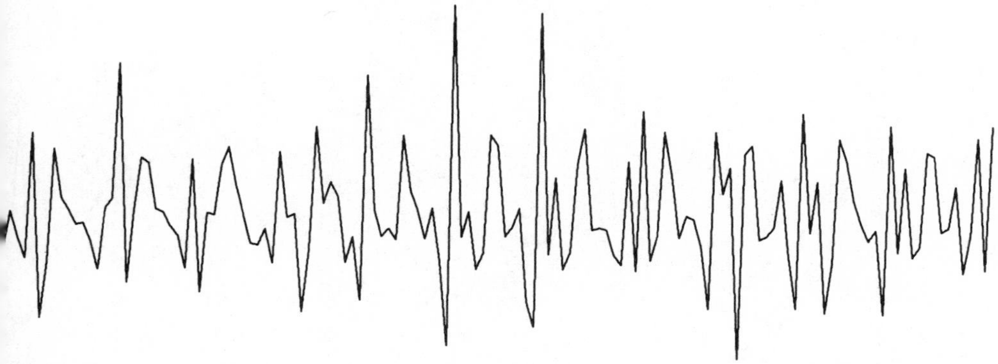

table 7.1 PDQ output for automobile registration data

US AUTO REGISTRATIONS IN THOUS MONTHLY 1947-01 THROUGH 1968-12

AUTOCORRELATION AND PARTIAL AUTOCORRELATION FUNCTIONS OF VARIOUS DIFFERENCES
LOGGED DATA TO NATURAL BASE   T= 264

AUTOCORRELATIONS

DIFFERENCE	LAGS													EST. STD ERROR FOR ROW
0 12 0 (1-B) (1-B) VAR = 0.105E 00	1-12	0.86	0.78	0.73	0.70	0.68	0.66	0.63	0.61	0.57	0.55	0.57	0.62	0.06
	13-24	0.53	0.48	0.44	0.43	0.41	0.38	0.36	0.34	0.33	0.33	0.36	0.41	0.20
	25-36	0.34	0.29	0.25	0.24	0.24	0.23	0.24	0.23	0.24	0.24	0.25	0.30	0.24
	37-48	0.24	0.20	0.18	0.17	0.18	0.19	0.21	0.21	0.22	0.25	0.26	0.32	0.25
1 12 0 (1-B) (1-B) VAR = 0.251E-01	1-12	-0.21	-0.14	-0.05	-0.04	0.02	-0.03	0.02	0.01	-0.03	-0.11	-0.18	0.59	0.06
	13-24	-0.16	-0.02	-0.10	-0.05	0.07	-0.05	0.00	-0.03	-0.03	-0.07	-0.14	0.51	0.07
	25-36	-0.12	0.01	-0.09	-0.07	0.05	-0.05	0.04	-0.02	-0.05	-0.01	-0.15	0.44	0.09
	37-48	-0.12	0.01	-0.08	-0.07	-0.01	-0.00	0.05	-0.04	-0.05	0.02	-0.14	0.41	0.10
0 12 1 (1-B) (1-B) VAR = 0.505E-01	1-12	0.80	0.64	0.56	0.46	0.38	0.33	0.27	0.19	0.07	-0.05	-0.18	-0.30	0.06
	13-24	-0.25	-0.20	-0.21	-0.21	-0.21	-0.23	-0.25	-0.24	-0.19	-0.15	-0.10	-0.09	0.14
	25-36	-0.07	-0.07	-0.07	-0.07	-0.06	-0.07	-0.05	-0.06	-0.09	-0.11	-0.14	-0.15	0.16
	37-48	-0.16	-0.17	-0.16	-0.14	-0.12	-0.08	-0.05	-0.03	-0.00	0.02	0.02	0.05	0.16
1 12 1 (1-B) (1-B) VAR = 0.201E-01	1-12	-0.09	-0.20	0.04	-0.05	-0.06	0.04	0.02	0.11	0.02	0.01	-0.03	-0.41	0.06
	13-24	0.01	0.13	-0.05	0.00	0.07	-0.02	-0.08	-0.07	0.02	-0.02	0.09	-0.02	0.07
	25-36	0.04	0.01	0.00	-0.03	0.05	-0.06	0.05	-0.05	-0.00	-0.00	-0.02	-0.03	0.08
	37-48	-0.00	-0.01	-0.05	0.01	-0.03	0.03	0.02	-0.01	0.06	0.06	-0.06	-0.02	0.08

PARTIAL AUTOCORRELATIONS

DIFFERENCE	LAGS													EST. STD ERROR FOR ROW
0 12 0 (1-B) (1-B)	1-12	0.86	0.14	0.14	0.12	0.09	0.02	0.04	0.00	-0.03	0.04	0.13	0.27	0.06
1 12 0 (1-B) (1-B)	1-12	-0.21	-0.20	-0.14	-0.13	-0.07	-0.09	-0.04	-0.02	-0.05	-0.16	-0.33	0.47	0.06
0 12 1 (1-B) (1-B)	1-12	0.80	0.00	0.12	-0.06	0.04	0.01	-0.05	-0.06	-0.20	-0.14	-0.20	-0.14	0.06
1 12 1 (1-B) (1-B)	1-12	-0.09	-0.21	-0.00	-0.09	-0.07	-0.01	-0.00	0.13	0.04	0.08	-0.00	-0.42	0.06

Sample autocorrelations of the log series appear in Table 7.1 as prepared by program PDQ. The correlogram for the undifferenced log series is plotted in Fig. 7.4 and displays both a failure to die out, which we may associate with nonstationarity, and peaks at the seasonal lags as expected. The correlogram of the first difference series $(1 - B)^1 z_t$ (where by z_t we shall mean the log series) in Fig. 7.5 is most notable for very conspicuous correlation at lags 12, 24, 36, and 48, suggesting that seasonal differencing is necessary. Finally, the correlogram for the series $(1 - B)^1(1 - B^{12})^1 z_t$ in Fig. 7.6 shows little remaining serial correlation except at lags 1, 2, 12, and 14.

We note that since the autocorrelations cut off, our model will be of moving-average form, and since 14 is the lag at which the cutoff occurs, the maximum power of B appearing in the model will be 14. Now, in terms of the multiplicative moving-average model, that maximum power of B would be consistent with $s = 12$, and values of Q and q of 1 and 2, respectively. Our tentative model for the log series z_t is then

$$(1 - B)(1 - B^{12})z_t = (1 - \theta_1 B - \theta_2 B^2)(1 - \Delta_1 B^{12})u_t \qquad (7.5.1)$$

which was the first example presented in Sec. 7.4. Since the mean of the differenced series is very small, about $.28 \times 10^{-4}$, it seems unlikely that we shall need to include a constant term in the model.

Preliminary estimates of parameters may be found as follows. Starting with θ_2, we have from (7.4.9)

$$\rho_2 = \frac{-\theta_2}{1 + \theta_1^2 + \theta_2^2} \qquad (7.5.2)$$

Now, in view of the size of r_1 and r_2, both θ_1 and θ_2 must be fairly small, so as a working approximation we may solve

$$r_2 \approx \frac{-\hat{\theta}_2}{1} \qquad (7.5.3)$$

for an estimate of $\hat{\theta}_2$, yielding

$$\hat{\theta}_2 = -r_2 = .20 \qquad (7.5.4)$$

Now, for θ_1 we have

$$\rho_1 = \frac{-\theta_1(1 - \theta_2)}{1 + \theta_1^2 + \theta_2^2} \qquad (7.5.5)$$

suggesting the approximation

$$r_1 \approx \frac{-\hat{\theta}_1(.8)}{\cdot \ 1} \qquad (7.5.6)$$

or

$$\hat{\theta}_1 = .12 \qquad (7.5.7)$$

sec. 7.5   example: monthly automobile registrations

figure 7.4 Sample correlograms for logs of automobile registration data, PDQ output.

US AUTO REGISTRATIONS IN THOUS MONTHLY 1947-01 THROUGH 1968-12

AUTOCORRELATION FUNCTION OF THE SERIES   (1-B) (1-B)
                                                       0   12 0
                                                      (1-B)

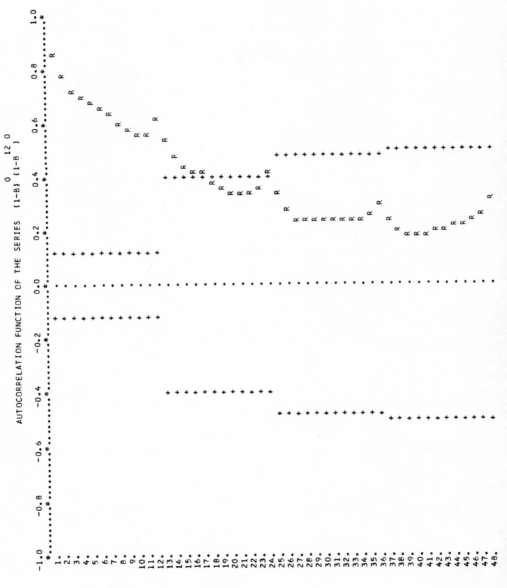

figure 7.5 Sample correlogram for first differences of logs of automobile registration data, PDA output.

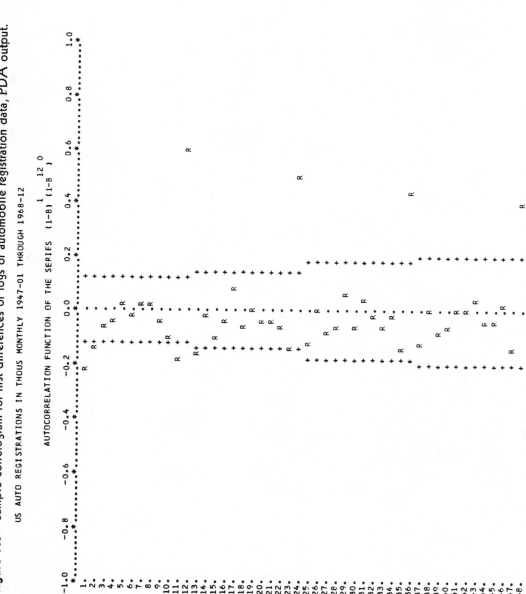

figure 7.6 Sample correlogram for seasonal differences of first differences of logs of automobile registration data, PDQ output.

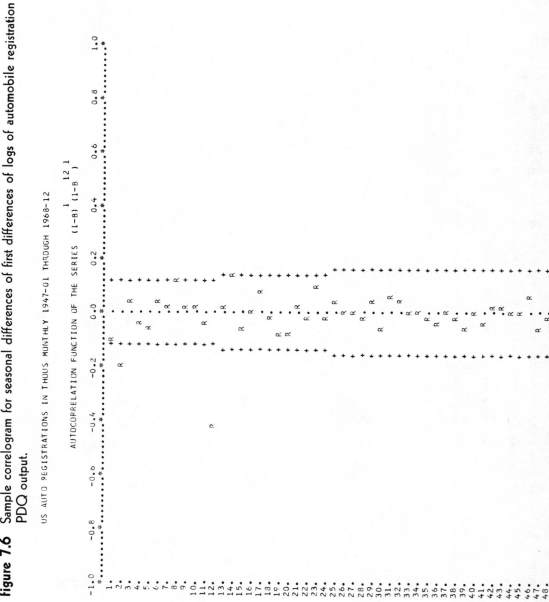

US AUTO REGISTRATIONS IN THOUS MONTHLY 1947-01 THROUGH 1968-12

AUTOCORRELATION FUNCTION OF THE SERIES $(1-B)^1 (1-B^{12})^1$

as a preliminary estimate of $\hat{\theta}_1$. Finally, for Δ_1 we have

$$\rho_{12} = \frac{-\Delta_1}{1 + \Delta_1{}^2} \tag{7.5.8}$$

therefore solving

$$r_{12} = \frac{-\hat{\Delta}_1}{1 + \hat{\Delta}_1} = -.41 \tag{7.5.9}$$

We have the preliminary estimate

$$\hat{\Delta}_1 = -\frac{1}{2r_{12}} \pm \left\{ \frac{1}{(2r_{12})^2} - 1 \right\}^{1/2}$$
$$= +1.22 \pm .70$$
$$= +.52 \tag{7.5.10}$$

taking the invertible value. Our tentative model is then

$$(1 - B)(1 - B^{12})z_t = (1 - .12B - .20B^2)(1 - .52B^{12})u_t \tag{7.5.11}$$

or $\quad (1 - B)(1 - B^{12})z_t = u_t - .12u_{t-1} - .20u_{t-2}$
$$- .52u_{t-12} + .06u_{t-13} + .10u_{t-14} \tag{7.5.12}$$

estimation

Maximum-likelihood estimation of multiplicative seasonal models is carried out under the same computational procedures as the simpler nonseasonal models. There are just additional parameters over which the sum-of-squares function must be minimized. Figure 7.7 presents program ESTIMATE output for the automobile registration model (7.5.1). The model with ML parameter estimates inserted is

$$(1 - B)(1 - B^{12})z_t = (1 - .21B - .26B^2)(1 - .85B^{12})u_t \tag{7.5.13}$$

which is quite close to model (7.5.11), which was based on preliminary estimates. All the parameters are highly significant. The ML estimate of the variance of the disturbances u_t is

$$\hat{\sigma}_u{}^2 = .012 \tag{7.5.14}$$

diagnostic checks

We note that the autocorrelations of residuals are generally quite small, exceptions being at lags 10 and 11. As an overall measure of the smallness

figure 7.7 ESTIMATE output for automobile registration data; model $d = 1$, $D = 1$, $q = 2$, $Q = 1$.

US AUTO REGISTRATIONS IN THOUS MONTHLY 1947-01 THROUGH 1968-12

NUMBER OF OBSERVATIONS = 264

INITIAL VALUE(S) OF MOVING AVERAGE PARAMETER(S)

   0.1200E 00   0.2000E 00

INITIAL VALUE(S) OF SEASONAL MA PARAMETER(S)

   0.8200E 00

MAXIMUM NUMBER OF ITERATIONS = 50

ORDER OF DIFFERENCING = 1

PERIODS PER SEASONAL CYCLE = 12

ORDER OF SEASONAL DIFFERENCING = 1

OPTIONS USED

   CONSTANT SUPPRESSED
   LOGS OF RAW DATA
   NEW RAW SERIES USED

DATA FROM CARDS

0.209E 03	0.265E 03	0.214E 03	0.290E 03	0.287E 03	0.270E 03	0.263E 03	0.265E 03	0.252E 03	0.281E 03
0.259E 03	0.275E 03	0.312E 03	0.250E 03	0.312E 03	0.331E 03	0.256E 03	0.247E 03	0.291E 03	0.318E 03
0.296E 03	0.313E 03	0.291E 03	0.311E 03	0.273E 03	0.258E 03	0.361E 03	0.391E 03	0.446E 03	0.433E 03
0.449E 03	0.460E 03	0.479E 03	0.466E 03	0.410E 03	0.415E 03	0.382E 03	0.409E 03	0.496E 03	0.471E 03
0.488E 03	0.610E 03	0.584E 03	0.684E 03	0.626E 03	0.580E 03	0.444E 03	0.552E 03	0.473E 03	0.431E 03
0.513E 03	0.470E 03	0.467E 03	0.455E 03	0.406E 03	0.424E 03	0.406E 03	0.373E 03	0.332E 03	0.310E 03
0.301E 03	0.333E 03	0.296E 03	0.374E 03	0.422E 03	0.424E 03	0.341E 03	0.216E 03	0.319E 03	0.383E 03
0.360E 03	0.386E 03	0.400E 03	0.397E 03	0.486E 03	0.528E 03	0.541E 03	0.542E 03	0.534E 03	0.502E 03
0.454E 03	0.450E 03	0.505E 03	0.414E 03	0.341E 03	0.370E 03	0.481E 03	0.508E 03	0.521E 03	0.597E 03
0.474E 03	0.408E 03	0.440E 03	0.396E 03	0.381E 03	0.657E 03	0.440E 03	0.477E 03	0.637E 03	0.652E 03
0.661E 03	0.647E 03	0.681E 03	0.659E 03	0.655E 03	0.576E 03	0.509E 03	0.631E 03	0.432E 03	0.448E 03
0.545E 03	0.560E 03	0.564E 03	0.540E 03	0.535E 03	0.568E 03	0.421E 03	0.424E 03	0.404E 03	0.514E 03
0.437E 03	0.573E 03	0.439E 03	0.549E 03	0.556E 03	0.517E 03	0.543E 03	0.492E 03	0.495E 03	0.464E 03
0.409E 03	0.382E 03	0.512E 03	0.334E 03	0.401E 03	0.418E 03	0.424E 03	0.411E 03	0.400E 03	0.371E 03
0.317E 03	0.335E 03	0.321E 03	0.511E 03	0.421E 03	0.425E 03	0.498E 03	0.575E 03	0.584E 03	0.586E 03
0.567E 03	0.458E 03	0.534E 03	0.535E 03	0.429E 03	0.431E 03	0.430E 03	0.494E 03	0.597E 03	0.647E 03
0.647E 03	0.547E 03	0.596E 03	0.525E 03	0.459E 03	0.548E 03	0.543E 03	0.544E 03	0.414E 03	0.375E 03
0.480E 03	0.544E 03	0.496E 03	0.572E 03	0.501E 03	0.471E 03	0.371E 03	0.550E 03	0.558E 03	0.526E 03
0.506E 03	0.592E 03	0.473E 03	0.635E 03	0.644E 03	0.602E 03	0.614E 03	0.540E 03	0.374E 03	0.678E 03
0.638E 03	0.554E 03	0.644E 03	0.498E 03	0.624E 03	0.759E 03	0.715E 03	0.692E 03	0.706E 03	0.553E 03
0.404E 03	0.640E 03	0.715E 03	0.712E 03	0.612E 03	0.552E 03	0.637E 03	0.812E 03	0.781E 03	0.754E 03
0.724E 03	0.565E 03	0.649E 03	0.659E 03	0.564E 03	0.757E 03	0.667E 03	0.631E 03	0.799E 03	0.896E 03
0.841E 03	0.834E 03	0.842E 03	0.767E 03	0.590E 03	0.746E 03	0.794E 03	0.909E 03	0.607E 03	0.722E 03
0.879E 03	0.777E 03	0.823E 03	0.753E 03	0.833E 03	0.744E 03	0.574E 03	0.767E 03	0.732E 03	0.8C8E 03
0.616E 03	0.671E 03	0.539E 03	0.786E 03	0.822E 03	0.806E 03	0.753E 03	0.726E 03	0.550E 03	0.710E 03
0.643E 03	0.658E 03	0.738E 03	0.605E 03	0.725E 03	0.859E 03	0.824E 03	0.801E 03	0.872E 03	0.744E 03
0.705E 03	0.757E 03	0.800E 03	0.977E 03						

MEAN OF SERIES = 0.5276E 03

VARIANCE OF SERIES = 0.2646E 05

figure 7.7 (continued)

US AUTO REGISTRATIONS IN THOUS MONTHLY 1947-01 THROUGH 1968-12

LOGGED SERIES   US AUTO REGISTRATIONS   IN THOUS MONTHLY

0.534E 01	0.537E 01	0.558E 01	0.567E 01	0.566E 01	0.560E 01	0.557E 01	0.558E 01	0.553E 01	0.564E 01
0.556E 01	0.574E 01	0.562E 01	0.552E 01	0.574E 01	0.580E 01	0.554E 01	0.551E 01	0.567E 01	0.576E 01
0.569E 01	0.567E 01	0.575E 01	0.574E 01	0.561E 01	0.555E 01	0.589E 01	0.597E 01	0.610E 01	0.607E 01
0.611E 01	0.617E 01	0.613E 01	0.614E 01	0.602E 01	0.603E 01	0.594E 01	0.601E 01	0.621E 01	0.616E 01
0.619E 01	0.637E 01	0.641E 01	0.653E 01	0.644E 01	0.636E 01	0.610E 01	0.631E 01	0.616E 01	0.607E 01
0.624E 01	0.615E 01	0.615E 01	0.612E 01	0.601E 01	0.605E 01	0.601E 01	0.592E 01	0.581E 01	0.574E 01
0.571E 01	0.569E 01	0.581E 01	0.593E 01	0.605E 01	0.605E 01	0.583E 01	0.537E 01	0.576E 01	0.595E 01
0.589E 01	0.599E 01	0.596E 01	0.598E 01	0.619E 01	0.627E 01	0.629E 01	0.630E 01	0.628E 01	0.622E 01
0.612E 01	0.622E 01	0.611E 01	0.603E 01	0.583E 01	0.591E 01	0.618E 01	0.623E 01	0.626E 01	0.639E 01
0.616E 01	0.609E 01	0.601E 01	0.598E 01	0.594E 01	0.649E 01	0.609E 01	0.617E 01	0.646E 01	0.648E 01
0.649E 01	0.652E 01	0.647E 01	0.649E 01	0.648E 01	0.636E 01	0.623E 01	0.645E 01	0.607E 01	0.610E 01
0.630E 01	0.634E 01	0.633E 01	0.629E 01	0.628E 01	0.634E 01	0.604E 01	0.605E 01	0.600E 01	0.624E 01
0.608E 01	0.608E 01	0.635E 01	0.631E 01	0.632E 01	0.625E 01	0.630E 01	0.620E 01	0.620E 01	0.614E 01
0.601E 01	0.624E 01	0.595E 01	0.581E 01	0.599E 01	0.604E 01	0.605E 01	0.602E 01	0.599E 01	0.592E 01
0.576E 01	0.577E 01	0.581E 01	0.624E 01	0.604E 01	0.605E 01	0.621E 01	0.635E 01	0.637E 01	0.637E 01
0.634E 01	0.628E 01	0.613E 01	0.628E 01	0.606E 01	0.607E 01	0.606E 01	0.620E 01	0.639E 01	0.647E 01
0.617E 01	0.639E 01	0.630E 01	0.626E 01	0.613E 01	0.631E 01	0.630E 01	0.630E 01	0.602E 01	0.593E 01
0.623E 01	0.621E 01	0.630E 01	0.635E 01	0.622E 01	0.615E 01	0.591E 01	0.631E 01	0.632E 01	0.626E 01
0.646E 01	0.616E 01	0.638E 01	0.645E 01	0.647E 01	0.640E 01	0.642E 01	0.629E 01	0.592E 01	0.652E 01
0.600E 01	0.647E 01	0.632E 01	0.621E 01	0.644E 01	0.663E 01	0.657E 01	0.654E 01	0.656E 01	0.632E 01
0.659E 01	0.657E 01	0.646E 01	0.657E 01	0.642E 01	0.631E 01	0.646E 01	0.670E 01	0.666E 01	0.663E 01
0.674E 01	0.674E 01	0.634E 01	0.649E 01	0.633E 01	0.663E 01	0.650E 01	0.645E 01	0.668E 01	0.680E 01
0.678E 01	0.671E 01	0.673E 01	0.664E 01	0.638E 01	0.661E 01	0.668E 01	0.681E 01	0.641E 01	0.658E 01
0.642E 01	0.629E 01	0.666E 01	0.662E 01	0.672E 01	0.661E 01	0.635E 01	0.664E 01	0.660E 01	0.669E 01
0.647E 01	0.660E 01	0.651E 01	0.667E 01	0.671E 01	0.669E 01	0.662E 01	0.659E 01	0.631E 01	0.657E 01
0.656E 01	0.678E 01	0.663E 01	0.688E 01	0.659E 01	0.676E 01	0.671E 01	0.669E 01	0.677E 01	0.661E 01

MEAN OF SERIES = 0.6218E 01

VARIANCE OF SERIES = 0.1052E 00

VARIANCE OF RESIDUALS(BACK FORECAST RESIDUALS INCLUDED) =   0.1243E-01 ,   248 DEGREES OF FREEDOM

VARIANCE OF RESIDUALS(BACK FORECAST RESIDUALS EXCLUDED) =   0.1234E-01 ,   248 DEGREES OF FREEDOM

MOVING AVERAGE PARAMETERS

0.211405E 00   0.261258E 00

SEASONAL MA PARAMETERS

0.847089E 00

CONSTANT TERM

0.0

95% CONFIDENCE LIMITS (+ & - TWO STD. ERRORS)

1	2	3
0.3343E 00	0.3841E 00	0.9108E 00
0.8854E-01	0.1384E 00	0.7834E 00

STANDARD ERROR FOR EACH PARAMETER (ON LINEAR HYPOTHESIS)

1	2	3
0.6143E-01	0.6143E-01	0.3184E-01

figure 7.7 (continued)

US AUTO REGISTRATIONS IN THOUS MONTHLY 1947-01 THROUGH 1968-12

T-STATISTIC FOR EACH PARAMETER   248 DEGREES OF FREEDOM

1	2	3
0.3441E 01	0.4253E 01	0.2660E 02

CORRELATION MATRIX OF PARAMETERS

	1	2	3
1	1.0000		
2	-0.2859	1.0000	
3	0.0250	0.0295	1.0000

AUTOCORRELATIONS OF RESIDUALS   T = 251

LAGS	AUTOCORRELATIONS												EST. S. E
1-12	-0.02	-0.01	0.05	-0.00	-0.01	0.08	-0.03	0.07	0.03	-0.15	-0.12	0.08	0.06
13-24	-0.09	-0.01	-0.06	-0.05	0.04	-0.03	-0.10	-0.06	0.04	-0.10	0.01	0.02	0.07
25-36	0.00	0.01	-0.03	-0.07	0.06	-0.02	0.00	0.02	0.04	-0.00	-0.05	-0.04	0.07

US AUTO REGISTRATIONS IN THOUS MONTHLY 1947-01 THROUGH 1968-12

CHI-SQUARE TEST OF AUTOCORRELATIONS

Q(12) = 15.0   9 DEGREES OF FREEDOM

Q(24) = 25.7   21 DEGREES OF FREEDOM

Q(36) = 29.5   33 DEGREES OF FREEDOM

CHI-SQUARE VALUES FROM TABLE

CHI-SQUARE = 29.6   10% LEVEL OF SIGNIFICANCE   21 DEGREES OF FREEDOM

CHI-SQUARE = 32.7   5% LEVEL OF SIGNIFICANCE   21 DEGREES OF FREEDOM

CROSS CORRELATIONS OF RESIDUALS AND DIFFERENCED SERIES

CROSS CORRELATION ZERO LAG = 0.72

CROSS CORRELATIONS U(T),W(T+K)

LAGS												
1-12	-0.10	-0.12	-0.02	-0.07	0.02	0.02	-0.02	0.05	-0.01	-0.12	-0.07	-0.53
13-24	0.08	0.17	-0.05	-0.03	0.06	-0.07	-0.06	-0.05	0.04	0.03	0.08	-0.07
25-36	0.05	0.01	-0.00	-0.03	0.02	0.00	0.06	0.04	-0.02	0.04	-0.05	-0.06

CROSS CORRELATIONS U(T+K),W(T)

LAGS												
1-12	0.03	-0.03	0.08	0.02	-0.06	0.05	0.02	0.10	0.03	-0.04	-0.09	0.07
13-24	-0.07	-0.01	-0.03	0.01	0.01	0.02	-0.08	-0.04	0.01	-0.10	0.02	0.03
25-36	0.02	0.03	-0.00	-0.02	0.07	-0.06	0.02	0.01	0.03	-0.05	-0.00	-0.00

table 7.2 theoretical autocorrelations of fitted model $(1 - B^{12})(1 - B)z_t = (1 - .21B - .26B^2)$ $(1 - .85B^{12})u_t$ and corresponding sample autocorrelations for natural logs of automobile registration data

Lag, months	ρ_i of fitted model	γ_i of data
1	$-.14$	$-.09$
2	$-.23$	$-.20$
10	.12	.01
11	.07	$-.03$
12	$-.49$	$-.41$
13	.07	.01
14	.12	.13

of the autocorrelations, the Q statistic is barely significant at the 10 percent level for the first 12 lags and is well within the 10 percent bound for lags 24 and 36.

Thus, although we do not reject the model on the basis of general adequacy with regard to transformation of the observations to random disturbances, it is well to understand why r_{10} and r_{11} are relatively large in view of the properties of the model fitted and the data at hand. Table 7.2 compares the autocorrelation function of the fitted model (7.5.13) at selected lags with the estimated autocorrelations of the transformed data. The discrepancies between these are quite small, the exception being at lag 10 months, where autocorrelation in the data sample is not as strong as the implied theoretical value. The result is that when we generate the residuals $\hat{u}_t$ by transforming the raw observations according to the fitted model, we find slight negative correlation at the same lag.

Residuals $\hat{u}_t$ are correlated with the current and future values of the differenced data but essentially uncorrelated with past observations as required by the specification of the model.

forecasting

Just as for any linear process of integrated autoregressive–moving-average form, the conditional expectation forecasts implied by a multiplicative seasonal model may be evaluated directly from the difference-equation form of

process. In the case of our model for automobile registrations, the current value of z_t is given by

$$z_t = z_{t-1} + z_{t-12} - z_{t-13} + u_t - .21u_{t-1} - .26u_{t-2} - .85u_{t-12}$$
$$+ .18u_{t-13} + .22u_{t-14} \quad (7.5.15)$$

The forecasts are then

$$\hat{z}_t(1) = z_t + z_{t-11} - z_{t-12} - .21u_t - .26u_{t-1} - .85u_{t-11}$$
$$+ .18u_{t-12} + .22u_{t-13}$$
$$\hat{z}_t(2) = \hat{z}_t(1) + z_{t-10} - z_{t-11} - .26u_t - .85u_{t-10} + .18u_{t-11} + .22u_{t-12} \quad (7.5.16)$$
$$\cdots\cdots\cdots\cdots\cdots\cdots\cdots\cdots\cdots\cdots\cdots$$
$$\hat{z}_t(l) = \hat{z}_t(l-1) + \hat{z}_t(l-12) + \hat{z}_t(l-13) \quad l > 14$$

It is clear that computation of forecasts is straightforward, although it is perhaps more informative to think in terms of forecasting the first differences $(z_t - z_{t-1})$ and then regard forecasts of the level z_t as the accumulation of the forecasted first differences. Following this alternative approach, we write the fitted model in terms of the first differences denoted w_t:

$$w_t = w_{t-12} + u_t - .21u_{t-1} - .26u_{t-2} - .85u_{t-12} + .18u_{t-13} + .22u_{t-14} \quad (7.5.17)$$

Forecasts of the first differences are then

$$\hat{w}_t(1) = w_{t-11} - .21u_t - .26u_{t-1} - .85u_{t-11} + .18u_{t-12} + .22u_{t-13}$$
$$\hat{w}_t(2) = w_{t-10} - .26u_t - .85u_{t-10} + .18u_{t-11} + .22u_{t-12}$$
$$\cdots\cdots\cdots\cdots\cdots\cdots\cdots\cdots\cdots\cdots\cdots$$
$$\hat{w}_t(12) = w_t - .85u_t + .18u_{t-1} + .22u_{t-2} \quad (7.5.18)$$
$$\hat{w}_t(13) = \hat{w}_t(1) + .18u_t + .22u_{t-1}$$
$$\hat{w}_t(14) = \hat{w}_t(2) + .22u_t$$
$$\hat{w}_t(l) = \hat{w}_t(l-12) \quad l > 14$$

We see then that forecasted changes are affected by the moving-average terms through horizon 14 months, the longest lag present in the moving average. Thereafter, the successive forecasted changes are simply the changes forecasted for 12 months previous. The profile of these forecasts repeats, then, at intervals of 12 months, beginning with horizon 15 months. This pattern is evident in the plot in Fig. 7.8 of forecasted changes through $l = 24$ months from origin 1968-12. Recall that changes in natural logs are approximately percentage changes (divided by 100), so the profile in Fig. 7.8 may be read as the sequence of forecasted percentage changes in automobile registrations. Note that subsequent actual changes follow the profile quite closely, the largest errors ocurring in the Januarys of 1969 and 1970.

figure 7.8 Log change in automobile registrations, 1968-01 through 1970-12 (solid line), and forecasted changes, 1969-01 through 1970-12 (dashed line), from origin 1968-12.

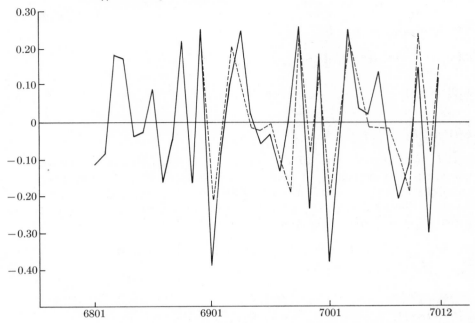

Figure 7.9 presents program FORECAST output for the levels of the log series and Fig. 7.10 the plot of forecasts and actuals. The effect on registrations of the automobile strike of 1970 and the worsening of the 1969–1970 economic recession is very evident in Fig. 7.10 from the substantial negative forecast errors in late 1970. Forecasts of the level of the series are of course simply the sum of the forecasted changes plotted in Fig. 7.7; that is,

$$\hat{z}_t(l) = z_t + \hat{w}_t(1) + \cdots + \hat{w}_t(l) \tag{7.5.19}$$

Consequently, errors in forecasting the level of the series are the sum of errors in forecasting the changes.

Standard errors for the forecasts, estimates of SD $[e_t(l)]$, are computed as for any linear process; that is, we write z_t in random-shock form

$$z_t = u_t + \Psi_1 u_{t-1} + \Psi_2 u_{t-2} + \cdots \tag{7.5.20}$$

by successive substitution for past z_{t-j} in (7.5.15), obtaining the familiar expression

$$\text{SD } [e_t(l)] = \sigma_u (1 + \Psi_1^2 + \cdots + \Psi_{l-1}^2)^{1/2} \tag{7.5.21}$$

figure 7.9 Program FORECAST output for automobile registration data.

```
FORECASTS FOR MODEL  1  OF  1  TENTATIVE MODELS FOR SERIES   MONTHLY AUTO REGISTRATIONS IN US

STARTING AT ORIGIN DATE 200,  FORECASTS ARE COMPUTED UP TO  24  STEPS AHEAD.

FOR THIS MODEL

   LOGGED DATA USED
   DEGREE OF DIFFERENCING =  1
   SPAN OF SEASONAL DIFFERENCING = 12
   DEGREE OF SEASONAL DIFFERENCING =  1
   NUMBER OF AUTOREGRESSIVE PARAMETERS =  0
   NUMBER OF SEASONAL AUTOREGRESSIVE PARAMETERS =  0
   NUMBER OF MOVING AVERAGE PARAMETERS =  2
   NUMBER OF SEASONAL MOVING AVERAGE PARAMETERS =  1

WITH PARAMETER VALUES

MOVING AVERAGE PARAMETER(S)

    1         2
0.211400  0.261200

SEASONAL MOVING AVERAGE PARAMETER(S)

    1
0.847100

CONSTANT =    0.0
```

figure 7.9 (continued)

```
FORECASTS FOR MODEL   1   OF   1   TENTATIVE MODELS FOR SERIES    MONTHLY AUTO REGISTRATIONS IN US

STARTING AT ORIGIN DATE 200,    FORECASTS ARE COMPUTED UP TO   24   STEPS AHEAD.

STEPS AHEAD    STD. ERROR IN FORECASTING      PSI WEIGHTS
     1            0.112719E 00                0.78860E 00
     2            0.143552E 00                0.52740E 00
     3            0.155374E 00                0.52740E 00
     4            0.166359E 00                0.52740E 00
     5            0.176662E 00                0.52740E 00
     6            0.186396E 00                0.52740E 00
     7            0.195646E 00                0.52740E 00
     8            0.204479E 00                0.52740E 00
     9            0.212945E 00                0.52740E 00
    10            0.221088E 00                0.52740E 00
    11            0.228941E 00                0.52740E 00
    12            0.236533E 00                0.68030E 00
    13            0.248653E 00                0.64798E 00
    14            0.259158E 00                0.60804E 00
    15            0.268068E 00                0.60804E 00
    16            0.276691E 00                0.60804E 00
    17            0.285053E 00                0.60804E 00
    18            0.293176E 00                0.60804E 00
    19            0.301081E 00                0.60804E 00
    20            0.308783E 00                0.60804E 00
    21            0.316298E 00                0.60804E 00
    22            0.323639E 00                0.60804E 00
    23            0.330816E 00                0.60804E 00
    24            0.337841E 00                0.76094E 00
```

STARTING AT ORIGIN DATE 200, FORECASTS ARE COMPUTED UP TO 24 STEPS AHEAD.

ORIGIN OBSERVATION

264

OBSERVATION	LOWER CONF. LIMIT	FORECAST	UPPER CONF. LIMIT	ACTUAL	ERROR
265	0.645803E 01	0.667896E 01	0.689899E 01	0.648860E 01	-0.190360E 00
266	0.633218E 01	0.561354E 01	0.689493E 01	0.640935E 01	-0.204188E 00
267	0.651442E 01	0.681895E 01	0.712349E 01	0.652386E 01	-0.295096E 00
268	0.659575E 01	0.692181E 01	0.724787E 01	0.677537E 01	-0.146444E 00
269	0.656352E 01	0.699377E 01	0.725603E 01	0.679021E 01	-0.119563E 00
270	0.652243E 01	0.588776E 01	0.725310E 01	0.673566E 01	-0.152102E 00
271	0.650019E 01	0.588365E 01	0.726712E 01	0.670356E 01	-0.180097E 00
272	0.638730E 01	0.678808E 01	0.718886E 01	0.657758E 01	-0.210500E 00
273	0.618674E 01	0.560411E 01	0.702148E 01	0.659769E 01	-0.641727E-02
274	0.640803E 01	0.684136E 01	0.727469E 01	0.586234E 01	0.209770E-01
275	0.631327E 01	0.576200E 01	0.721072E 01	0.663002E 01	-0.131974E 00
276	0.644371E 01	0.591232E 01	0.737592E 01	0.681619E 01	-0.961304E-01
277	0.623125E 01	0.571861E 01	0.720597E 01	0.642827E 01	-0.290344E 00
278	0.617105E 01	0.567900E 01	0.718695E 01	0.636027E 01	-0.318734E 00
279	0.635900E 01	0.584441E 01	0.740982E 01	0.660814E 01	-0.276277E 00
280	0.644496E 01	0.597727E 01	0.752958E 01	0.666431E 01	-0.342959E 00
281	0.641653E 01	0.597523E 01	0.753393E 01	0.666492E 01	-0.310313E 00
282	0.637860E 01	0.695322E 01	0.757285E 01	0.680339E 01	-0.149828E 00
283	0.635899E 01	0.694911E 01	0.753923E 01	0.673066E 01	-0.218451E 00
284	0.624833E 01	0.585594E 01	0.745876E 01	0.652679E 01	-0.326755E 00
285	0.604962E 01	0.566957E 01	0.728951E 01	0.641690E 01	-0.252672E 00
286	0.627249E 01	0.590682E 01	0.754115E 01	0.657786E 01	-0.328959E 00
287	0.617906E 01	0.587746E 01	0.747586E 01	0.628637E 01	-0.541087E 00
288	0.631561E 01	0.597778E 01	0.763995E 01	0.640803E 01	-0.569743E 00

figure 7.10 Logs of automobile registrations 1968-01 through 1970-12 (solid line) and forecasts 1969-01 through 1970-12 (dashed line) from origin 1968-12.

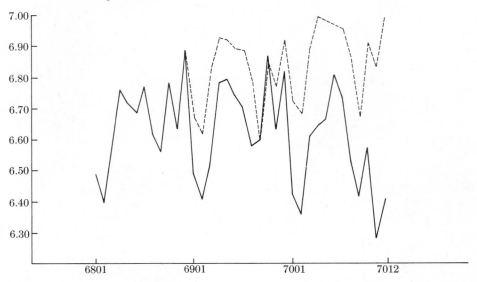

The Ψ_i needed to evaluate (7.5.21) are listed in Fig. 7.9 beside the resulting standard errors for horizons 1 to 24 months. The standard error at horizon 1 month is about 11 percent, at 12 months 24 percent, and at 24 months 34 percent. Since the series is nonstationary we know that the standard errors will increase with horizon without limit.

Exercises

7.1 Verify expressions (7.4.9), and provide corresponding expressions for autocorrelations. Compute autocorrelations for parameter values $\theta_1 = .4$, $\theta_2 = -.6$, $\Delta_1 = -.7$, and plot the correlogram.

7.2 Verify expressions (7.4.11) to (7.4.13), and provide corresponding expressions for autocorrelations. For $s = 12$ compute autocorrelations through lag 26 for parameter values $\Gamma = .6$, $\theta_1 = -.8$.

7.3 The model developed in Chap. 4 for tool sales series B may be reinterpreted as a seasonal model. Discuss the nature of the seasonality displayed by that series and the way in which it is reflected in the model.

7.4 (a) Compute standard errors for forecasted *log changes* in automobile registrations for horizons 1 to 12. Compute the implied 95 percent confidence limits and plot them in Fig. 7.9.

chap. 7 models for seasonal time series

(b) Compute and plot conditional expectation forecasts of the absolute numerical (antilog) changes in automobile registrations from origin data 1968-12 for the period 1969-01 through 1970-12. Provide 95 percent confidence intervals for those forecasts. (To answer this question you will need to use the forecasts of the log of sales provided in Fig. 7.9 and the fact that the log of sales in 1968-12 was 6.885.)

7.5 The velocity of money is defined to be national income during a given time period divided by the supply of money prevailing during the period. A quarterly series of velocity figures was constructed for the period 1947–1970 using data that had not undergone seasonal adjustment. The 96 raw observations exhibited non-stationarity as well as seasonality, and the first differences exhibited strong seasonality. The sample autocorrelations of the transformation $(1 - B)(1 - B^4)z$ were as follows:

lag	1	2	3	4	5	6	7	8	9	10	11	12
r_j	.19	.05	$-.15$	$-.53$	$-.19$	$-.11$	$-.03$	.08	.16	.15	.05	.03

with standard error .10 under the hypothesis $q = 0$. Suggest a model to account for these autocorrelations, and compute preliminary estimates of the parameters.

Additional Readings

Box, G. E. P., and G. M. Jenkins: "Time Series Analysis, Forecasting and Control," Holden-Day, Inc., San Francisco, 1970. The general multiplicative seasonal model is developed in chap. 9.

Grether, D. M., and M. Nerlove: Some Properties of "Optimal" Seasonal Adjustment, *Econometrica*, **38**:682–703 (September 1970).

Kendall, M. G., and A. Stuart: "The Advanced Theory of Statistics," vol. 3, Hafner Publishing Company, Inc., New York, 1966. Chapter 46 outlines the traditional analysis of seasonality and "trend."

Leuthold, R. M. et al.: Forecasting Daily Hog Prices and Quantities—A Study of Alternative Forecasting Techniques, *Journal of the American Statistical Association*, 90–107 (March 1970). The multiplicative seasonal model provides the basis for evaluation of forecasts of a structural model of the hog market.

Thompson, Howard E. and George C. Tiao: Analysis of Telephone Data: A Case Study of Forecasting Seasonal Time Series, *The Bell Journal of Economics and Management Science*, **2**:515–541 (Autumn 1971).

8
Forecast
Evaluation:
A Case Study

In Chap. 1 we discussed the wide range of forecasting techniques available for use in operational decision-making. As a result of this diversity, the decision-maker is very frequently confronted with the problem of choosing between or among alternative forecasts. The alternatives may take the form of different statistical techniques: a structural model versus a time series model, or statistical as opposed to subjective forecasts (for example, your sales manager's forecast versus that of a statistical model); or the alternatives may be simply the range of subjective forecasts offered by different individuals. The particular case we consider in this chapter is one of a structural model versus time series models. It illustrates, however, the fundamental aspects of the evaluation problem. We shall argue that forecast evaluation should not be regarded as a procedure for accepting one forecasting method or model to the exclusion of others. Rather, each alternative forecast almost always contains a unique component of information that may be usefully exploited by combining *all* available forecasts into a composite forecast.

8.1 The Federal Reserve Board-MIT-Penn (FMP) Model of the United States Economy

The FMP model is a large-scale, structural, and quarterly econometric model of the United States economy consisting of 171 equations, each of which describes the relationship of one variable, say, a short-term interest rate, to other variables included in the model. The 171 variables that are explained by the model are referred to as the *endogenous* variables of the equation system, and other variables that appear, but which are not explained by the model, are referred to as the *exogenous* variables. Continuing development of the FMP model has resulted in a succession of revisions, the subject of this chapter being version 4.1, which was released during the summer of 1969. This version has been thoroughly checked out and has been the subject of considerable interest in academic, corporate, and governmental contexts.[1]

This evaluation focuses on the one-quarter-ahead predictions of 14 endogenous variables of general interest, namely, nominal GNP, its endogenous components, the unemployment rate, two price indices, and three interest rates. Predictions are obtained from the model by simultaneous solution of the equation system. This requires as inputs the historical values of endogenous and exogenous variables and projected *future* values of exogenous variables.[2] In order to avoid ambiguity in interpretation of results because of the particular method for projecting exogenous variables, these were set at the future values subsequently realized. These actual future values provide ex post information to the model, which is exploited by the behavioral relationships and provides some of the accounting components of GNP. Such predictions may be thought of as forecasts that *would* have been made by a user of the model who was endowed with *perfect* foresight with regard to future values of exogenous variables.

The computation of predictions from the FMP model amounts to evaluation of the conditional expectations of future endogenous variables implied by the equation system since future values of the stochastic disturbances in the system are set at their expected values of zero. If the observed data being predicted were generated by the FMP system, then the conditional expectation predictions being computed would constitute minimum mean-square-error predictions among those conditioned on the same set of information. In this case, that information set includes historical data on all the endogenous and exoge-

---

[1] Version 4.1 has been described in more technical detail in articles by Franco Modigliani, Robert Rasche, and J. Phillip Cooper (1970); Frank de Leeuw and Edward Gramlich (1964); and Robert Rasche and Harold Shapiro (1968), all listed in the Additional Readings at the end of the chapter.

[2] Recall from Chap. 1 that computation of forecasts from structural models generally requires that projected future values of exogenous variables be supplied to the model.

nous variables of the system as well as *actual* future values of exogenous variables. Clearly, the latter is never available to an operational forecaster, so these forecasts represent "ideal" forecasts for this model.

The motivation for evaluating the forecasting performance of the FMP model is twofold. First, we are interested in the utility of the model for operational forecasting and policy design. Second, the quality of forecasts provides a measure of the success of the model in simulating the behavior of the economy. As an alternative to the FMP model, we pose the time series models of integrated autoregressive–moving-average form, which was the subject of Chaps. 2 through 7 of this book. Although the alternatives are both statistical models, they do offer considerable contrasts in many respects. One is very expensive and computationally complex, and the other is relatively inexpensive and simple. One is structural in concept, relying heavily on economic theory to specify causal relationships. The other is devoid of economic theory and purely extrapolative. The fact that the information set utilized by the FMP model, that is, the histories of *all* variables in the system, as well as actual future values of exogenous variables, subsumes the set available to the ARIMA models, just the past history of the variable being forecast, also motivates the choice of the time series models as a relevant alternative. To the extent that the economy behaves "as if" it were being generated by the FMP model, then the larger information set used by the model should be useful in reducing mean square prediction error relative to the ARIMA models. Furthermore, if FMP and ARIMA predictions are combined in a composite prediction to minimize mean square error, we would expect little contribution from the ARIMA predictions. On the other hand, if FMP predictions prove to be relatively inaccurate and ARIMA predictions contribute substantially to a composite prediction, then we would be led to conclude that the FMP model had underutilized the information available to it, presumably because of statistical and economic errors of specification and sampling error in parameter estimates.

8.2 ARIMA Models for 14 Endogenous Variables of the FMP Model

The criterion of model selection followed in this study has been the representation of each series in the most parsimonious form that is consistent with its stochastic structure. The parameters included in the models are those for which estimates are significant or which are required to eliminate serial correlation in residuals. Thus the procedure has not been to minimize the variance of prediction errors over the general class of ARIMA models; it has been to obtain the simplest adequate representations. The objective has been to apply the methodology in the most straightforward fashion so that these models could presumably be duplicated, except for minor differences, by another investigator. This objective required that prior information of various sorts be disregarded. For example, logs rather than levels of output variables presumably exhibit spatial stochastic homogeneity. Logs were not used, however, since the postwar data to which the study was confined do not by themselves provide strong evidence against homogeneity in the raw levels. Also, inclusion of a constant term in models for interest rates would clearly have improved both sample and postsample period performance. These terms were omitted, however, because they were not, interestingly enough, statistically significant.

Most equations of version 4.1 were estimated through 1966-04. To maintain comparability with respect to data base, the ARIMA models were also estimated through 1966-04. Models for the 14 endogenous variables included in the study are displayed in Table 8.1. It suffices to note that the models generally involve rather few parameters and few lagged values. The range of models represented is quite broad, including both pure AR and pure MA models as well as mixed models. An interesting by-product of fitting the models was evidence from the autocorrelations of residuals of a *negatively* seasonal component in some of the standard seasonally adjusted series. In the cases of consumer expenditures on nondurable goods, housing expenditures, and the GNP deflator and, to a lesser extent, GNP itself, the residual $\hat{u}_t$ for a given quarter tended to be negatively related to the residual appearing four quarters later. The implication of this finding is that the seasonal adjustment procedures in general use may "overadjust" series with particular stochastic structures and thereby introduce a negative seasonal relationship. This would tend to reinforce the idea expressed in Chap. 8 that unadjusted data should be utilized wherever possible and that seasonality should be accommodated by the econometric or statistical model under construction.

Two of the series are those used as examples in Chaps. 4 and 5, namely, GNP and EPD, and the other is the unemployment rate analyzed in Chap. 5.†

8.3 Analysis of Sample-period Prediction Errors

The system of equations of the FMP model requires a substantial number of lagged observations for solution; thus 1956-01 is the first quarter for which one-quarter-ahead predictions may be computed. Housing expenditures are exogenous through 1956 and only become endogenous in 1957, providing a more restricted prediction sample that begins in 1957-01. Thus, we shall

† The slight differences in parameter values between those reported in Table 8.1 and Chap. 5 result from the fact that the backforecasting method was used for the latter but not the former.

table 8.1 ARIMA models for 14 endogenous variables of the FMP model based on quarters 1947-01 through 1966-04

Endogenous variables†	ARIMA models
1. Gross national product	$z_t = z_{t-1} + .615(z_{t-1} - z_{t-2})$, $\qquad + 2.76 + u_t$ $\hat{\sigma}_a = 4.77$
2. Consumers' expenditures on nondurable goods	$z_t = z_{t-1} + .190(z_{t-1} - z_{t-2})$ $\qquad + .504(z_{t-2} - z_{t-3}) + 1.06 + u_t$ $\hat{\sigma}_a = 1.72$
3. Consumers' expenditures on durable goods	$z_t = z_{t-1} + .666 + u_t$ $\hat{\sigma}_a = 1.92$
4. Nonfarm inventory investment	$z_t = .581_{t-1} + u_t + .0013u_{t-1}$ $\qquad + .742u_{t-2} + 1.69$ $\hat{\sigma}_a = 3.14$
5. Expenditures on producers' durables	$z_t = z_{t-1} + u_t + .347u_{t-1} + .517$ $\hat{\sigma}_a = 1.06$
6. Expenditures on producers' structures	$z_t = z_{t-1} + .303(z_{t-1} - z_{t-2})$ $\qquad + .216(z_{t-2} - z_{t-3})$ $\qquad + .297(z_{t-3} - z_{t-4})$ $\qquad - .442(z_{t-4} - z_{t-5})$ $\qquad + .159 + u_t$ $\hat{\sigma}_a = .47$
7. State and local government expenditures	$z_t = 2z_{t-1} - z_{t-2} + u_t - .695u_{t-1}$ $\hat{\sigma}_a = .52$
8. Housing expenditures	$z_t = z_{t-1} + .639(z_{t-1} - z_{t-2})$ $\qquad + .076(z_{t-2} - z_{t-3})$ $\qquad - .286(z_{t-3} - z_{t-4}) + u_t$ $\hat{\sigma}_a = .74$
9. Unemployment rate	$z_t = 1.46z_{t-1} - .612z_{t-2} + u_t$ $\qquad + .284u_{t-1} + .734$ $\hat{\sigma}_a = .33$
10. GNP deflator-price index	$z_t = z_{t-1} + .523(z_{t-1} - z_{t-2}) + u_t + .256$ $\hat{\sigma}_a = .46$
11. Consumer goods price index	$z_t = z_{t-1} + .414(z_{t-1} - z_{t-2}) + u_t + .244$ $\hat{\sigma}_a = .48$
12. Yield on United States treasury bills	$z_t = z_{t-1} + .608(z_{t-1} - z_{t-2})$ $\qquad - .425(z_{t-2} - z_{t-3}) + u_t$ $\hat{\sigma}_a = .29$
13. Yield on commercial paper	$z_t = z_{t-1} + .727(z_{t-1} - z_{t-2})$ $\qquad - .427(z_{t-2} - z_{t-3}) + u_t$ $\hat{\sigma} = .27$
14. Yield on corporate bonds	$z_t = z_{t-1} + .490(z_{t-1} - z_{t-2})$ $\qquad - .169(z_{t-2} - z_{t-3}) + u_t$ $\hat{\sigma} = .11$

† Variables 1 through 8 are in billions of current dollars, the remaining variables in percentage points. The z_t and u_t are understood to be general notation referring to the observed value and disturbance associated with each respective variable.

chap. 8   forecast evaluation: a case study

refer to 1956-01 through 1966-04 as the *sample period*, but both the FMP equations and the ARIMA models were generally fitted over periods that began before 1956-01. The analysis is confined to one-quarter-ahead predictions, although predictions of longer horizon are available from both the FMP and ARIMA models and are of considerable practical interest. The intention is to concentrate on a more thorough analysis of the one-step-ahead case than would be tractable if a wider range of horizons were included.

The mean squares, means, and standard deviations of sample-period prediction errors appear in Table 8.2 and indicate that the FMP model provided generally more accurate predictions during that 44-quarter interval, although the differences are surprisingly small. In the cases of state and local government expenditure and the unemployment rate, the ARIMA model predictions had smaller mean square errors. Mean errors were all small, suggesting that the prediction bias may be characterized as being minor.[1]

The correlation between FMP and ARIMA errors provides a measure of similarity between the two sets and is substantial for many of the variables, including GNP. The highest error correlations are for consumers' expenditures on nondurable goods, nonfarm inventory investment, and expenditure on producers' structures. The lowest correlations are for state and local government expenditures, where the FMP predictions did poorly, and for yields on United States treasury bills.

Among desirable properties for predictions are that their errors be successively uncorrelated and that the predictions themselves be uncorrelated with future errors. Failure to meet either condition implies underutilization of information; that is, predictions may be adjusted to reduce mean square error. If one-step-ahead errors are serially correlated, then predictions could have been improved upon by simply taking into account the relation between past and future errors. If predictions are correlated with corresponding future errors, then this relationship may be used to adjust predictions accordingly. Sample correlations between predictions and errors reported in Table 8.2 are small except for FMP predictions of expenditures on producers' durables and

---

[1] To investigate further the question of prediction bias, the actual values of endogenous variables were regressed on predictions. The predictions are properly regarded as the independent variables in these regressions since if they were correlated with their respective error terms then their prediction accuracy could be improved merely by exploitation of that correlation. The constant term was significant (at the 5 percent level) only in the case of FMP predictions of state and local government expenditures, for which it was $1.54 billion. Estimated slopes were significantly different from unity only for FMP predictions of expenditures on producers' structures (1.04) and state and local government expenditures (.97) and for ARIMA predictions of expenditures on producers' durables (1.05). Although these deviations from theoretical values are statistically significant, they are of rather small magnitude, thus reinforcing our previous conclusion that prediction bias is fairly small.

table 8.2 summary statistics for FMP model and ARIMA model sample-period prediction errors

Endogenous variable	FMP model errors†			ARIMA model errors†			Correlation between model errors	Correlation between predictions and errors		Serial correlation coefficients of prediction errors§							
										FMP				ARIMA			
	MSE	Mean	Standard deviation	MSE	Mean	Standard deviation		FMP	ARIMA	r_1	r_2	r_3	r_4	r_1	r_2	r_3	r_4
1. Gross national product	11.665	.695	3.344	25.330	.520	5.006	.468	.200	.263	.09	−.04	.05	.12	−.06	.03	−.05	−.14
2. Consumers' expenditures on nondurable goods	1.926	.008	1.388	2.671	.230	1.618	.673	.055	.174	−.19	.04	−.07	−.07	−.13	.00	.13	−.09
3. Consumers' expenditures on durable goods	1.278	−.034	1.130	3.258	.057	1.804	.581	.005	.161	−.21	.17	−.08	.00	−.09	.12	−.07	.06
4. Nonfarm inventory investment	6.710	.892	2.432	10.992	.376	3.294	.640	.191	−.096	.11	.01	−.08	−.12	.08	−.21	−.01	.04
5. Expenditures on producers' durables	.682	−.224	.795	1.050	.116	1.018	.238	−.152	.406	.38	.15	−.01	.14	.18	.25	−.07	.08
6. Expenditures on producers' structures	.249	.064	.495	.310	.013	.557	.627	.303	.032	.21	.26	.28	−.15	−.13	.02	.08	.05
7. State and local government expenditures	.570	.018	.755	.294	.136	.525	.121	−.555	.224	.44	.43	.44	.35	−.09	−.10	.05	.03
8. Housing expenditures‡	.206	.092	.445	.486	.006	.697	.297	.216	−.224	.34	.19	.24	.19	.09	−.01	.06	−.04
9. Unemployment rate	.134	−.087	.356	.089	.040	.296	.432	.120	−.039	.01	.12	−.08	−.14	−.03	−.03	−.07	−.16
10. GNP deflator-price index	.038	.022	.194	.053	.004	.230	.402	−.160	−.108	.31	.16	.24	.31	−.09	.28	−.05	.32
11. Consumer goods price index	.052	.018	.227	.062	.028	.247	.321	−.199	−.132	.10	.11	.25	.33	.00	.24	.09	.23
12. Yields on United States treasury bills	.061	.012	.247	.124	.015	.352	.173	−.058	−.179	−.23	−.20	.05	.09	−.01	−.11	−.17	.23
13. Yield on commercial paper	.053	.044	.227	.101	.048	.314	.324	.080	−.165	.07	−.18	.01	.15	.04	−.21	−.09	.27
14. Yield on corporate bonds	.010	.020	.097	.016	.034	.120	.568	−.067	−.204	.15	−.08	.10	.04	−.01	−.17	.01	.17

† Errors are in billions of current dollars for variables 1 to 8, and percentage points for the remaining variables.
‡ Sample period for housing expenditures is 1957-01 through 1966-04.
§ The estimated standard error of r_1 under the hypothesis that the errors are uncorrelated is .16.

state and local government expenditures, for which the mean square error was high. The sample correlation is also substantial for ARIMA predictions of expenditures on producers' durables. Sample autocorrelations of FMP errors are large at lag 1 quarter (relative to a standard error of .16 for sample autocorrelations of uncorrelated noise) for variables, expenditures on producers' durables, expenditures on producers' structures, state and local government expenditures, housing expenditures, and the GNP deflator. Results for the consumer goods price index show substantial correlation of FMP errors at longer lags (3 and 4 quarters). ARIMA model errors are relatively less autocorrelated but display strong correlation at lags 2 and 4 for the GNP deflator. By way of summarizing these results for the two sets of prediction errors, we note that 7 of the 56 autocorrelations for FMP errors lie outside the bounds ±.32 compared to one value of .32 for ARIMA model errors.

From the viewpoint of the operational forecaster, relationships between errors for different variables are important in prediction evaluation since his loss function will generally depend on such relationships. For example, in the case that his loss function is a quadratic form in the prediction errors, as we assume in Sec. 8.6, then expected loss is a weighted sum of covariances between errors as well as individual error variances. Correlations across variables for both FMP and ARIMA errors appear in Table 8.3. A large correlation between ARIMA errors for a pair of variables would suggest that factors accounting for their respective contemporaneous disturbances are common to both. Thus, it is not surprising to find substantial positive correlation between GNP errors (disturbances) and those for consumers' expenditures on durable goods, nonfarm inventory investment, and expenditures on producers' durables, and substantial negative correlation with those for the unemployment rate. Errors for expenditures in producers' durables are strongly correlated with those for consumers' expenditures on durable goods and nonfarm inventory investment. Perhaps surprisingly, these three investment categories show quite strong positive correlation with the disturbances in the three interest-rate series.

Correlations between contemporary errors of FMP predictions are generally indicative of the structure of the model and, of course, accounting relationships. Consequently, in Table 8.3 errors for GNP are positively related to those for its components and negatively to the unemployment rate errors. Errors for housing expenditures and expenditures on producers' structures are positively related. Where relationships are not so obvious on prior grounds, the correlations provide indications of structural interaction within the model and may help to locate problem areas. For example, it is surprising that GNP deflator and consumer price index errors are negatively related to those for GNP and expenditures on producers' durables. It is also interesting that errors for the three interest rates are positively related to errors for con-

table 8.3 correlation of sample-period prediction errors across variables: FMP errors above the diagonal, ARIMA errors below the diagonal

Endogenous variable	1	2	3	4	5	6	7	8	9	10	11	12	13	14
1. Gross national product	1.00	.20	.38	.74	.55	.28	.14	.34	−.35	−.16	−.27	.23	.33	.51
2. Consumers' expenditures on nondurable goods	.13	1.00	−.16	−.19	−.06	.08	−.08	.14	.03	.27	.28	−.09	−.07	.04
3. Consumers' expenditures on durable goods	.48	.09	1.00	.04	.22	.23	.03	.22	−.30	−.20	−.32	.22	.11	.30
4. Nonfarm inventory investment	.66	−.03	.18	1.00	.26	.12	−.14	.28	−.32	−.05	−.16	.22	.32	.38
5. Expenditures on producers' durables	.50	.18	.63	.35	1.00	−.06	.37	.11	.09	−.41	−.37	.02	.20	.26
6. Expenditures on producers' structures	.20	.04	.25	.19	.12	1.00	−.19	.35	−.22	−.00	−.02	−.05	−.00	−.02
7. State and local government	.06	.11	.13	.14	−.02	.12	1.00	.16	−.01	−.37	−.28	−.08	−.13	−.02
8. Housing expenditures†	.33	−.12	.30	.12	.03	.24	−.18	1.00	−.42	−.10	−.15	.03	.10	.05
9. Unemployment rate	−.62	−.17	−.32	−.60	−.37	−.41	−.12	−.18	1.00	−.14	−.07	−.31	−.20	−.18
10. GNP deflator-price index	−.05	−.06	−.03	.08	.06	.13	.21	−.13	−.23	1.00	.95	.16	.06	−.07
11. Consumer goods price index	−.33	−.20	−.29	−.00	−.08	.05	.16	−.42	.05	.65	1.00	−.00	−.09	−.29
12. Yield on United States treasury bills	.34	.29	.30	.26	.40	.11	−.22	.19	−.30	−.22	−.31	1.00	.86	.53
13. Yield on commercial paper	.34	.20	.24	.44	.45	.12	−.17	.12	−.39	−.06	−.10	.89	1.00	.65
14. Yield on corporate bonds	.40	.29	.16	.33	.40	.11	−.21	.13	−.40	−.05	−.10	.77	.74	1.00

† Sample period for housing expenditures entries is 1957-01 through 1966-04.

sumers' expenditures on durable goods, nonfarm inventory investment, and expenditures on producers' durables. These correlations may be indicative of the origin of shocks in the real sector and their impact on the financial sector. They may also, of course, be indicative of problems in the structure of the model. The chains of interaction in a model of this size are enormously complex, and examination of error correlations may facilitate otherwise unwieldy diagnostic analysis.

8.4 Turning-point Errors

The reader may have noted by this point the absence of analysis of *turning-point* errors, a topic that has practically become standard in analysis of prediction accuracy. The argument for the importance of turning-point errors, that is, errors in predicting the direction of change, is briefly as follows. Economic time series show strong systematic movements—trends and cycles. It should then be relatively easy to predict the continuation of a rise or fall. Consequently, to predict the end of the current movement and the beginning of the next appears to be a more crucial goal.

The crucial element in the argument for the importance of turning points is the view that cycles and trends in economic time series are *systematic*. However, as we have seen from simulations of the ARIMA representations of GNP, *cycles* are not necessarily systematic in nature but rather may be merely artifacts of random shocks working their way through the economy as Eugen Slutzky and Ragnar Frisch suggested some time ago. Thus, it appears ex post that if turning points had been foreseen, prediction errors for subsequent observations could have been reduced. Turning points are usually associated with the occurrence of unusually large shocks to the system, and presumably success in anticipating *any* large disturbance would contribute to the accuracy of predictions of subsequent observations. If that is the case, then we should not restrict our attention only to the large disturbances which produce turning points but rather should be interested in anticipation of all large disturbances. In other words, to say that turning points are important because they are difficult to predict is to say that only large disturbances are associated with large prediction errors. Statistical decision theory offers further clarification on this point; namely, once the loss associated with errors has been specified, then conditions for optimal predictions may be stated, for example, in minimization of mean square error. Thereafter, turning-point errors are of no special interest in and of themselves.

8.5 Composite Predictions for the Endogenous Variables

Predictions computed from the FMP model are essentially the conditional expectations of future realizations implied by the structure of the model and the information set available to it. If the FMP model makes efficient use of that information, that is, if it does in fact provide conditional expectation predictions, then the ARIMA models which draw on only a subset of the same information should not be able to contribute to the accuracy of composite predictions which combine both.

A linear composite prediction is of the form

$$A_t = \beta_1(FMP)_t + \beta_2(ARIMA)_t + \epsilon_t \tag{8.5.1}$$

where A_t = actual value for period t
β_1 and β_2 = fixed coefficients
ϵ_t = composite prediction error

Least-squares fitting of (8.5.1) requires minimization of $\Sigma \hat{\epsilon}_t^2$ over values of β_1 and β_2 and therefore provides the minimum mean-square-error linear composite prediction for the sample period. In the case that both FMP and ARIMA predictions are individually unbiased, then (8.5.1) may be rewritten simply as

$$A_t = \beta(FMP)_t + (1 - \beta)(ARIMA)_t + \epsilon_t \tag{8.5.2}$$

The least-squares estimate of β in (8.5.2) is then given by

$$\hat{\beta} = \frac{\Sigma[(FMP)_t - (ARIMA)_t][A_t - (ARIMA)_t]}{\Sigma[(FMP)_t - (ARIMA)_t]^2} \tag{8.5.3}$$

which is seen to be the coefficient of the regression of ARIMA prediction errors $[A_t - (ARIMA)_t]$ on the difference between the two predictions. As would seem quite reasonable, the greater the ability of the difference between the two predictions to account for errors committed by $(ARIMA)_t$, the larger will be the weight given to $(FMP)_t$.

Consider now the hypothetical case that the FMP predictions subsume the ARIMA predictions and contain additional information $(FMP')_t$ so that

$$(FMP)_t = (ARIMA)_t + (FMP')_t \tag{8.5.4}$$

Then
$$\hat{\beta} = \frac{\Sigma(FMP')_t[A_t - (FMP)_t + (FMP')]}{\Sigma(FMP')_t^2} \tag{8.5.5}$$

and it is readily shown that in large samples $\hat{\beta}$ will approach unity or that the probability limit (plim) of $\hat{\beta}$ is

$$\text{plim } \hat{\beta} = 1 \tag{8.5.6}$$

since FMP predictions are presumably uncorrelated with their associated errors. Thus, if FMP predictions do incorporate all the information provided by ARIMA predictions, then estimates $\hat{\beta}_1$ and $\hat{\beta}_2$ in (8.5.1) should be approximately unity and zero, respectively.

Further insight into the structure of composite predictions is provided by an analogy to asset portfolios; namely, composite predictions may be viewed as *portfolios* of predictions. If we denote individual FMP and ARIMA errors by u_1 and u_2, respectively, then from (8.5.2) composite prediction error is seen to be

$$\epsilon_t = \beta(u_{1t}) + (1 - \beta)(u_{2t}) \tag{8.5.7}$$

Thus, just as the return on a portfolio of assets is the weighted average of individual asset returns, the composite error is the weighted average of individual errors. In both cases the objective is to minimize the variance of the weighted average, given its expected value. Construction of efficient asset portfolios requires selection of weights that minimize variance for various values of expected return, but in the case of prediction portfolios the weighted average always has expectation zero if individual predictions are unbiased or may be given expectation zero by addition of an appropriate constant.

Minimizing composite error variance over a finite sample of observations leads to the estimate of β given by

$$\hat{\beta} = \frac{\Sigma u_{2t}^2 - \Sigma u_{1t}u_{2t}}{\Sigma u_{1t}^2 + \Sigma u_{2t}^2 - 2\Sigma u_{1t}u_{2t}} \tag{8.5.8}$$

For large samples, or in the case that the variances $V(u_{1t})$ and $V(u_{2t})$ and the covariance $C(u_{1t},u_{2t})$ are known, we have

$$\beta = \frac{V(u_{2t}) - C(u_{1t},u_{2t})}{V(u_{1t}) + V(u_{2t}) - 2C(u_{1t},u_{2t})} \tag{8.5.9}$$

Thus, the minimum variance weight β is seen to depend on the covariance between individual errors as well as on their respective variances, just as the analogous weight for a minimum-variance two-asset portfolio depends on the covariance of returns as well as on return variances. Holding covariance constant, the larger the variance of the ARIMA error relative to that of the FMP error, the larger the weight given to the FMP prediction. However, with the exception of the special case $C(u_{1t},u_{2t}) = V(u_{1t})$, β will always differ from unity, and therefore the weight given to the ARIMA prediction differs from zero no matter how extreme might be the ratio of their error variances. *In short, relative accuracy is not an appropriate basis for choosing one prediction to the exclusion of the other; rather, even a very inaccurate prediction would generally be included in a minimum-variance composite.*

Considering again the limiting case where the FMP prediction subsumes all the information in the ARIMA prediction, we see from expression (8.5.4) that the ARIMA error u_{2t} would be given by

$$u_{2t} = u_{1t} + (\text{FMP}')_t \tag{8.5.10}$$

Since errors are presumably uncorrelated with corresponding predictions we have

$$V(u_{2t}) = V(u_{1t}) + V[(FMP')_i] \qquad (8.5.11)$$

and

$$C(u_{1t}, u_{2t}) = V(u_{1t}) \qquad (8.5.12)$$

Expression (8.5.12) would imply, as noted, that $\beta = 1$. The portfolio analysis of composite predictions then also leads to the conclusion that if the FMP model succeeds in utilizing the larger information set available to it, subsuming the information contained in ARIMA predictions, estimates $\hat{\beta}_1$ and $\hat{\beta}_2$ in (8.5.1) should be approximately unity and zero.

table 8.4 composite sample-period predictions of endogenous variables

		Minimum square error composite predictions				*Weight given to ARIMA under constraint* $\beta_1 + \beta_2 = 1$
		Weights		*Standard deviation of error*	*DW†*	
Endogenous variables		*FMP*	*ARIMA*			
1.	Gross national product	.834	.167	3.27	1.87	.168
2.	Consumers' expenditures on nondurable goods	.722	.278	1.36	2.39	.264
3.	Consumers' expenditures on durable goods	.958	.042	1.14	2.41	.044
4.	Nonfarm inventory investment	.975	.194	2.38	1.81	.185
5.	Expenditures on producers' durables	.658	.340‡	.70	1.62	.369‡
6.	Expenditures on producers' structures	.670	.334‡	.47	1.99	.355‡
7.	State and local government expenditures	.290	.712‡	.46	2.35	.681‡
8.	Housing expenditures§	.794	.209‡	.42	1.44	.225‡
9.	Unemployment rate	.338	.662‡	.27	1.91	.659‡
10.	GNP deflator-price index	.641	.359‡	.18	1.70	.363‡
11.	Consumer goods price index	.561	.439‡	.19	2.00	.436‡
12.	Yield on United States treasury bills	.706	.301‡	.22	2.19	.292‡
13.	Yield on commercial paper	.736	.276‡	.21	1.86	.273‡
14.	Yield on corporate bonds	.750	.255¶	.09	1.85	.225

† Durbin–Watson statistic.
‡ Denotes weight for ARIMA prediction significant at the 5 percent level.
§ Sample period for housing expenditures is 1957-01 through 1966-04.
¶ Denotes weight for ARIMA prediction significant at the 10 percent level.

Least-squares estimates of β_1 and β_2 for each of the endogenous variables appear in Table 8.4. Values of $\hat{\beta}_1$ are significant at the 5 percent level for all the variables; values of $\hat{\beta}_2$ are significant at the 5 percent level for 9 of 14 variables and at the 10 percent level for a tenth. Durbin–Watson statistics, denoted DW, are generally close to 2, and in no case may the hypothesis that the errors of the composite prediction are uncorrelated be rejected at the 5 percent level.[1] These results suggest that the ARIMA predictions do embody information which is omitted by FMP predictions, in particular, information available from the history of the individual variables themselves.

Since individual predictions are essentially unbiased, we would expect that their coefficients in a composite would add to approximately unity. Tests of the hypothesis that $\beta_1 + \beta_2 = 1$ in each regression led to rejection only in the case of nonfarm inventory investment. The weights given to the ARIMA predictions when the weights are reestimated under the constraint $\hat{\beta}_1 + \hat{\beta}_2 = 1$ are also given in Table 8.4 and differ little from the unconstrained estimates.

8.6 Jointly Optimal Composite Predictions

The composite forecasts are of interest in assessing the utilization of information by the FMP model, but they may not be the optimal composites for a decision-maker whose objective is to select weights that minimize expected loss. In particular, the relationships between errors for different variables may be of crucial importance, as noted in Sec. 8.3. A class of loss functions which allows for such interaction is that of the quadratic forms

$$L = \varepsilon' W \varepsilon \tag{8.6.1}$$

where L is the loss associated with the vector of errors across variables ε and W is a symmetric matrix.[2] Enumeration of plausible choices of W is, of course, impossible. As an illustrative example, however, consider the particular loss function

$$L = \varepsilon' \Sigma^{-1} \varepsilon \tag{8.6.2}$$

where Σ is var (ε), the matrix of variances and covariances of composite errors. Minimization of average loss over a given sample period corresponds in this special case to Aitken's generalized least-squares estimation of parameters β_1 and β_2 for each of the composites over the set of endogenous variables of interest. The matrix Σ is, of course, in practice unknown and must be esti-

---

[1] When constants were added to the regressions, none were significantly different from zero.

[2] The reader who is unfamiliar with quadratic forms may refer to any basic text in matrix algebra.

mated. Zellner has suggested that Σ be estimated as the matrix of sample moments of residuals from ordinary least-square estimation of the individual equations, in this case the individual composite predictions.[1] Estimates of jointly optimal weights obtained by Zellner's procedure appear in Table 8.5. The weight assigned to the FMP prediction is significant at the 5 percent level for each variable. The weight assigned to the ARIMA prediction is significant at the 5 percent level for 10 of the 14 variables and at the 10 percent level for another 3. Thus, joint estimation of optimal weights for ARIMA predictions reinforces our conclusion that these predictions utilize information that is omitted by the FMP predictions.[2]

The general implication of stating the problem of composite weight selection

---

[1] See A. Zellner, An Efficient Method of Estimating Seemingly Unrelated Regressions and Tests for Aggregation Bias, *Journal of the American Statistical Association*, **57**:348–368 (June 1962).

[2] The weights given in Table 8.5 sum to approximately unity for each variable except non-farm inventory investment. Individual t statistics for the linear hypotheses $\beta_1 + \beta_2 = 1$ are not significant except in the case of the latter variable. However, the F statistic for

table 8.5 jointly optimal composite predictions

	Endogenous variable	Weights for jointly optimal composite predictions†		t statistic for hypothesis $\beta_1 + \beta_2 = 1$
		FMP	ARIMA	
1.	Gross national product	.881	.119‡	1.301
2.	Consumers' expenditures on nondura-ble goods	.807	.194§	.542
3.	Consumers' expenditures on durable goods	.936	.065	.056
4.	Nonfarm inventory investment	1.042	.091§	4.424
5.	Expenditures on producers' durables	.692	.306‡	−.903
6.	Expenditures on producers' structures	.659	.343‡	.720
7.	State and local government expenditures	.345	.656	.931
8.	Housing expenditures	.880	.123§	1.263
9.	Unemployment rate	.310	.698‡	1.052
10.	GNP deflator-price index	.791	.209‡	.302
11.	Consumer goods price index	.711	.289‡	.548
12.	Yield on United States treasury bills	.668	.354‡	.338
13.	Yield on commercial paper	.700	.310‡	1.121
14.	Yield on corporate bonds	.816	.187‡	.948

† Sample period for estimate of jointly optimal weights is 1957-01 through 1966-01.
‡ Denotes weight for ARIMA prediction significant at the 5 percent level.
§ Denotes weight for ARIMA prediction significant at the 10 percent level.

chap. 8   forecast evaluation: a case study

in a loss-function context is that from the viewpoint of the decision-maker the question of whether one set of predictions or the other is more accurate is irrelevant. Since his objective is to minimize expected loss, he will purchase any piece of information that reduces expected loss by more than its cost. Thus, the value of the ARIMA predictions, for example, is not measured by their individual errors but rather by the contribution which they are able to make to the reduction in expected loss associated with a composite prediction or a set of composite predictions. This is also true, of course, for the FMP predictions. Since the latter are relatively expensive relative to ARIMA predictions (including computational expense, updating, etc.), we might expect to find that many decision-makers would purchase the less accurate and less expensive set of predictions. Likewise, if the bum on the street corner offers free tips to the decision-maker on his way to the office, these will be incorporated in composite predictions if they result in any reduction in expected loss, regardless of presumably gross inaccuracy.

8.7 Analysis of Postsample Prediction Errors

It is scarcely surprising that both sets of predictors as well as their composites achieve reasonable accuracy during the period they were designed to explain. In the operational use of models, however, neither the forecaster nor the policy-maker enjoys the luxury of working within the period of fit. Rather, from their point of view it is postsample performance that is most relevant. Data for quarters 1967-01 through 1969-01 included in the FMP data deck provide only a short postsample record but nevertheless yield rather interesting and important results.

The mean squares, means, and standard deviations of postsample one-quarter-ahead errors for both FMP and ARIMA models appear in Table 8.6 (FMP predictions continue to be conditioned on *true* future values of exogenous variables). It is immediately apparent that the accuracy of both sets of predictions deteriorated substantially during the postsample period. However, mean square errors are smaller for ARIMA than for FMP predictions in the case of GNP, both categories of consumer expenditures, expenditures on producers' durables, state and local government expenditures, the unemployment rate, and all three interest rates. Differences are small for the GNP deflator and consumer goods price index. It would appear, then, that the accuracy of FMP predictions deteriorated relative to that of ARIMA pre-

---

the joint test of $\beta_1 + \beta_2 = 1$ for *all* variables is 4.03 with 14 and 532 degrees of freedom so that we may reject the joint hypothesis at the .01 level. Thus, although departures from unbiasedness over the sample period may not be large in absolute magnitude, they are sufficient to provide rejection of the joint hypothesis of unbiasedness.

table 8.6 summary statistics for FMP model and ARIMA model postsample prediction errors

Endogenous variables	FMP model errors			ARIMA model errors			Errors of jointly estimated composite predictions		
	MSE	Mean	Standard deviation	MSE	Mean	Standard deviation	MSE	Mean	Standard deviation
1. Gross national product	77.259	3.783	7.934	36.652	2.632	5.452	55.468	2.979	6.826
2. Consumers' expenditures on nondurable goods	25.540	−3.914	3.197	11.605	1.464	3.076	18.944	−3.050	3.105
3. Consumers' expenditures on durable goods	14.440	2.152	3.312	5.369	.990	2.095	13.270	2.065	3.001
4. Nonfarm inventory investment	11.161	1.474	2.998	49.589	−.166	7.040	12.285	.586	3.456
5. Expenditures on producers' durables	22.288	2.752	3.836	6.211	.668	2.401	15.939	2.261	3.291
6. Expenditures on producers' structures	1.038	.220	.995	4.427	.337	2.077	1.596	.349	1.214
7. State and local government expenditures	8.065	.693	2.754	.766	.001	.875	1.414	.118	1.183
8. Housing expenditures	1.935	1.002	.965	2.646	.764	1.436	1.572	.873	.899
9. Unemployment rate	.412	−.522	.374	.081	−.141	.247	.114	−.287	.178
10. GNP deflator-price index	.068	−.016	.260	.120	.237	.253	.051	.025	.225
11. Consumer goods price index	.098	−.191	.249	.200	.295	.336	.068	−.074	.249
12. Yield on United States treasury bills	.425	.176	.628	.305	.091	.545	.280	.132	.512
13. Yield on commercial paper	.240	.282	.400	.190	.085	.427	.168	.172	.372
14. Yield on corporate bonds	.066	.156	.204	.055	.116	.205	.058	.133	.200

dictions during the postsample period. In particular, the FMP model appears to have overestimated the effect of the federal tax surcharge enacted in 1968 and applied to personal income taxes in the third quarter of 1968 and to corporate income taxes retroactively to the first quarter of 1968. The FMP prediction of GNP was low by $4.9 billion and $4.4 billion in the third and fourth quarters of 1968 compared to $0.5 billion and $2.4 billion, respectively, for the ARIMA model. In the first quarter of 1969 the FMP model got very seriously off-track with a prediction that was too low by $23.2 billion when the ARIMA prediction was high by $1.9 billion.

The results described suggest that the simple ARIMA models are relatively more robust with respect to postsample prediction than the complex FMP model is. It is interesting that this comparison generalizes to a considerable extent to relative performance among ARIMA models for different variables. In particular, the ratios of postsample to sample MSE are large for the fairly complex models for expenditures on producers' structures and housing expenditures. Among the best performers are the very simple models for GNP and consumers' expenditures on durable goods, although the four-parameter model for the unemployment rate is the best of all and is the only model with a postsample MSE smaller than its sample period MSE.

Finally, it is interesting to compare the postsample performance of FMP and ARIMA predictions with that of the composite predictions constructed using the jointly estimated weights of Table 8.5. The relative magnitudes of mean square errors given in Table 8.6 indicate that composite predictions were more accurate than FMP predictions for 12 of the 14 variables, the exceptions being nonfarm inventory investment and housing expenditures, for which the ARIMA component had suffered considerable postsample deterioration. Composite predictions were more accurate than ARIMA predictions, however, in only seven cases, reflecting the generally severe deterioration in FMP performance. Composite predictions were more accurate than *either* individual prediction in five cases. If we score each of the three predictions by number of first places, the ARIMA models earn seven points, the composites five, and the FMP model only two. Thus, if mean square error were an appropriate measure of loss, an unweighted assessment clearly indicates that a decision-maker would have been best off relying simply on ARIMA predictions in the postsample period. To have ignored the information available from the simple time series models altogether would have been costly indeed.

Exercises

8.1 Use the definition of correlation to rewrite expression (8.5.8) for the estimated minimum-variance composite weight $\hat{\beta}$ in terms of the sample standard deviations of u_{1t} and u_{2t} and the correlation between them.

8.2　Mr. A is the bond portfolio manager for a large financial institution and is therefore concerned about forecasting the future course of short-term interest rates. His two brokers have given him their forecasts of bill yields over a considerable period of time, and Mr. A. would like to evaluate their forecasts on the basis of this past record. His calculations show that broker 1's forecast errors have variance .20 percent points, broker 2's have variance .16 percent points, and the covariance between their errors is .10 percent points.

(a)　An associate of Mr. A glances at the results of his calculations and declares "I wouldn't pay any further attention to broker 1, if I were you. It is clear that you should just listen to broker 2—his forecasts are 20 percent more accurate!" How would you answer this associate if you were Mr. A?

(b)　Both sets of forecasts are essentially unbiased. Compute minimum-variance composite weights for the broker's forecasts. What is the variance of the composite forecast error? What increase in variance would be the consequence of Mr. A's taking his associate's advice?

8.3　Suppose that the token seller in the subway also gives Mr. A tips on bill yields. He is a terrible forecaster. His forecast errors are unbiased, but their variance is .81. They are essentially uncorrelated with either broker's forecasts. Should Mr. A ignore the token seller? What weight would you give his forecasts in a three-way composite with the forecasts of the two brokers?

Additional Readings

The FMP model, version (4.1), is described in:

de Leeuw, Frank and Edward Gramlich: The Federal Reserve-MIT Econometric Model, *Federal Reserve Bulletin*, **54**:11–40 (January 1964).

Modigliani, Franco, Robert Rasche, and J. Phillip Cooper: Central Bank Policy, the Money Supply and the Short-term Rate of Interest, *Journal of Money, Credit and Banking*, **2**:116–218 (May 1970).

Rasche, Robert, and Harold Shapiro: The FRB-MIT Econometric Model: Its Special Features, *American Economic Review*, Papers and Proceedings, **58**:123–149 (May 1968).

The following are studies in the evaluation of economic forecasts and represent a range of views and approaches:

Moore, G. H.: Forecasting Short-term Economic Change, *American Statistical Association*, **64**:1–22 (March 1969).

Steckler, H. O.: Forecasting with Econometric Models: An Evaluation, *Econometrica*, **36**:437–463 (1968).

Theil, H.: "Applied Economic Forecasting," North-Holland Publishing Company, Amsterdam, 1966.

Zarnowitz, V.: "An Appraisal of Short-Term Economic Forecasts," National Bureau of Economic Research, New York, 1967.

The reader should also look again at Leuthold et al. (Additional Readings, chap. 7) and at Chambers et al. (Additional Readings, chap. 1).

In the following, the concept of a linear composite or "combined" forecast is introduced, and various methods besides least squares for arriving at weights for alternative extrapolative forecasts of monthly airline passenger miles are evaluated:

Bates, J. M., and C. W. J. Granger: The Combination of Forecasts, *Operational Research Quarterly*, **20**:451–468 (December 1969).

additional readings

Appendix
Computer Programs
for
Identification,
Estimation,
and Forecasting

Application of time series analysis to operational forecasting requires a substantial amount of computing at each stage of the modeling process—identification of an appropriate model, estimation of the parameters of the model, and computation of forecasts. Discussion of these procedures was accompanied in the text by illustrative output from computer programs in the belief that facility in working with such programs is essential to successful implementation. The programs have been designed with the objective of offering maximum flexibility to nonprogramming users. They are written in FORTRAN IV for the IBM 360 and inquiries concerning their availability should be directed to the author. The capabilities of the programs are described below.

A.1 Program PDQ

The task of PDQ is to compute sample statistics required for identification of a tentative model or models, in particular sample autocorrelations and partial autocorrelations. Generally it will not be apparent a priori what degrees of consecutive and/or seasonal differencing will be necessary to render a particular series stationary. The program therefore requires the user to specify an ultimate transformation and then supplies results for all differences up to and including the ultimate transformation. In other words, if the ultimate transformation is the dth consecutive difference of the Dth seasonal difference (for specified seasonal span s), that is,

$$(1 - B)^d(1 - B^s)^D z_t$$

then sample statistics for each of the series

$$(1 - B)z_t$$

$$\cdot \quad \cdot \quad \cdot \quad \cdot \quad \cdot$$

$$(1 - B)^d z_t$$
$$(1 - B)(1 - B^s)z_t$$

$$\cdot \quad \cdot \quad \cdot \quad \cdot \quad \cdot \quad \cdot \quad \cdot \quad \cdot \quad \cdot \quad \cdot$$

$$(1 - B)^d(1 - B^s)z_t$$
$$(1 - B)(1 - B^s)^2 z_t$$

$$\cdot \quad \cdot \quad \cdot \quad \cdot \quad \cdot \quad \cdot \quad \cdot \quad \cdot \quad \cdot \quad \cdot$$

$$(1 - B)^d(1 - B^s)^D z_t$$

are supplied. In economic contexts, d and D may both be set at 2 unless it is obvious that stationarity will be achieved at lower orders of differencing or that a series is not seasonal. The user may also entertain the possibility that logs rather than the raw data will exhibit spatial homogeneity. In this case, transformation of the raw data to logs is specified and all statistics for both the raw and log data are presented.

Standard output also includes the sample variances of each series and standard errors for the sample autocorrelations and partial autocorrelations. Plots of the series themselves and of their autocorrelations and partial autocorrelations are produced by option. The program requires 90K of storage capacity for a maximum of 1,000 observations.

A.2 Program ESTIMATE

Any model of general multiplicative autoregressive–moving-average form is fully specified by the values of p, the number of ordinary autoregressive parameters; P, the number of seasonal autoregressive parameters; q, the number of ordinary moving-average parameters; Q, the number of seasonal moving-average parameters; d, the degree of consecutive differencing; s, the number of periods per seasonal cycle; D, the degree of seasonal differencing; and whether a constant term δ is to be included. By providing the program with these dimensions for his model, the user tells the program exactly what the model looks like and what parameters are to be estimated, namely, $\phi_1, \ldots, \phi_p; \Gamma_1, \ldots, \Gamma_P; \theta_1, \ldots, \theta_q; \Delta_1, \ldots, \Delta_Q$; and δ if it is included. The estimates provided by the program are those that minimize the unconditional sum-of-squares function through backforecasting of presample observations. The minimum is located by use of Marquardt's iterative procedure, which amounts to a compromise between the methods of Gauss–Newton and steepest descent.[1] Initial guess values

[1] See D. W. Marquardt, An Algorithm for Least-Squares Estimation of Nonlinear Parameters, *Journal of the Society for Industrial and Applied Mathematics*, **2**: 431–441 (1963).

provided by the user are needed to start the iterations. Although convergence occurs rapidly in almost all cases even if guess values are quite far from the final estimates, computational expense is reduced if the preliminary estimates implied by the sample autocorrelations are used.

An option available to the user is that of suppressing any subset of the ordinary autoregressive and moving-average parameters. This is often useful in reducing the number of parameters to be estimated when it is apparent that only terms at specified lags are required. The user may also indicate transformation of the raw data to logs.

Standard output includes listing of the raw series and of its transformation via logging and/or differencing; the succession of parameter values and sums of squares resulting from each iteration; listing of residuals and the implied one-step-ahead forecasts; the final point estimates of parameters with their standard errors, t ratios, 95 percent confidence intervals, and estimated correlation matrix; estimates of the variance of disturbances alternatively including and excluding presample residuals; the sample autocorrelations of the residuals and the Q statistics for lags 1 to 12, 1 to 24, and 1 to 36; and the sample cross correlations of the residuals with the differenced data. The residuals and their cumulative periodogram are plotted by option. Storage requirement of the program is 130K under the constraint (number of observations + 104) × (number of parameters to be estimated) $\leq$ 9,624.

A.3 Program FORECAST

Subsequent to estimation of parameters by ESTIMATE, the user will generally be interested in computing point forecasts as well as confidence intervals for future observations. Direct evaluation of point forecasts from the difference-equation form of the process requires only that the dimensions p, P, q, Q, d, s, and D be specified along with the parameter estimates. Because values of the residuals are required for forecast computation if moving-average terms are present and the residuals are just one-step-ahead forecast errors, the program computes first the sequence of one-step-ahead forecasts and corresponding errors. Then using those errors, forecasts for subsequent horizons through the maximum specified by the user are computed recursively. The residuals also provide the estimate of the variance of the disturbances needed to compute standard errors for the forecasts and confidence intervals. If the data series submitted to FORECAST extends beyond the sample period over which the model was estimated, then computation of the variance of residuals is restricted to the sample period so that any postsample deterioration in the fit of the model will not be reflected in standard errors and confidence intervals. Finally, the weights Ψ_i in the random-shock form of the model are computed from the given parameters, completing the information needed for evaluation of the standard error

$$\text{SE}\,[e_t(l)] = \sigma_u (1 + \Psi_1{}^2 + \cdots + \Psi_{l-1}^2)^{1/2}$$

Standard output includes forecasts for the origin dates specified by the user, corresponding 95 percent confidence intervals, actuals, and implied errors, and for the range of horizons specified, the values of SE $[e_t(l)]$ and the Ψ_i used to compute them.

If the raw data have been transformed to logs, forecasts of the raw data as well as forecasts of logs may be of interest.   As pointed out in Chap. 6, merely taking antilogs of the log forecasts will not produce conditional expectation forecasts.   Rather, an adjustment is required based on the log-normal distribution of the raw series.   When requested by the user, these adjusted forecasts are presented along with 95 percent confidence intervals, corresponding actuals, and the implied errors.

Plots of the undifferenced data together with the forecast profiles for specified origin dates and associated confidence bounds are available by option.   Storage requirement of the program is 100K for a maximum series length of 1,500.

Index